P9-CEH-121

Teddy Bears
&
All the
Trimmings

by Jodie Davis

WILLIAMSON PUBLISHING CO.
Charlotte • Vermont 05445

Copyright © 1988 by Jodie Davis

All Rights reserved.
No portion of this book may be reproduced mechanically,
electronically or by any other means including
photocopying — without written permission of the
publisher.

Library of Congress Cataloging-in-Publication Data

Davis, Jodie, 1959–
     Easy-to-make teddy bears & all the trimmings.

Bibliography: p.
     1. Soft toy making.   2. Teddy bears.   I. Title.
     TT174.3.D375   1988   745.592'4   88–28022
     ISBN 0–913589–40–3

Cover, interior design & typesetting: Trezzo–Braren Studio

Printing: Capital City Press

Williamson Publishing Co.
Charlotte, Vermont 05445

Manufactured in the United States of America

10   9   8   7   6   5   4   3   2

Notice: The information contained in this book is true,
complete and accurate to best of our knowledge. All
recommendations and suggestions are made without any
guarantees on the part of the author or Williamson
Publishing. The author and publisher disclaim all liability
incurred in connection with the use of this information.

CONTENTS

DEDICATION

To my Grandmother, Bobbie,
for the generous gift of her creative genes;
To my Mom,
for nurturing and believing in me;
and to Lee,
for giving me the opportunity
and support to find my own way.

INTRODUCTION

Welcome to the world of the teddy bear!
Since Clifford Berryman put pen to paper to draw the cartoon destined to immortalize the beseeching bear cub who caused Teddy Roosevelt's expedition of 1902 to be not just another hunting trip, the teddy bear has made our hearts its permanent home. Soon after this event the Ideal Toy Company requested permission from Mr. Roosevelt to sell "Teddy" bears. Permission granted, the shop displayed the bears in the store window and subsequently sold out of them.

The teddy bear rage made a short leap of the Atlantic Ocean, and soon became the subject of some wonderfully classic, and decidedly English literature. Most familiar to Americans is Pooh who made his debut in 1924 with his friend Christopher Robin in A.A. Milne's **When We Were Very Young**. Paddington arrived, in his rain gear of course, in 1956. Less well known to Americans is Rupert, who has been a regular in London's **Daily Express** since his first appearance on November 8, 1920. **The Rupert Annual**, now a fondly anticipated British Christmas tradition, sells 250,000 copies each year, keeping the third generation of Rupert artists and writers busy with his antics in Nutwood, Rupert's fictional home town.

Whether British or American, Chinese or Australian, 6 years old or a senior citizen, there's just something magically irresistible about teddy bears, pulling on our heartstrings as if we were their marionettes, rather than they, our stuffed friends.

The romanticized version of that lucky little bear whose life was saved by the kindness of our then president sparked a mania which still surges today. A new, even stronger resurgence of teddy bear mania draws ever-growing numbers of arctophiles to teddy bear conventions, picnics, sales, and club meetings. Adults satisfy their teddy bear love under the guise of the label "Teddy Bear Collector," hugging their bears ever closer. In fact, teddy bear collecting rivals stamps and dolls as America's favorite collecting hobby, which certainly proves just how grown up we really are!

And this book is your invitation to join the fun.

Teddy Bears and All The Trimmings *is a one-book source for creating your very own bears and their world. Here are patterns and instructions for many bears, both jointed and non-jointed, including a large and huggable bear to a tiny teddy eager to be carried in one's pocket; an all-occasion wardrobe for both boy and girl bears; a complete birthday party; a fun-filled year of bear paraphernalia for holiday celebrations; and furniture, sure to please your bear at bed and play time.*

Just turn the page and enter the enchanting world of the teddy bear—with all the trimmings!

CHAPTER • 1

THE
BEAR
BASICS

This brief overview of techniques gives you the essentials for constructing the bears and their clothes in this book. If you feel the need for more complete how-to-do-it information, there are some excellent general sewing reference books listed in the bibliography which you will find in your local library or bookstore. Most of these patterns are very easy to make and beginning sewing technique is all that is required to complete these projects satisfactorily. Just take your time, assemble all of the tools and materials listed for your project first, and then follow the instructions one step at a time.

GENERAL SUPPLIES

Essential

Bent-handle dressmaker's shears: Best for cutting fabrics, fur, and felt. A good quality shear, 7" or 8" in length is recommended for general sewing purposes. Reserve these shears for cutting fabrics only, as paper will dull them quickly. (Use regular kitchen scissors instead for paper cutting.)

Dressmaker's tracing paper: Used for transferring markings from patterns to fabric.

Dressmaker's tracing wheel: A device used with the tracing paper.

Straight pins or pattern weights: To hold paper pattern pieces in place as you cut the fabric out.

Hand-sewing needles: For general hand sewing. Choose a fine, size 10–8, sharp for lightweight fabrics such as calico, and a medium, size 8–6, sharp for heavier fabrics such as corduroy, flannel, and denim. When hand-sewing bears, choose between medium, a size 8–6.

Long sewing needle such as a doll maker's needle: For installing glass eyes on bears.

Tapestry needle: For embroidering bear faces.

Glue: A general purpose white glue made for fabric, felt, wood, and paper is available at any dime, crafts, or fabric store under a variety of brand names.

General purpose thread: The all-purpose size 50 will fill most of your general hand and machine sewing needs. Some people insist on cotton thread but I find that polyester or cotton-wrapped polyester are stronger and slide through the fabric more easily.

Button and carpet thread: Has the strength required to withstand the tugging needed to pull the necks of your jointed bears closed.

Paper: For clothing and other patterns.

Cardboard, empty cereal boxes, or oak tag: For bear patterns.

Wire cutters: For installing the glass eyes.

Wooden spoon or dowel: For stuffing the bears.

Needle nose pliers: For tightening joints of jointed bears.

Felt tip pen

Nice to Have

Seam ripper: A sharp, pointed tool used to tear out temporary basting stitches and seams. I list this as non-essential because you can substitute the thread clipper listed below.

Pinking shears: Cut a ravel-resistant, zigzag used for finishing seams. A good choice is the $7^1/2$" size.

Thread clippers: A variation on a small pair of scissors, thread clippers are made by a number of companies and are handy for clipping threads at the sewing machine, for clipping into seam allowances, and for making buttonholes. If you do much sewing, I recommend a pair highly.

Thimble: This is listed as non-essential though many, including myself, will argue that a thimble is essential in guiding the needle. When hand-sewing the bears, I find that I need to push the needle through the fabric with the thimble rather than with my sore fingers.

Awl: A sharp instrument, sort of like a pointed screwdriver, used to make small round holes in fabric, as in holes for joints for the arms and legs of the bears. I use my thread clipper or seam ripper for this purpose.

Sewing machine: It is not essential that you use a sewing machine for any of the projects in this book. In fact, you will have better results when making the small bears if you do hand-sew them. For general hand-sewing, use a small running stitch. For constructing the bears by hand, use tiny $1/16$"-long backstitches, pulling the thread tight after each stitch. In some cases, I do say "machine stitch," but that is only for convenience, not necessity.

HOW TO TRANSFER PATTERNS

All of the patterns in this book are drawn to their actual size. It is suggested that you make your bear patterns out of heavy cardboard, such as oak tag or cereal boxes. By tracing around the cardboard pieces, you will transfer the patterns very accurately. Heavy paper will suffice for the clothing patterns, as you will pin the patterns to the fabric and cut out the pieces.

MATERIALS

Dressmaker's tracing paper

Dressmaker's tracing wheel or pencil

Cardboard or paper for patterns

INSTRUCTIONS

1. Lay a piece of tracing paper over the pattern in the book. Carefully trace the pattern onto the tracing paper, including all pattern markings.

2. Lay the cardboard or, for clothing patterns, heavy paper on your work surface (not the dining room table!). Place a sheet of carbon paper on top and your tracing over that. To avoid the possibility of slippage, you may wish to tape the two top sheets to the bottom cardboard or paper, or to the work surface. With a pencil or dressmaker's wheel, trace the pattern, pressing firmly. Pick up a corner of the two top layers to be sure that the pattern is being transferred clearly to the bottom surface. Transfer all markings to the pattern.

3. Cut out your pattern. Mark the name of the pattern piece and the name of the bear or garment on it.

4. To avoid mistakes later, when you are cutting your fur, turn over the leg, arm, paw pad, body front, body back, and head patterns now and make a reverse pattern of each so that you have a right and a left. Mark each leg piece "cut two". If you now have two arm pattern pieces (for a bear with no paw pad) mark each of the two pattern pieces "cut two". If you have four pattern pieces (for a bear with paw pads) mark them "cut one". Mark each paw pad, body front, body back, and head pattern piece "cut one".

TIP: Letter-size envelopes and zip lock sandwich bags are great places to store your individual patterns. Place these inside a large well-marked manila envelope, and store. These patterns are meant to get a lot of use!

SEWING TECHNIQUES

Darts

Fold the fabric along the center line of the dart, right sides together. Beginning at the raw edges, or widest point of the dart, sew the dart along the broken lines to the point. Back-stitch to secure the stitching. For clothing, press the completed dart to one side. For heavy fabrics such as bear fur, slash the fabric along the center line to within $1/2$" of the point of the dart. Press the dart flat with your fingers.

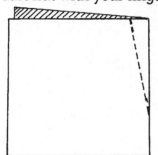

Gathering

Using a long stitch, make two parallel rows of stitching in the seam allowance between the marks indicated on the pattern, leaving the thread tails long enough to grasp so that you can pull them. The first row should be a thread's width into the seam allowance, and the second row should be $1/4$" above the first, into the seam allowance. Place the stitched edge against the ungathered edge you wish to sew it to, right sides together, matching the dots on the two pattern pieces as indicated. Pin the two pieces together at the dots. Pull up the threads to gather the fabric and loop the thread tails around the pins at either end. Even the gathers between the two pins. Pin the gathers in place. Baste the seam. Stitch the seam.

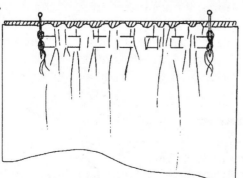

Trimming and Clipping Seams

After stitching a seam, seam allowances are trimmed and clipped for a number of reasons. For clothing, trimming with pinking shears will reduce the bulk of the seam and, in some fabrics, prevent ravelling of the raw edges. For both clothing and bears, clipping into the seam allowances of convex (outward) curves permits the edges to spread when the item is turned right side out. Notching the seam allowances on concave (inward) curves allows the edges to draw in when the item is turned right side out. Trimming across corners insures a smooth, finished seam and square, crisp corners.

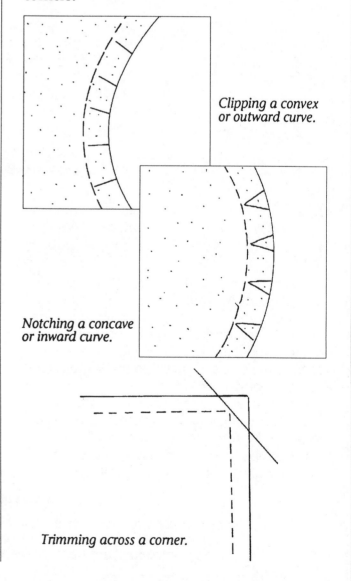

Clipping a convex or outward curve.

Notching a concave or inward curve.

Trimming across a corner.

Elastic Casings

The casing is a tunnel of turned-under fabric enclosing flat elastic which is stretched to fit snugly around the body.

To make an elastic casing, the raw edge of the garment is pressed under $1/4$ inch. Then the edge is turned and pressed under again to the desired amount. The lower edge of the casing is then machine-stitched in place, leaving a $1/2$-inch wide opening for threading the elastic. Machine-stitch a second row of stitching close to the top fold.

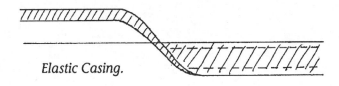

Elastic Casing.

Cut a length of elastic as indicated in the instructions for the garment. Attach a safety pin to one end of the elastic, push it into the casing and work it through the casing, being careful not to twist the elastic.

Safety pin the two ends of the elastic together, overlapping them $1/2$ inch. Try the garment on the bear. Adjust the elastic if necessary. Your bear's measurements may vary according to how you stuff him, so it is best to double check the fit. Machine-stitch the ends of the elastic together, back and forth to secure them. Pull the elastic into the casing. Stitch the opening closed, being careful not to catch the elastic in the stitching.

STITCH DICTIONARY

Basting Stitch

This long—$1/4$" by hand or longest possible by machine—temporary stitch is used for marking and for stitching two pieces of fabric to make sure they fit properly before the final stitching.

Running Stitch

This stitch is similar to the basting stitch, though it is a shorter, even stitch for fine, permanent seaming.

Topstitch

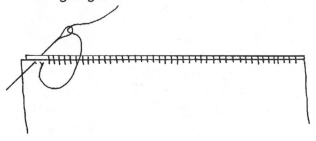

Longer than a regular sewing stitch, the topstitch is sewn onto the right side of the finished item. It is used decoratively as well as functionally to secure casings, zippers, facings, and more.

Overhand or Whipstitch

This stitch is used to join two finished edges, as when closing the turned under edges of the ear. We will also use this stitch for our felt projects in chapter 5 since felt has a non-ravelling edge.

Satin Stitch

This is an embroidery stitch consisting of long stitches placed next to one another so that the desired area is filled with parallel stitches of embroidery floss which touch one another, hiding the fabric beneath.

Backstitch

A very strong stitch, the backstitch is made by inserting the needle just behind the point where the thread comes out of the fabric from the preceding stitch. You will use this stitch in constructing the bears, in which case you will insert your needle $1/16$ of an inch behind the emerging thread.

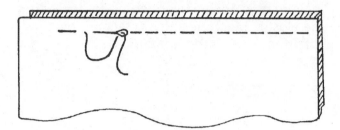

FUR FABRICS

Fur Fabrics

The fur you choose for your teddy has a lot to do with determining his personality and the quality of the finished product. Considering all the time, love, and care someone will give this new friend, it is wise to choose the best material possible for constructing your bear. There are two general types of fur available today: the natural fiber furs such as mohair, wool, and alpaca, and the synthetic furs.

Mohair, the traditional fur, is found on many old bears and is the choice of many teddy bear artists today. With its firm, woven backing and dense pile, this smooth, shiny fur is quite durable and is always an excellent choice.

Wool and *alpaca furs* share the dense pile and firm backing of the mohair but have their own special qualities which are attracting the attention of many bearmakers.

Synthetics offer a wide range of colors, textures, and pile lengths. Less expensive than the natural fiber furs by a factor of as much as ten, these fabrics have the added advantage for the beginning bearmaker of being easier to work with than the natural fabrics which are more difficult to coax into the shape you desire. Therefore, a synthetic fabric is a good choice for your first bear. In fact, the quality of the synthetics is so high that you may never venture out of the many choices available to you with this wonderful man-made fabric. There are two types of backings used in making synthetic fabrics. The furs made with woven backings don't "give" as much as those with knit backings and are therefore suitable for patterns designed for mohair. The fabrics made with knit backings are well-suited to soft-stuffed bears, producing a soft, huggable bear with a wonderfully rounded tummy.

Whatever your choice, all of these furs come in an array of colors, from the many browns and tans to pink and red. And when considering fur color remember to be creative in your choice of embroidery floss or pearl cotton for your bear's nose and mouth. How about a gray or white bear with a pink or mauve nose? Or a black bear with a brown nose?

Bears can also be made of many commonly available fabrics. The Patchwork Bear in this book was made from scraps left over from the two wall quilts and the bear pillow I made for the bedroom. Velveteen or velvet is perfect for tiny bears. Wool and corduroy are old favorites, especially for homemade-looking bears.

Be creative in your choice of fabrics— upholstery fabric launched one bear artist's career!

Cutting Out the Fur

Stroke the fur to find the *nap* or the direction in which the fur wants to lay naturally. This is just like stroking your dog. You know when you go against the grain of the fur.

Lay the fur right side down with the nap of the fur running toward you so that if you were to stroke the fur from the top to the bottom you would be stroking with the fur. Arrange the pattern pieces on the wrong side of the fabric, making sure that the arrows on the pattern pieces indicating the nap are pointing down in the direction of the nap. Count all the pattern pieces to be sure that you have included all of them. Be sure that you have both left and right arm, leg, body, and head pieces.

Trace around the pattern pieces with a felt tip pen. Check to be sure that the ink is not bleeding through to the fur side of the fabric. Mark all darts and dots, and eye, ear, and joint placements.

Double check to be sure that you have included all of the pattern pieces and that the nap of each piece is running in the correct direction. Carefully cut out the pattern pieces. With short strokes, cut through the backing only, sliding the tip of the scissors close to the backing as you go. In this way you will avoid cutting the actual fur itself, but will cut the backing only.

Marking

After you cut out the fabric pieces, transfer the markings from the patterns to the fabric. Cut a small hole through the pattern where a dot or an X appears, and make a mark with your felt tip pen through this dot onto the backing of the fur fabric. Make a series of holes in the pattern where the darts are, and connect your penned dots to form guidelines for sewing the darts. To see the X's on the right side of the fabric for joint, eye, and ear placement, make tailor's tacks. (With a long length of double unknotted thread, push the needle through the fabric from the right to the wrong side and back up through the fabric to the right side again, leaving about an inch of thread tails.)

PAW & FOOT PADS

Suede, felt, short-pile fur, and velvet are all suitable choices for paw pads and soles. If felt is your choice, a heavy wool felt is recommended. If you choose velvet, interfacing the paw and foot pads is recommended. You may also choose to make the pads out of the same fur you used for the rest of the bear, as for the Pookie Bear.

STUFFING

Good quality, polyester fiberfill is recommended for stuffing your bear. Choose a brand which is fluffy and of even consistency. A perfectly stuffed bear will have no lumps or hard bulges, will stand evenly, and will have no hollow areas.

Jointed bears are stuffed firmly, almost hard to the touch rather than huggable like the soft-stuffed bears. Stuff irregular areas such as the nose first. When stuffing arms and legs start by pushing a handful of stuffing into the feet or paws. Using the handle end of a wooden spoon or a tool made just for this purpose, pack the stuffing hard. Continue adding stuffing and packing it, checking for lumps and molding the body parts, especially the head, as you go. Make sure that seams lie flat and straight, and that rounded seamlines are smooth and even. Stuffing should not be rushed. Stuff the entire bear, pin the openings of the various body parts closed, and study the bear to be sure that he or she is evenly stuffed with no bumps, that the seams are flat, and that he or she is symmetrical. Slipstitch the seams closed.

Since they are meant to be soft and huggable, the non-jointed bears are stuffed a little less firmly than the jointed bears. Stuff the head, arms, and legs first, making sure you are happy with them before you stuff the body. Pin the back opening closed and squeeze your bear to be certain that he or she has the feel you desire. Stitch the back opening closed.

EYES, NOSE, & MOUTH

While the bear patterns in this book all have eye, ear, nose, and mouth placements marked on them, the bearmaker may wish to create his or her own bear personality by varying the position of these features, size of the eyes, or slant of the mouth.

Eyes

Together with the nose and mouth, a bear's eyes determine his or her character. Both the placement of the eyes on the face and the choice of eye materials provide many variables for your bear's expression.

The eyes are usually placed at the curve or bridge of the nose along the side head/gusset seamline. By positioning the eyes closer or farther away from the nose, or above or below the side head/gusset seamline, you will find your bear's expression changing from sweet and innocent to sad and even comical.

If you are making the bear for a child, plastic safety eyes are the only choice. Widely available and simple to install, these eyes are secured to the wrong side of the fur with a washer which cannot be pulled out by a child. These eyes are installed before the head is stuffed. Black or amber are always good choices, and other colors are available.

Many old bears have black glass shoe buttons for eyes. These can still be found and may be just the thing for a special bear. Glass eyes are a perfectly appropriate substitute.

Always an excellent choice, glass eyes have sparkle to them, giving a bear that lively look. Many sizes and colors are available. They may arrive prelooped or on a straight wire, one eye on each end. In the latter case, you must cut the wire with wire cutters to about 3/4" from the eye. Using needle-nose pliers, bend the wire into a small double circle close to the back of the eye.

These eyes are installed after the head is stuffed, but before it is attached to the body. Using small, pointed scissors, cut a hole at the eye mark. Double-thread a long needle with heavy-duty thread. Push the needle through the head at the base of the neck. Come up through the eye hole. Pull the needle up out of the head. Thread the shank of the eye onto the needle. Push the needle into the hole, through the head, and out through the base of the neck. Pull on the thread to seat the eye firmly and flatly against the head. Using an awl or knitting needle, stretch the hole for the eye if it doesn't want to fit. Pull tightly on the thread again and make a few stitches in the fabric at the base of the neck to secure.

Nose and Mouth

Clip the fur where the nose is to go so that stray hairs won't poke through your stitching. Cut a piece of felt according to the nose pattern, the same color as your embroidery floss. Glue the felt in place.

Thread a length of embroidery thread or pearl cotton on a tapestry needle. Make a knot in one end of the thread. Push the needle into the middle of the nose and bring it up at a top corner. Pull up on the thread so that the knot is snug. Push the needle back into the fabric at the bottom corner below the point where you just came up.

Continue working across the nose area using satin stitches. When you reach the other side, take your final stitch, coming up at just under the center of the bottom of the nose. Push the needle into the fabric at one of the marks indicating the corner of the mouth. Bring the needle out of the fabric on the seamline at the mark so that it runs between the yarn and the first corner of the mouth.

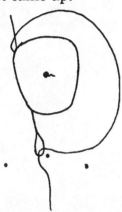

Push the needle back into the fabric at the other corner of the mouth and out through the center of the nose.

Fasten the thread with tiny stitches under the embroidery on the nose. Clip the thread close to the fabric.

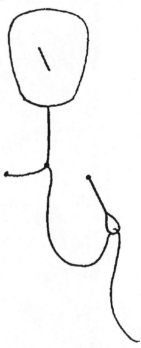

Ears

To give your bear's ears have an indentation in the front, push a pin into one side of the bottom edge of the ear, one quarter of the way from the outside edge of the ear, and out one quarter of the way from the other bottom outside of the ear. This will have the effect of bending the ear towards the front so that the inside of the ear is concave. After stitching the ear in place, remove the pin.

C H A P T E R • 2

MEET THE BEARS

Here they are, from the soft and cuddly 19"
soft-stuffed bear to the demure 5½" pocket
bear, this bevy of bears includes individuals
to suit every taste.

There are two basic types of construction
of teddy bears: non-jointed and jointed.
Simply put, crown joints are the devices
which allow your bear to turn his head, lift
his arms, sit, and stand. They are composed
of two hardboard disks, two washers, and
either a cotter pin or a bolt and nut. While
the cotter pin is the more common of the
two, tightening the nut and bolt is much
easier on the hands.

Take your time when installing joints.
Check for tightness by shaking hands (or leg)
with the bear. The joint should be quite tight
since it will loosen with time. A wobbly
jointed bear will have difficulty sitting and
holding up its arms. Jointed bears are usually
more firmly stuffed than non-jointed bears,
the latter, therefore, being more suitable for
snugly bears for children.

NON–JOINTED BEARS

These soft, cuddly friends are designed to wear the clothes in the next two chapters. Synthetic fur with knit backing gives these bears their plump look and their squeezeable softness. Made with safety eyes, these bears are perfect for children.

16" NON–JOINTED BEAR

MATERIALS

¹/₃ yard synthetic fur

Matching thread

Heavy duty thread

Two 14-mm eyes

Embroidery floss

18" NON–JOINTED BEAR

MATERIALS

¹/₂ yard synthetic fur

Matching thread

Heavy duty thread

Two 18-mm eyes

Embroidery floss

GENERAL INSTRUCTIONS FOR NON–JOINTED BEARS

Note: All seam allowances are ¹/₄" unless otherwise indicated.

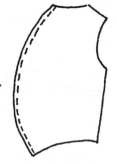

1. Cut the patterns per instructions in chapter 1.

2. Pin the two fronts together along the center front seam, right sides together. Stitch.

3. Pin the two backs together along the center back seam, right sides together. Stitch from the top to the first dot, backstitching at both ends to secure. Stitch from the second dot to the bottom, backstitching at both ends to secure.

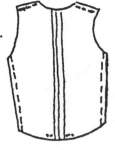

4. Pin front to back, right sides together, matching front left side to back left side and front right side to back right side. Stitch side seams and shoulder seams.

5. Matching the bottom edges and the center front to the center back seam, stitch between the dots on the bottom body opening.

6. Pin paw pad to inner arm, right sides together. Stitch. Open out the paw pad and pin the seam allowances open so they will lie flat.

7. Pin the arms to the inner arms, right sides together, with the paw pads open. Stitch, starting at one dot, all the way around the paw and ending at the other dot, leaving an opening for attaching the arm to the body. Turn the arms right side out.

8. With right sides facing, pin the legs together. Stitch from the top of the front of the leg, down the leg, around the toes, ending at the bottom of the foot. Stitch from the top of the back of the leg down to the bottom of the back of the foot.

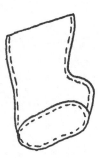

9. Pin the foot pads to the bottom of the foot, right sides together, matching the large dot to the front leg seam and the small dot to the back leg seam. Stitch. Turn the foot right-side out.

10. Make darts in the two head pieces. Pin the two head pieces, right sides together, from the nose to the neck opening. Stitch from the dot at the nose, under the chin to the neck opening.

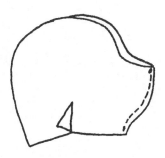

11. Pin the dot on the gusset to the dot on the seam where the two head pieces meet. Pin the neck opening edges together. Pin between these points, easing the gusset to fit as you go. Stitch.

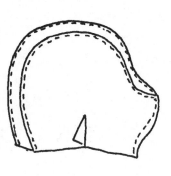

12. With the body inside out and the legs right side out, pin the legs to the leg holes. Be sure that the toes are facing the front. Match the dots to the outside and inside seams. Stitch. You may wish to baste or handstitch first, especially when making the small bear, to facilitate easier and more accurate machine stitching.

13. With the arms turned right side out, pin the arms to the body matching the dot at the top of the arm with the shoulder seam and the dot on the curve of the inner arm with the body side seam. Make sure that the arms are facing the front of the body. Stitch, easing the top of the arm.

14. With the head turned right side out, pin the head to the body, matching the center front seams of the head and body, the darts to the side seam, and the dot at the middle of the gusset to the center back seam of the body. Stitch.

15. Pin and sew the rounded part of the ears, right sides together, leaving the bottom edges open. Clip the curves. Turn. Turn the bottom edges under 1/4" and handstitch closed.

16. Turn the bear right side out. Install the eyes and ears as described in chapter 1. Stuff and close the back opening of the bear, and embroider the nose and mouth as instructed in chapter 1.

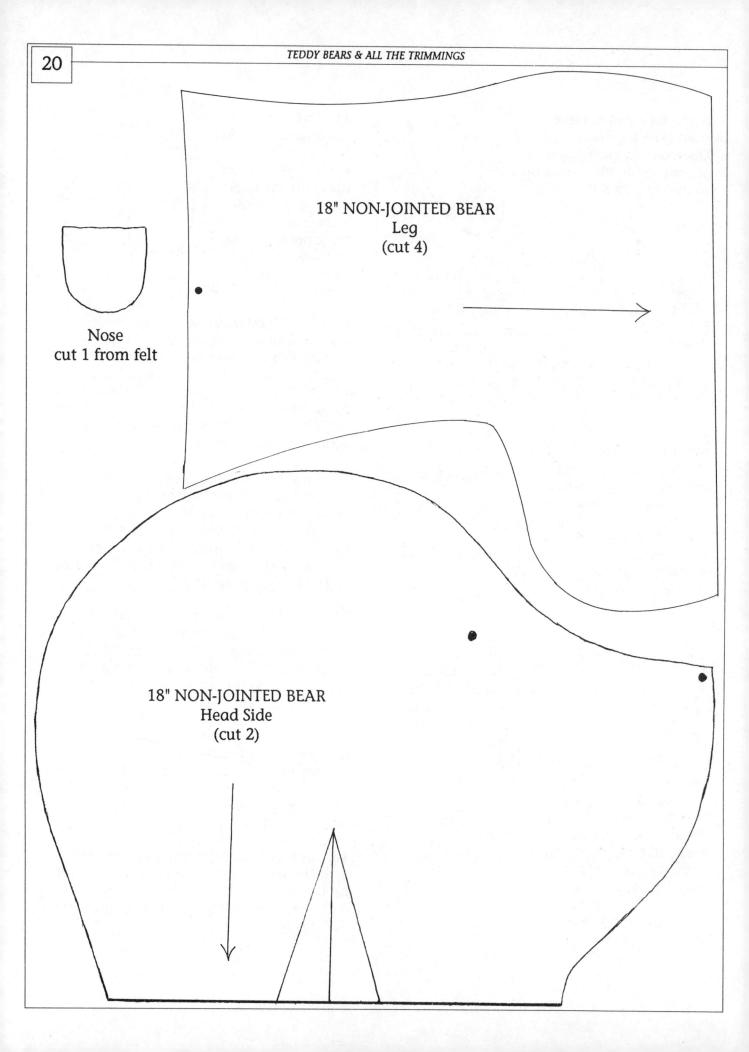

Nose
cut 1 from felt

18" NON-JOINTED BEAR
Leg
(cut 4)

18" NON-JOINTED BEAR
Head Side
(cut 2)

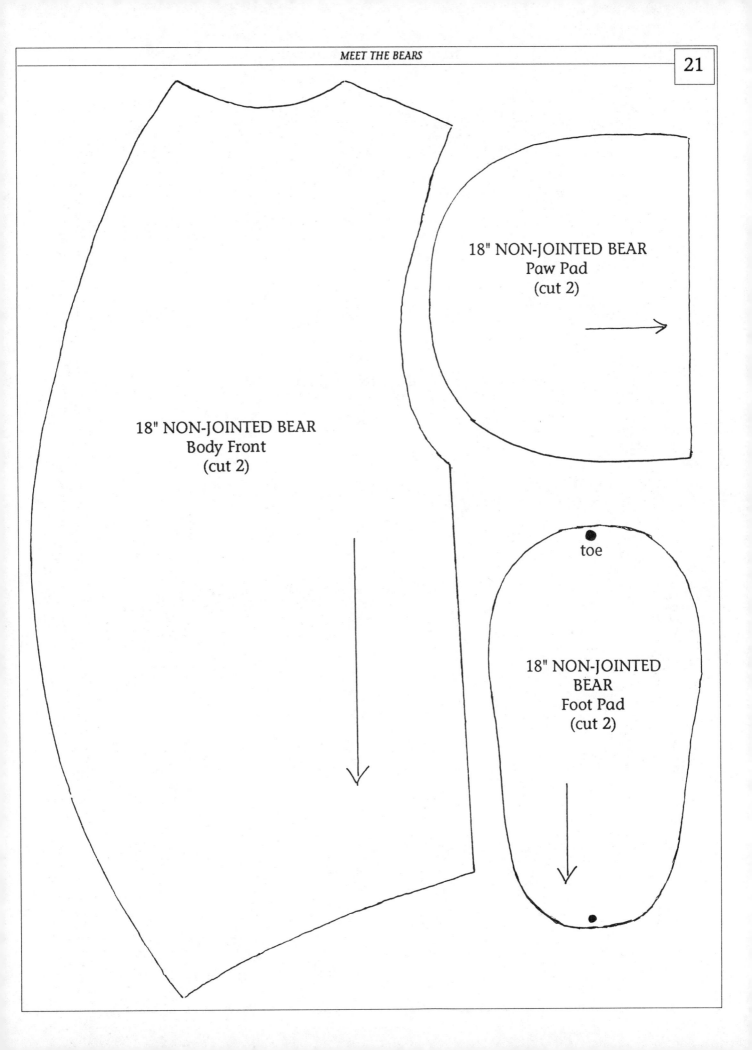

18" NON-JOINTED BEAR
Paw Pad
(cut 2)

18" NON-JOINTED BEAR
Body Front
(cut 2)

toe

18" NON-JOINTED
BEAR
Foot Pad
(cut 2)

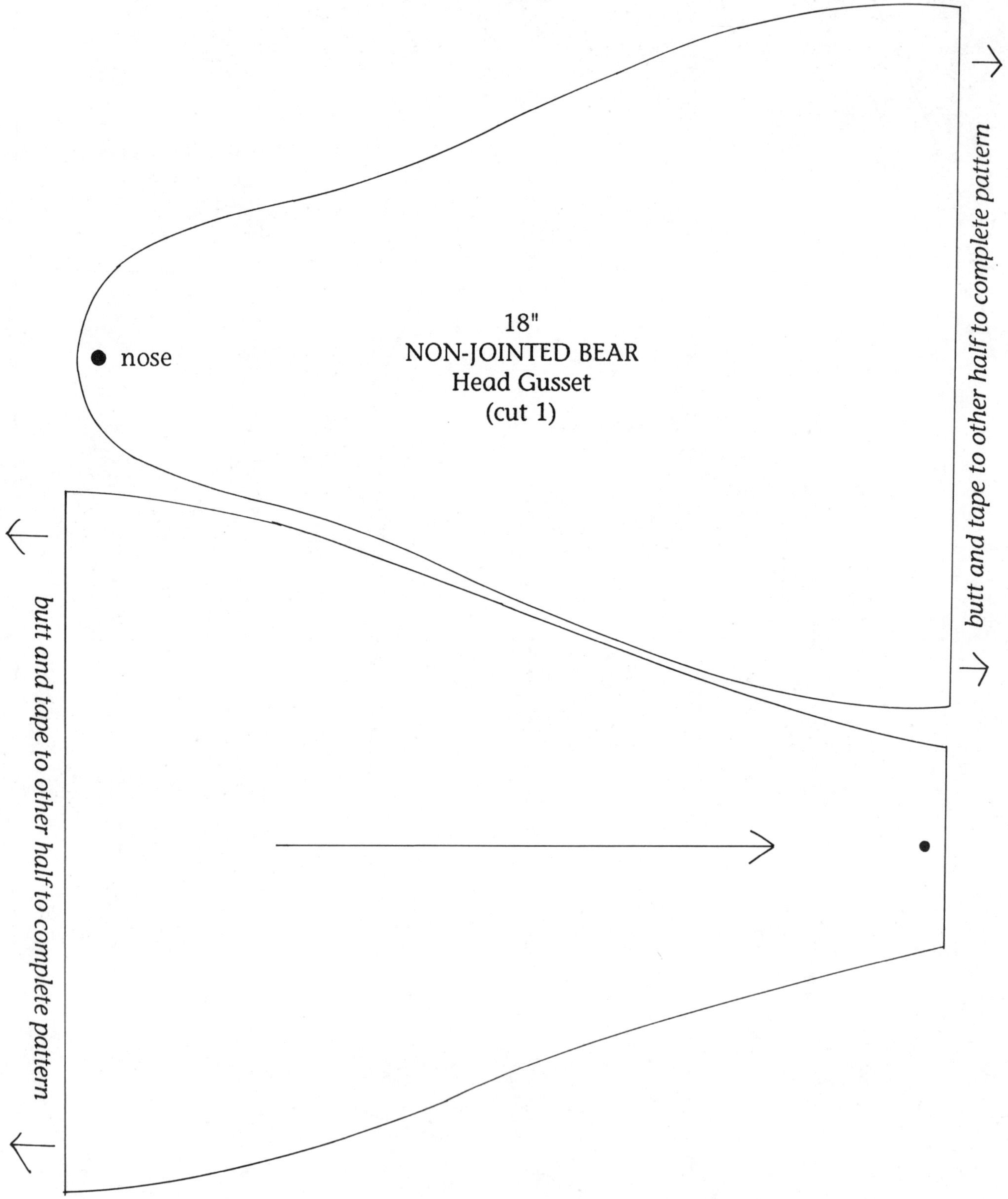

● nose

18"
NON-JOINTED BEAR
Head Gusset
(cut 1)

butt and tape to other half to complete pattern

butt and tape to other half to complete pattern

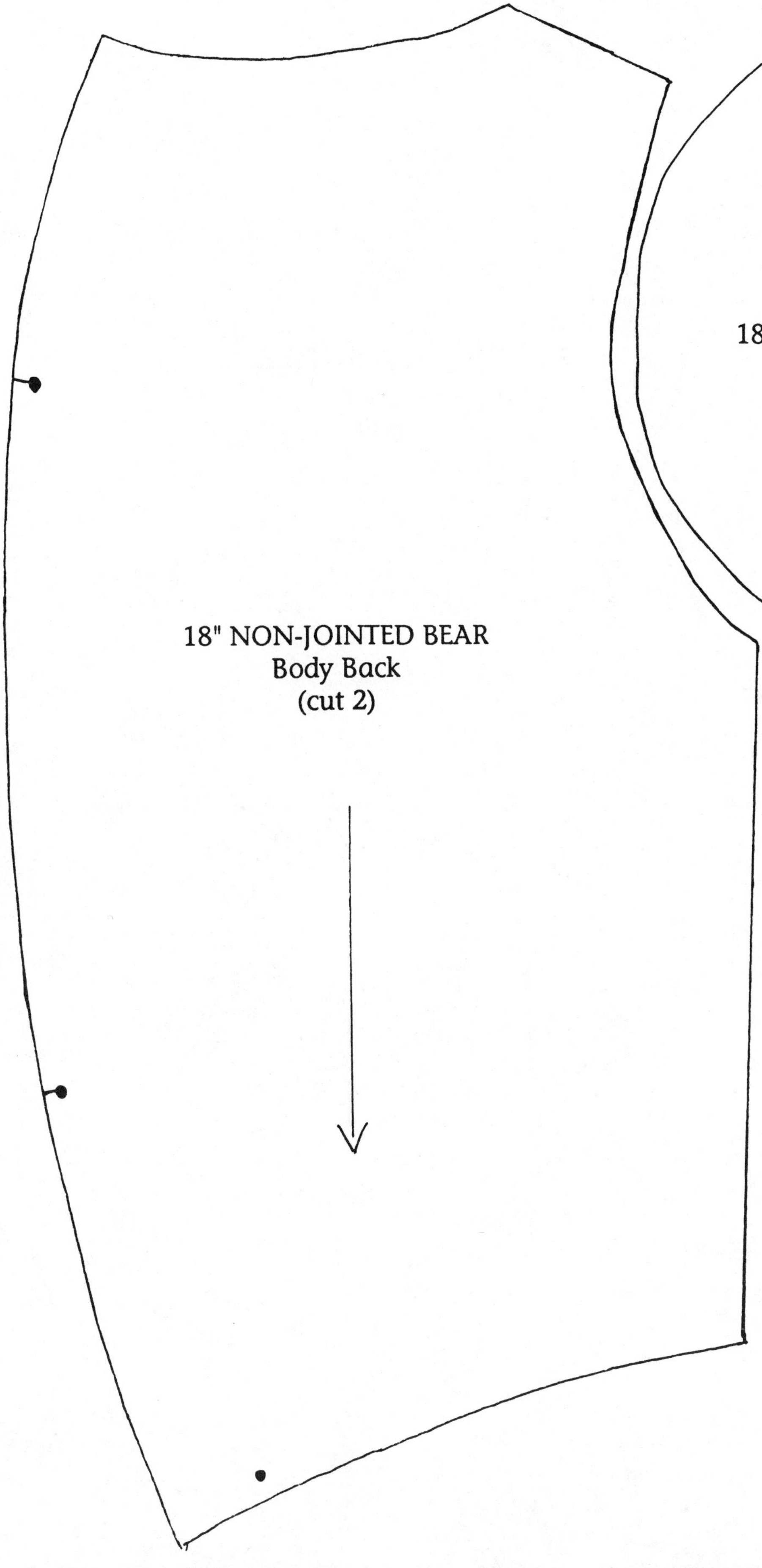

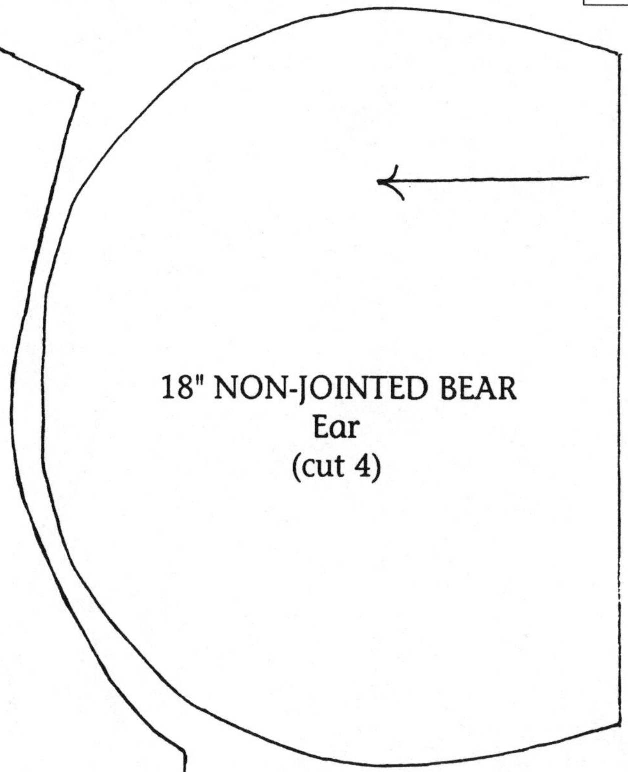

18" NON-JOINTED BEAR
Ear
(cut 4)

18" NON-JOINTED BEAR
Body Back
(cut 2)

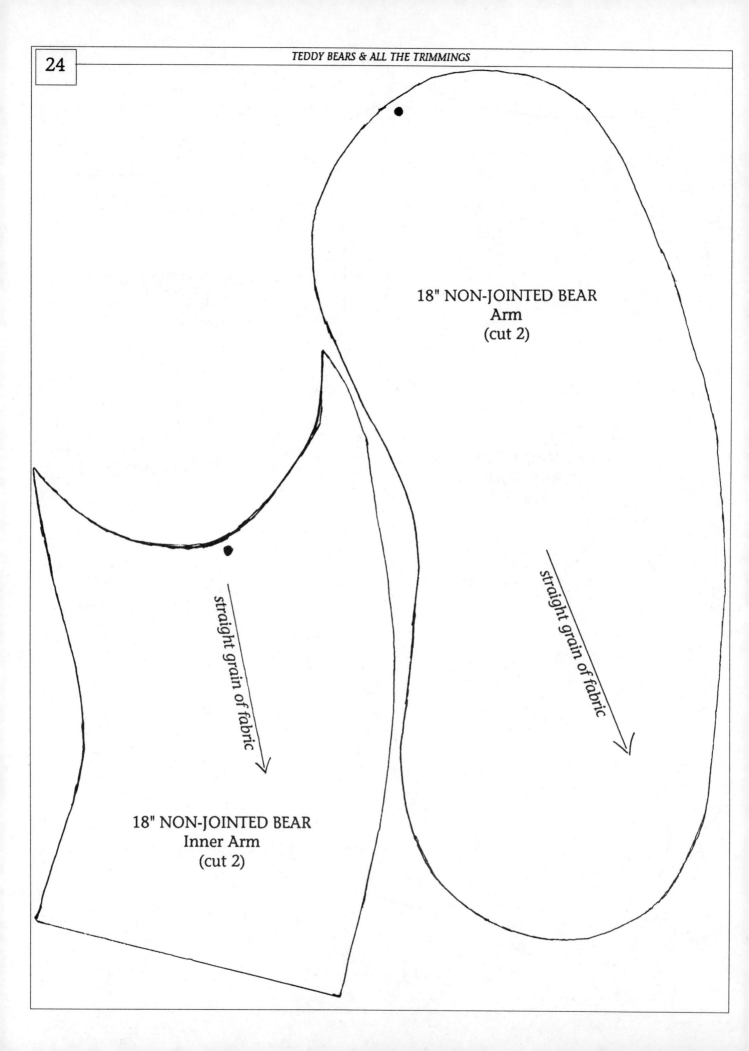

18" NON-JOINTED BEAR
Arm
(cut 2)

straight grain of fabric

straight grain of fabric

18" NON-JOINTED BEAR
Inner Arm
(cut 2)

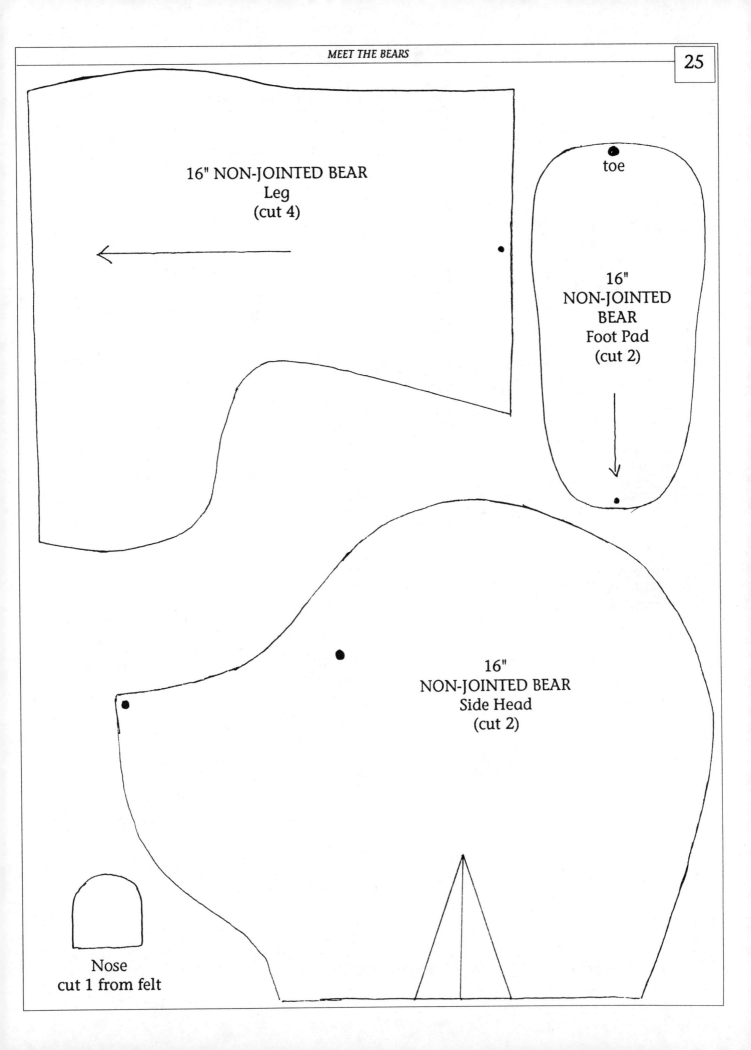

16" NON-JOINTED BEAR
Leg
(cut 4)

toe

**16"
NON-JOINTED
BEAR**
Foot Pad
(cut 2)

**16"
NON-JOINTED BEAR**
Side Head
(cut 2)

Nose
cut 1 from felt

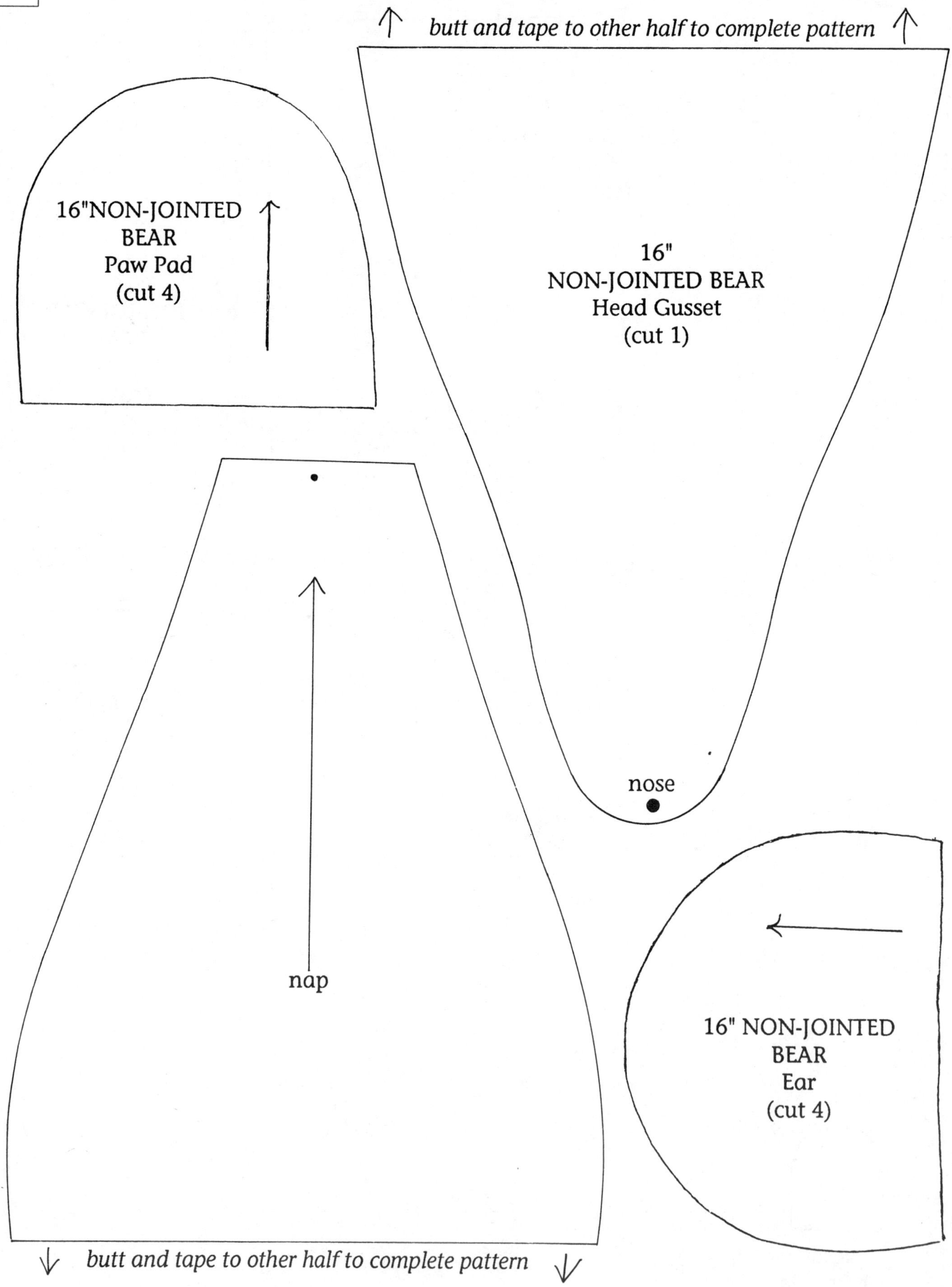

butt and tape to other half to complete pattern

16"NON-JOINTED
BEAR
Paw Pad
(cut 4)

16"
NON-JOINTED BEAR
Head Gusset
(cut 1)

nose

nap

16" NON-JOINTED
BEAR
Ear
(cut 4)

butt and tape to other half to complete pattern

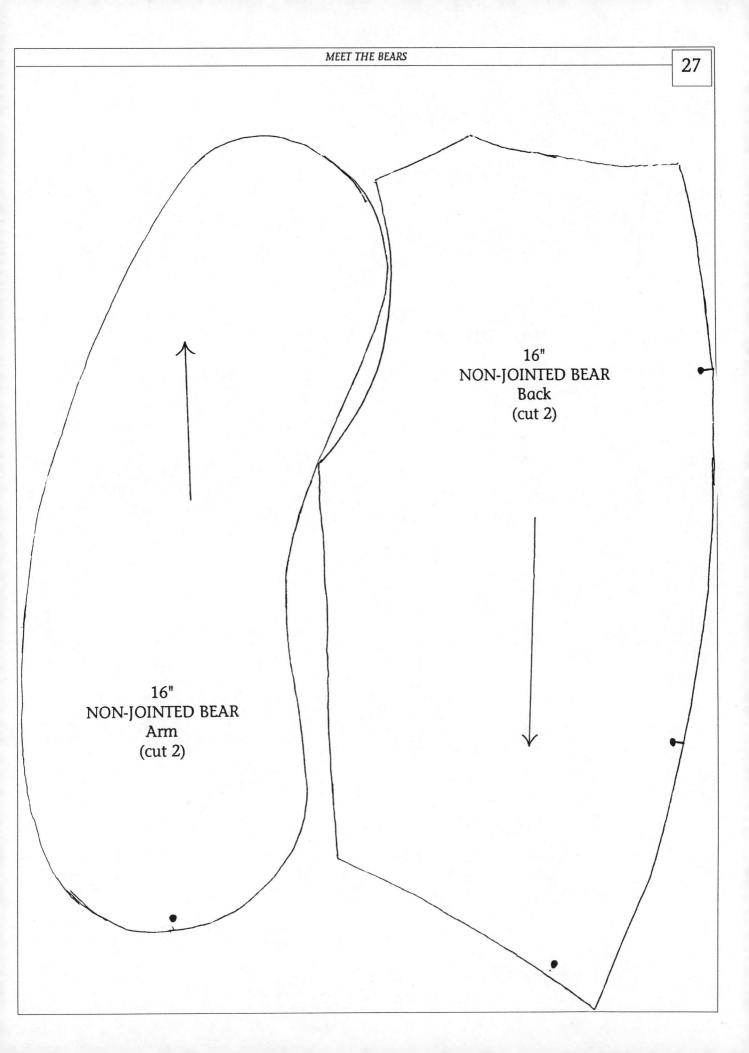

16"
NON-JOINTED BEAR
Back
(cut 2)

16"
NON-JOINTED BEAR
Arm
(cut 2)

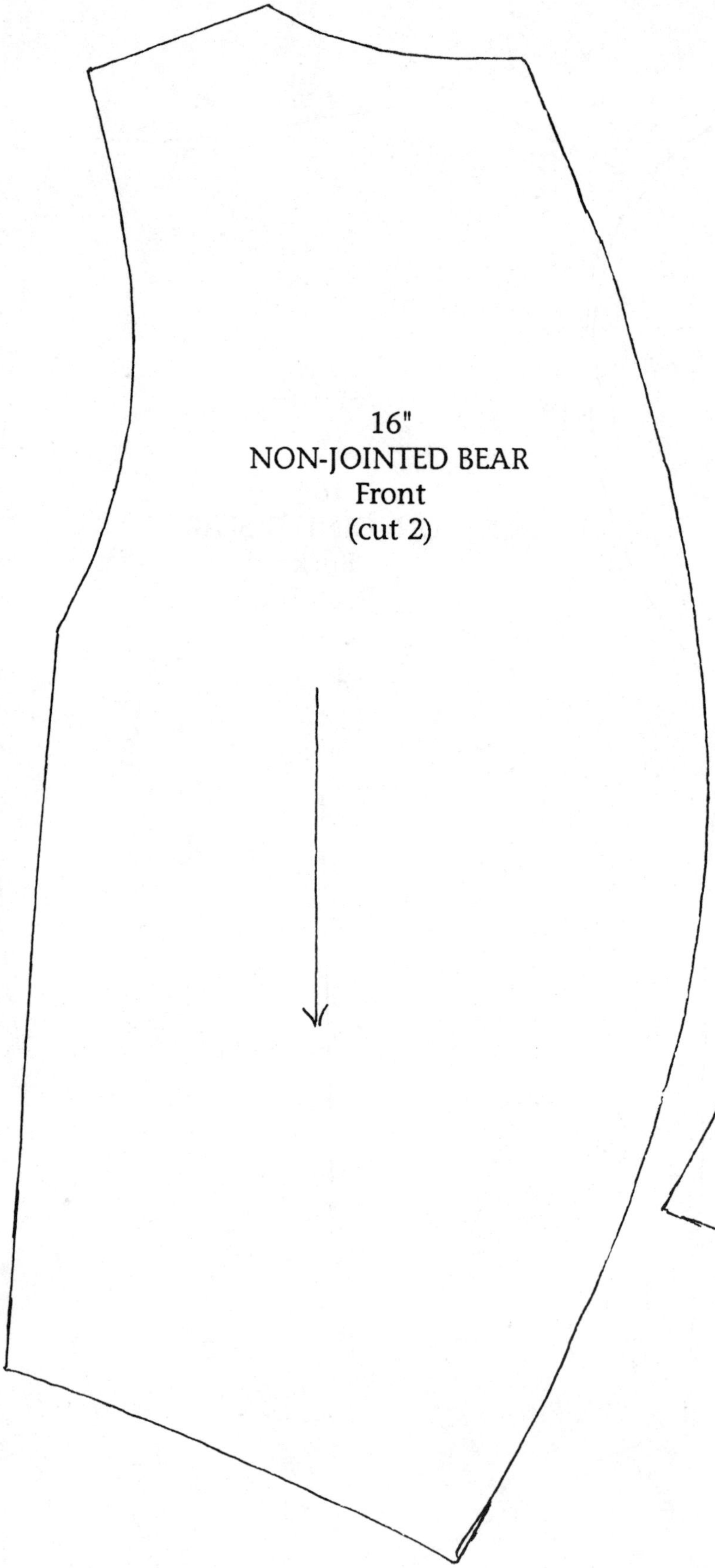

16"
NON-JOINTED BEAR
Front
(cut 2)

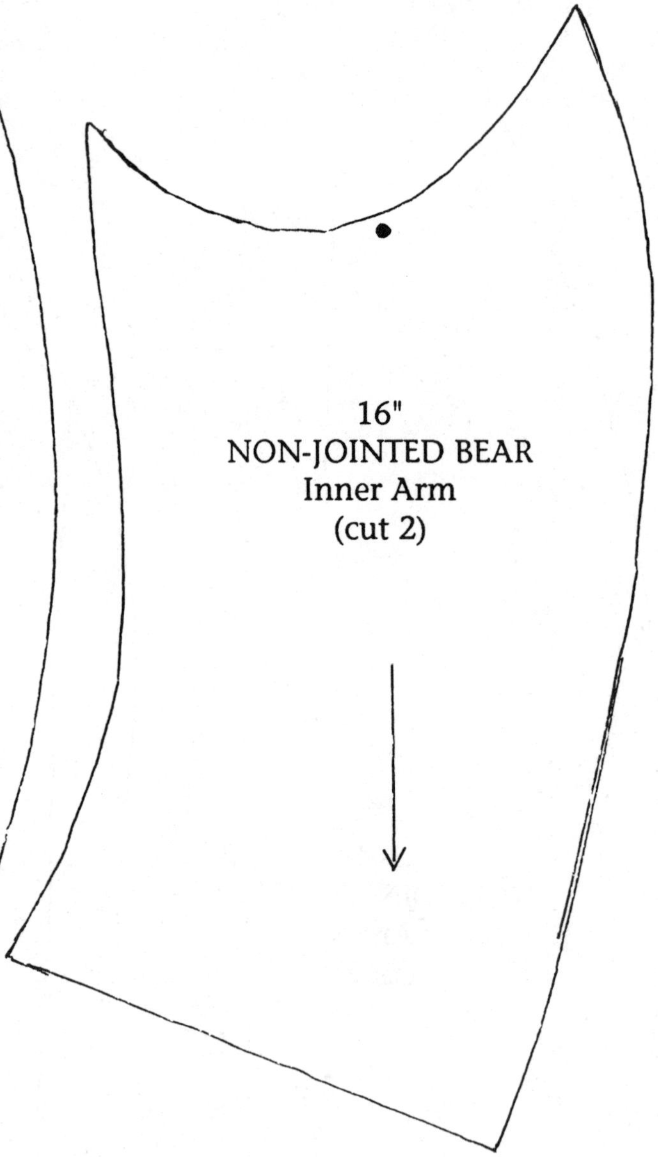

16"
NON-JOINTED BEAR
Inner Arm
(cut 2)

17" JOINTED MOHAIR BEAR

Made of mohair, wool, alpaca, or a woven-backed synthetic, this bear, with his classic look and traditional hump, is sure to be a hit.

MATERIALS

$^1/_2$ yard of mohair, wool, alpaca, or woven-backed synthetic fur

Matching thread

Heavy duty thread

Polyester fiberfill

Five 2$^1/_2$" joint sets

Pair of 14-mm eyes

Embroidery floss

8" x 8" piece of fabric, felt, or suede for paw and foot pads

INSTRUCTIONS

Note: All seam allowances are $^1/_4$" unless otherwise indicated.

1. Cut pattern per instructions in chapter 1.

2. Pin the two body fronts together along the center front. Stitch.

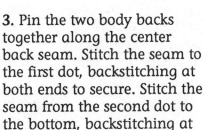

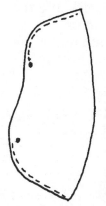

3. Pin the two body backs together along the center back seam. Stitch the seam to the first dot, backstitching at both ends to secure. Stitch the seam from the second dot to the bottom, backstitching at both ends to secure. The gap left in the stitching between the two dots will provide access to the body cavity for jointing and stuffing the bear.

4. Pin the body sides together, matching front left side to back left side and front right side to back right side. Stitch between the dots, backstitching at both ends. This small gap will allow room for a cotter pin or bolt for the neck joint. Turn body right side out.

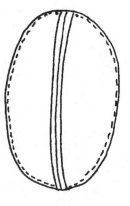

5. Pin paw pad to inner arm, right sides together. Stitch. Open out the paw pad and pin the seam allowances open so they will lie flat.

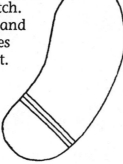

6. Pin the arms to the inner arms, right sides together, with the paw pads opened. Stitch between the dots, all the way around the paw. Turn the arms right side out.

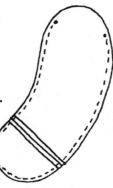

7. With right sides facing, pin the legs together. Stitch from the dot at the front of the thigh down the leg, around the toes, ending at the bottom of the foot. Stitch from the dot at the back of the thigh down to the bottom of the back of the foot. Clip curves.

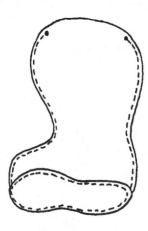

8. Pin the foot pads to the bottom of the foot, right sides together, matching the large dot to the front leg seam and the small dot to the back leg seam. Stitch. Turn the foot right side out.

9. Pin the two side head pieces, right sides together, from the nose to the base of the neck. Stitch from the dot at the nose under the chin to the base of the neck.

10. Pin the dot on the gusset to the seam where the two head pieces meet at the tip of the nose. Pin from the tip of the nose to the base of the neck at the back of the head, easing the gusset to fit as you go. Stitch. Repeat for the other side. Turn right side out. Stuff the head lightly.

11. Attach the eyes to the head as instructed in the general bearmaking instructions at the beginning of chapter 1.

12. Restuff the head firmly, beginning at the nose. Using a long running stitch and heavy duty thread, stitch along the neck opening. Insert a cotter pin and a washer or a bolt through a joint disk. Insert the disk into the head opening with the cotter pin or the threaded end of the bolt pointing out of the bottom of the head. Pull up the thread to tighten the neck opening around the joint post. Sew around the neck opening a few times, tightening up on the thread as you go, to secure the fabric around the disk.

13. Pin and sew the rounded part of the ears, right sides together, leaving the bottom edges open. Clip the curves. Turn. Turn the bottom edges under ¹/₄" and handstitch closed.

14. With small scissors or an awl make holes for the joints in the arms, legs, and body as marked. Make sure you have a right and a left arm and leg. Put a washer and then a hardboard disk on a cotter pin or bolt. Insert the cotter pins or bolts through the holes you made for them in the arms and legs so that the post is sticking out.

An inside look at a finished bear arm.

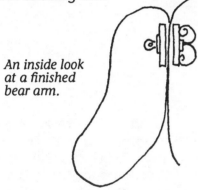

15. To join the bear, begin with the head. Push the pin or bolt through the small gap in the stitching at the top of the body. Slip another disk over the pin or bolt, and then a washer. Bend the cotter pin as shown or tighten the bolt. Check to be sure that the disks are seated properly and that no fabric is caught between them.

16. Install the arms and legs to the body as you did the head, inserting the cotter pins or bolts through the holes on the body that you made for them with the awl. Double check the direction of the limbs— taking apart a completed bear is no fun!

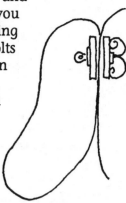

17. Stuff the arms and legs tightly. Turn under ¹/₄" at the top openings and sew them closed so that no raw edges show.

18. Decide where you want the ears. Pin them in place. Whipstitch.

19. Stitch the nose and mouth as instructed in the general bearmaking section at the beginning of chapter 1.

20. With a seam ripper or other pointed object, pick out any fur caught in the seams.

17" PATCHWORK BEAR

Whether you choose calico fabrics to match a quilt or an entire bedroom, or the traditional shiny silks and rich velvets of the Victorian crazy quilts, your Patchwork Bear will be the ultimate expression of the bearmaker's art as you will make not only the bear, but the fabric, too!

MATERIALS

Fabric scraps

8" x 8" scrap of corduroy for paw and foot pads

$1/3$ yard muslin

Quilt or craft batting

Polyester fiberfill

Two 14-mm eyes

Embroidery floss

Five $2^1/2$" joint sets

INSTRUCTIONS

Note: All seam allowances are $1/4$" unless otherwise indicated.

1. Prepare the pattern pieces as instructed in chapter 1. Lay the pattern pieces on the muslin. Trace around the shapes. Cut out.

2. Using the muslin pieces as a guide, cut batting to fit each piece, excluding paw and foot pads.

3. Piece calico (or silk, or velvet) over the muslin pieces as illustrated, sandwiching the batting between the muslin and the calico.

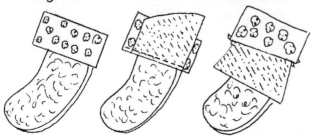

4. Baste all around the pieces, $1/4$" from raw edges, through all layers.

5. Pin the two body fronts together along the center front seam. Stitch.

6. Pin the two body backs together along the center back seam. Stitch the seam to the first dot, backstitching at both ends to secure. Stitch the seam from the second dot to the bottom, backstitching at both ends to secure. The gap left in the stitching between the two dots will provide access to the body cavity for jointing and stuffing the bear.

7. Pin the body sides together, matching front left side to back left side and front right side to back right side. Stitch between the dots, backstitching at both ends. This small gap will allow room for a cotter pin or bolt for the neck joint. Turn body right side out.

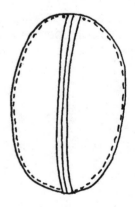

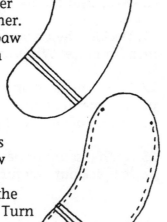

8. Pin paw pad to inner arm, right sides together. Stitch. Open out the paw pad and pin the seam allowances open so they will lie flat.

9. Pin the arms to the inner arms, right sides together, with the paw pads opened. Stitch between the dots, all the way around the paw. Turn the arms right side out.

10. With right sides facing, pin the legs together. Stitch from the dot at the front of the thigh down the leg, around the toes, ending at the bottom of the foot. Stitch from the dot at the back of the thigh down to the bottom of the back of the foot. Clip curves.

11. Pin the foot pads to the bottom of the foot, right sides together, matching the large dot to the front leg seam and the small dot to the back leg seam. Stitch. Turn the foot right side out.

12. Pin the two side head pieces, right sides together, from the nose to the base of the neck. Stitch from the dot at the nose under the chin to the base of the neck.

13. Pin the dot on the gusset to the seam where the two head pieces meet at the tip of the nose. Pin from the tip of the nose to the base of the neck at the back of the head, easing the gusset to fit as you go. Stitch. Repeat for the other side. Turn right side out. Stuff the head lightly.

14. Attach the eyes to the head as instructed in the general bearmaking instructions at the beginning of chapter 1.

15. Restuff the head firmly, beginning at the nose. Using a long running stitch and heavy duty thread, stitch along the neck opening. Insert a cotter pin and a washer or a bolt through a joint disk. Insert the disk into the head opening with the cotter pin or the threaded end of the bolt pointing out of the bottom of the head. Pull up the thread to tighten the neck opening around the joint post. Sew around the neck opening a few times, tightening up on the thread as you go, to secure the fabric around the disk.

16. Pin and sew the rounded part of the ears, right sides together, leaving the bottom edges open. Clip the curves. Turn. Turn the bottom edges under 1/4" and handstitch closed.

17. With small scissors or an awl make holes for the joints in the arms, legs, and body as marked. Make sure you have a right and a left arm and leg. Put a washer and then a hardboard disk on a cotter pin or bolt. Insert the cotter pins or bolts through the holes you made for them in the arms and legs so that the post is sticking out.

18. To join the bear, begin with the head. Push the pin or bolt through the small gap in the stitching at the top of the body. Slip another disk over the pin or bolt, and then a washer. Bend the cotter pin as shown or tighten the bolt. Check to be sure that the disks are seated properly and that no fabric is caught between them.

19. Install the arms and legs to the body as you did the head, inserting the cotter pins or bolts through the holes on the body that you made for them with the awl. Double check the directions of the limbs; taking apart a completed bear is no fun.

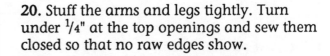

20. Stuff the arms and legs tightly. Turn under 1/4" at the top openings and sew them closed so that no raw edges show.

21. Decide where you want the ears. Pin them in place. Whipstitch.

22. Stitch the nose and mouth as instructed in the general bearmaking section at the beginning of chapter 1.

23. With a seam ripper or other pointed object, pick out any fur caught in the seams.

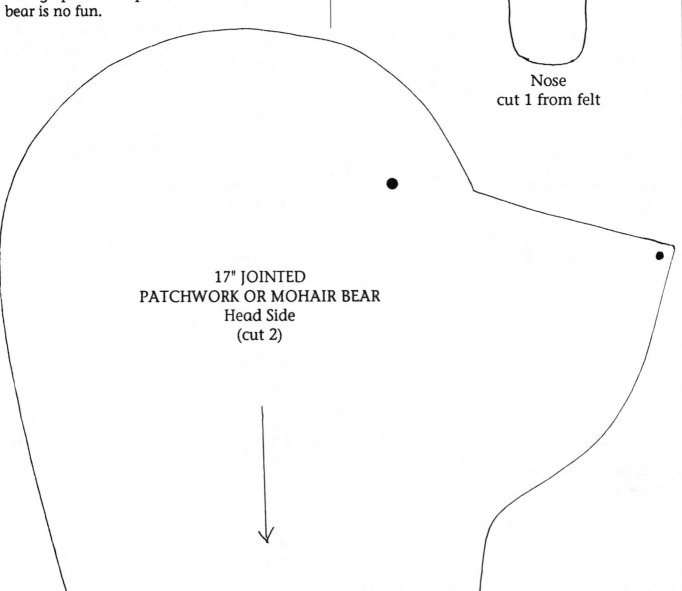

Nose
cut 1 from felt

17" JOINTED
PATCHWORK OR MOHAIR BEAR
Head Side
(cut 2)

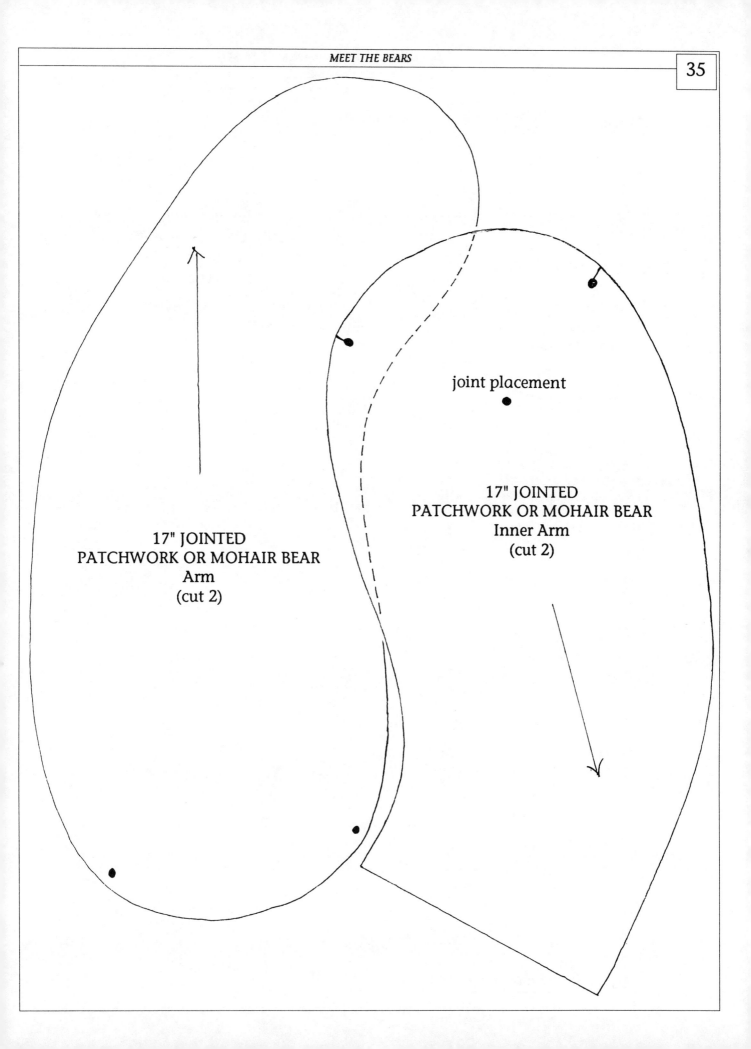

17" JOINTED
PATCHWORK OR MOHAIR BEAR
Arm
(cut 2)

joint placement

17" JOINTED
PATCHWORK OR MOHAIR BEAR
Inner Arm
(cut 2)

butt and tape to other half to complete pattern

17"
JOINTED PATCHWORK
OR
MOHAIR BEAR
Ear
(cut 4)

17" JOINTED
PATCHWORK OR MOHAIR BEAR
Head Gusset
(cut 1)

nose

butt and tape to other half to complete pattern

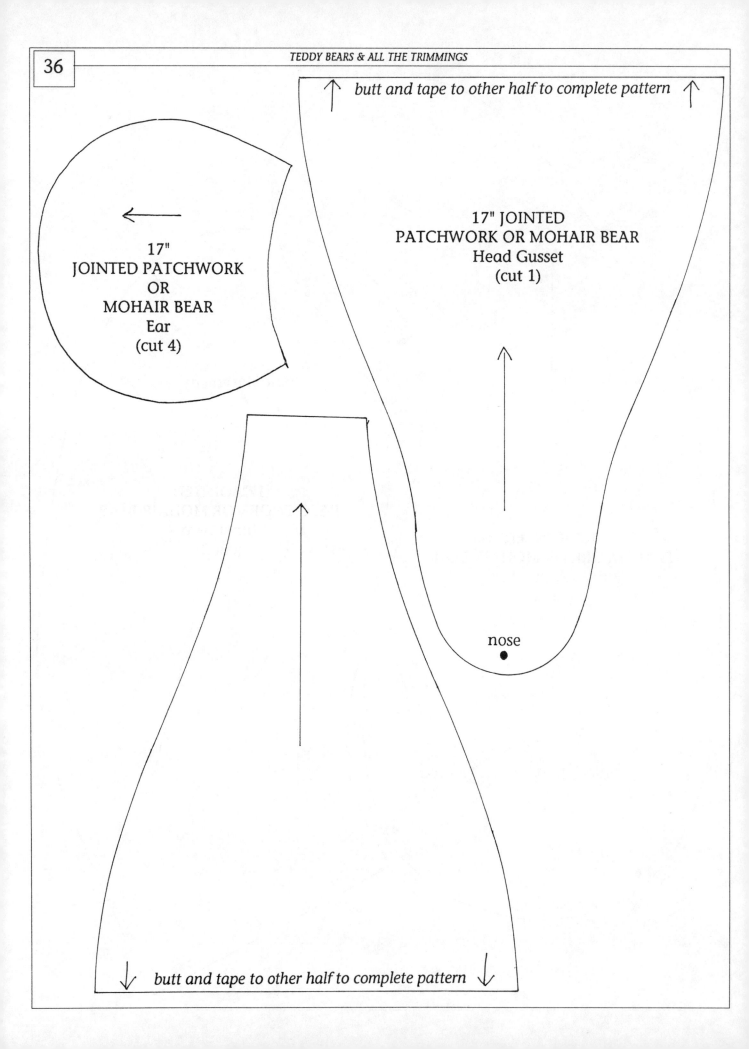

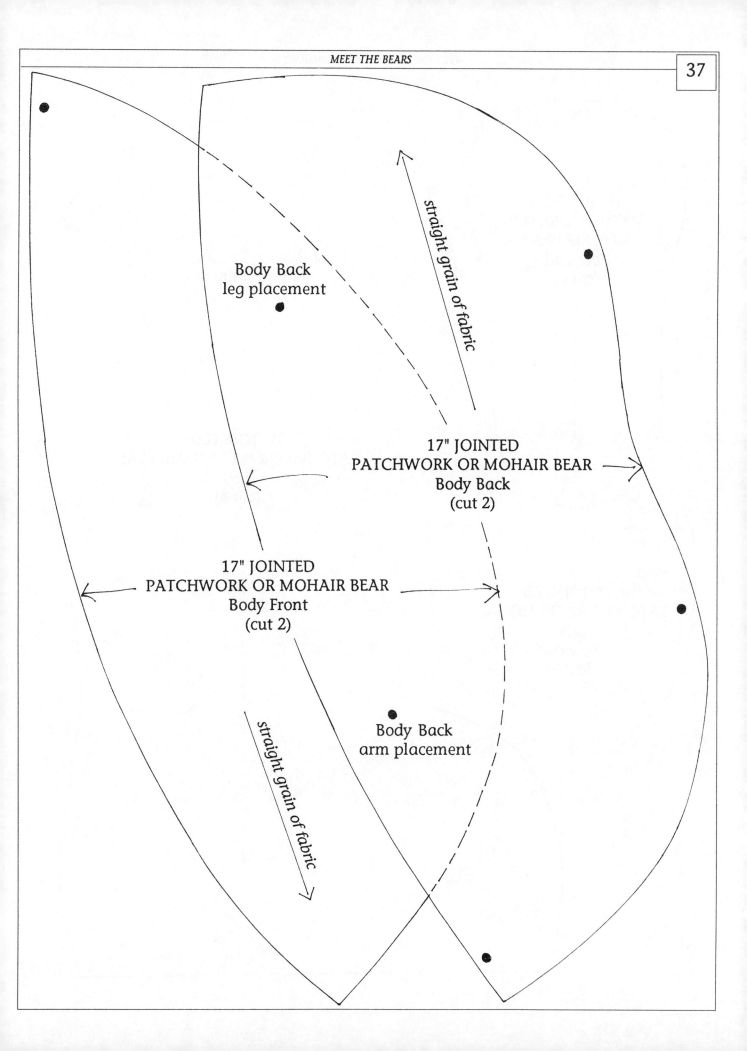

Body Back
leg placement

straight grain of fabric

17" JOINTED
PATCHWORK OR MOHAIR BEAR
Body Back
(cut 2)

17" JOINTED
PATCHWORK OR MOHAIR BEAR
Body Front
(cut 2)

Body Back
arm placement

straight grain of fabric

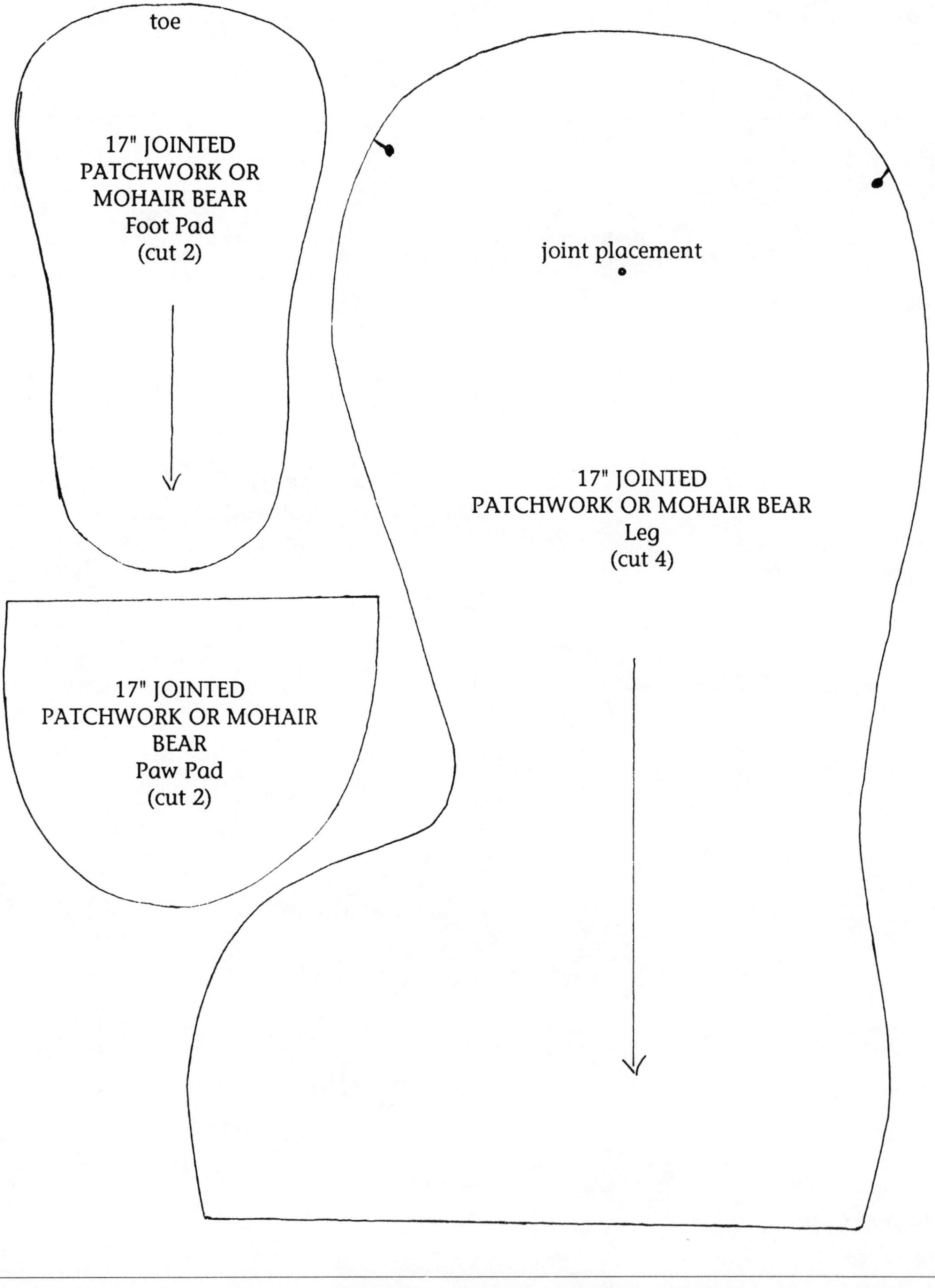

toe

17" JOINTED
PATCHWORK OR
MOHAIR BEAR
Foot Pad
(cut 2)

17" JOINTED
PATCHWORK OR MOHAIR
BEAR
Paw Pad
(cut 2)

joint placement

17" JOINTED
PATCHWORK OR MOHAIR BEAR
Leg
(cut 4)

13" POOKIE BEAR

Named after my sister, this bear is as full of fun as she is. Reminiscent of Winnie the Pooh, this bear, when made of golden synthetic fur, holds special appeal for young children and toddlers.

MATERIALS

¼ yard of synthetic fabric

Matching thread

Heavy duty thread

Polyester fiberfill

Five 2" joint sets

Two 12-mm eyes

Embroidery floss

INSTRUCTIONS

Note: All seam allowances are ⅛" unless otherwise indicated.

1. Cut pattern per instructions in chapter 1.

2. Pin the two body fronts together along the center front seam. Stitch.

3. Pin the two body backs together along the center back seam. Stitch the seam to the first dot, backstitching at both ends to secure. Stitch the seam from the second dot to the bottom, backstitching at both ends to secure.

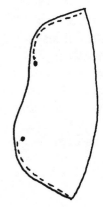

The gap left in the stitching between the two dots will provide access to the body cavity for jointing and stuffing the bear.

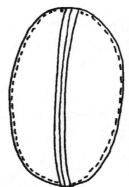

4. Pin the body sides together, matching front left side to back left side and front right side to back right side. Stitch between the dots, backstitching at both ends. This small gap will allow room for a cotter pin or bolt for the neck joint. Turn body right side out.

5. Pin paw pad to inner arm, right sides together. Stitch. Open out the paw pad and pin the seam allowances open so they will lie flat.

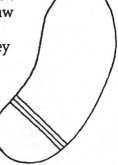

6. Pin the arms to the inner arms, right sides together. Stitch between the dots, all the way around the paw. Turn the arms right side out.

7. With right sides facing, pin the legs together. Stitch from the dot at the front of the thigh down the leg, around the toes, and ending at the bottom of the foot. Stitch from the dot at the back of the thigh down to the bottom of the back of the foot. Clip curves.

8. Pin the foot pads to the bottom of the foot, right sides together, matching the large dot to the front leg seam and the small dot to the back leg seam. Stitch. Turn the foot right side out.

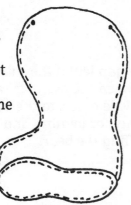

9. Stitch the darts in the head sides, right sides together.

10. Stitch the two head gusset pieces together at the crown of the head, matching dots and having right sides facing.

11. Pin the two side head pieces, right sides together, from the nose to the base of the neck. Stitch from the dot at the nose under the mouth to the base of the neck.

12. Pin the dot on the gusset to the seam where the two head pieces meet at the tip of the nose. Pin from the tip of the nose to the base of the neck at the back of the head, easing the gusset to fit as you go. Stitch. Repeat for the other side.
Turn right side out.
Stuff the head lightly.

13. Pin and sew the rounded part of the ears, right sides together, leaving the bottom edges open. Clip the curves. Turn. Turn the bottom edges under 1/4" and handstitch closed.

14. Attach the eyes to the head as instructed in the general bearmaking instructions at the beginning of chapter 1.

15. Restuff the head firmly, beginning at the nose. Using a long running stitch and heavy duty thread, stitch along the neck opening. Insert a cotter pin and a washer or a bolt through a joint disk. Insert the disk into the head opening with the cotter pin or the threaded end of the bolt pointing out of the bottom of the head. Pull up the thread to tighten the neck opening around the joint post. Sew around the neck opening a few times, tightening up on the thread as you go, to secure the fabric around the disk.

16. With small scissors or an awl make holes for the joints in the arms, legs, and body as marked. Make sure you have a right and a left arm and leg. Put a washer and then a hardboard disk on a cotter pin or bolt. Insert the cotter pins or bolts through the holes you made for them in the arms and legs so that the post is sticking out.

17. To join the bear, begin with the head. Push the pin or bolt through the small gap in the stitching at the top of the body. Slip another disk over the pin or bolt, and then a washer. Bend the cotter pin as shown or tighten the bolt. Check to be sure that the disks are seated properly and that no fabric is caught between them.

18. Install the arms and legs to the body as you did the head, inserting the cotter pins or bolts through the holes on the body that you made for them with the awl. Double check the direction of the limbs—taking apart a completed bear is no fun!

19. Stuff the arms and the legs tightly. Turn under ¼" at the top openings and sew them closed so that no raw edges show.

20. Match the outer edges of the ears with the outside point of the top head side darts. Pin them in place. Whipstitch.

21. Stitch the nose and mouth as instructed in the general bearmaking section at the beginning of chapter 1.

22. With a seam ripper or other pointed object, pick out any fur caught in the seams.

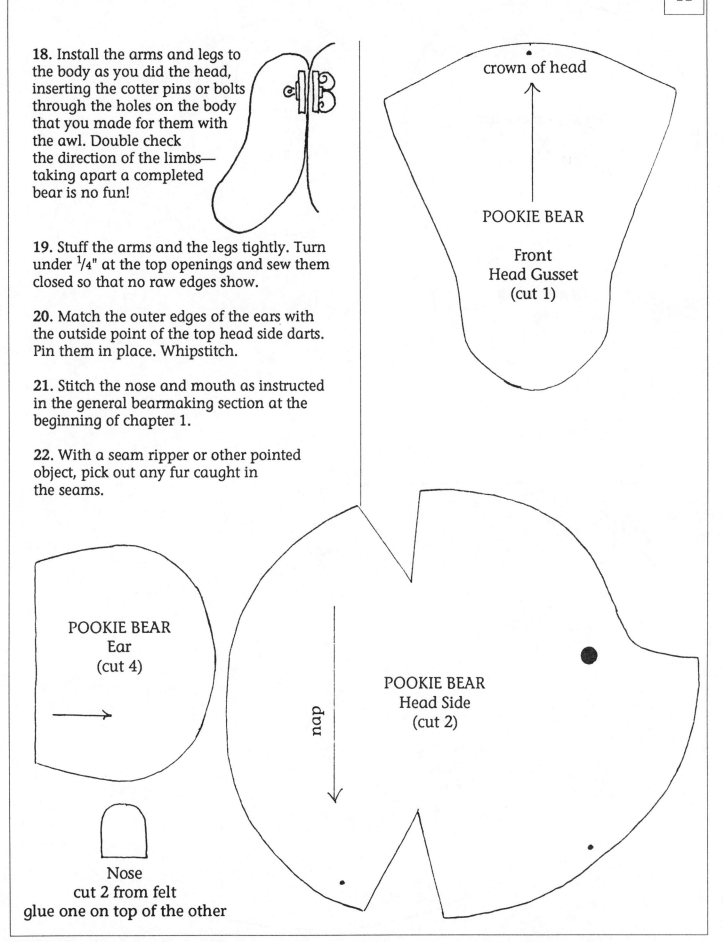

crown of head

POOKIE BEAR

Front
Head Gusset
(cut 1)

POOKIE BEAR
Ear
(cut 4)

POOKIE BEAR
Head Side
(cut 2)

nap

Nose
cut 2 from felt
glue one on top of the other

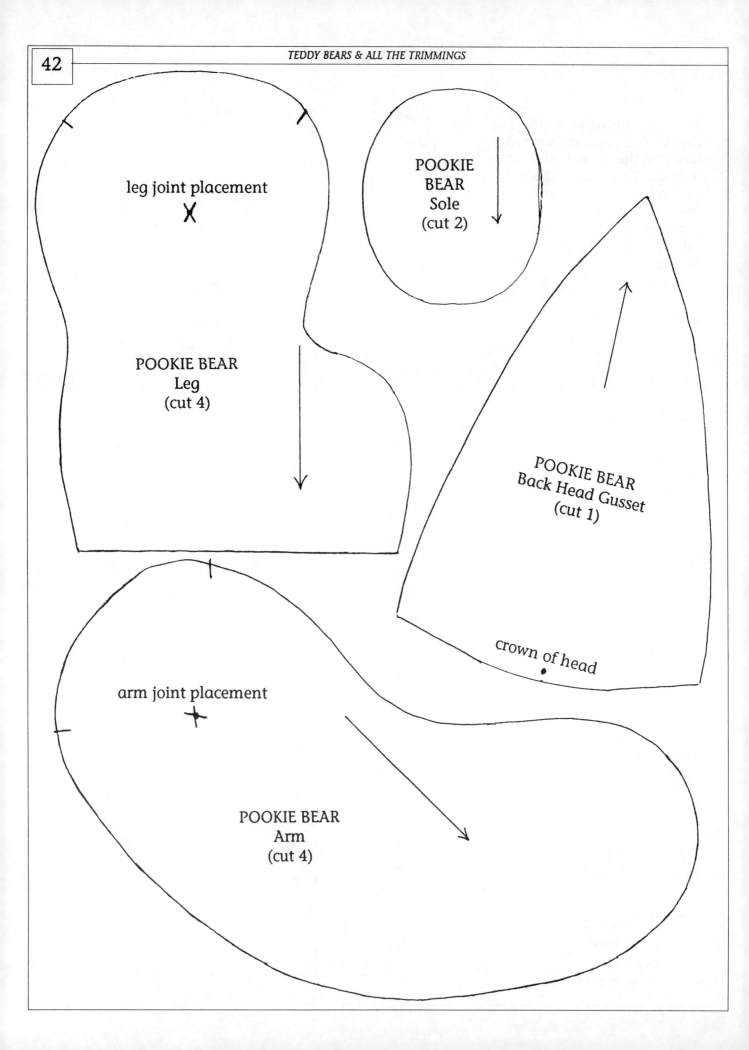

leg joint placement

POOKIE BEAR
Sole
(cut 2)

POOKIE BEAR
Leg
(cut 4)

POOKIE BEAR
Back Head Gusset
(cut 1)

crown of head

arm joint placement

POOKIE BEAR
Arm
(cut 4)

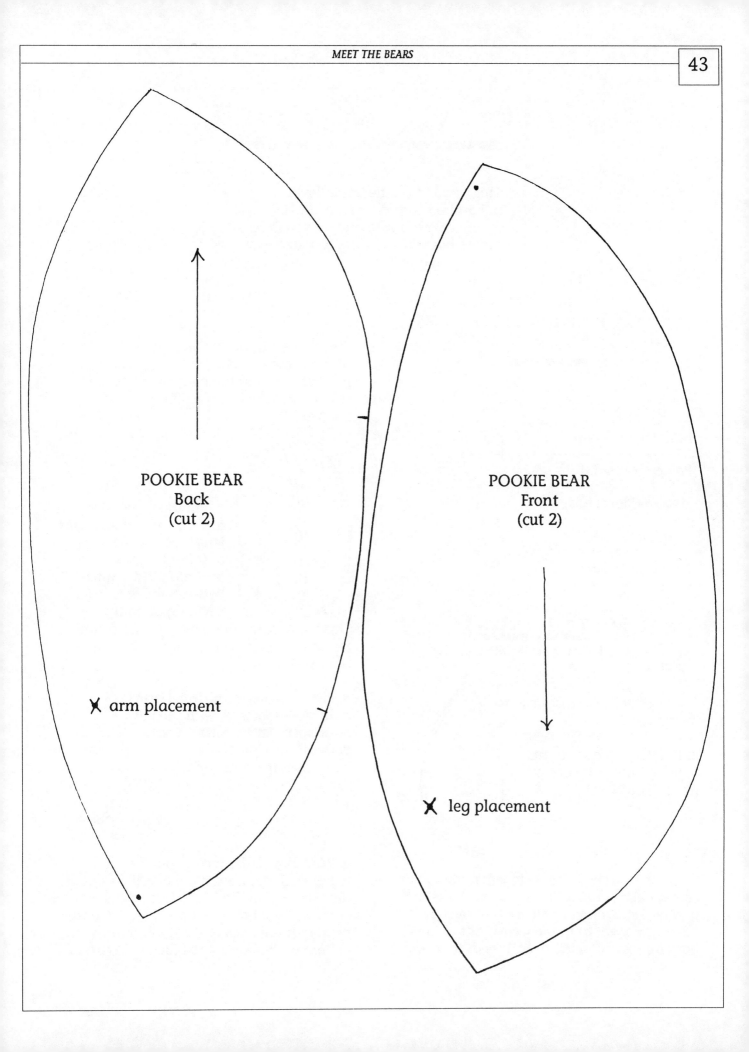

POOKIE BEAR
Back
(cut 2)

✗ arm placement

POOKIE BEAR
Front
(cut 2)

✗ leg placement

BABY BEAR

This wonderful little friend loves to pal around with a larger bear. He is very easy to make and uses so little fabric that you will want to make more than one.

MATERIALS

12" x 20 " piece of synthetic fur

Matching thread

Polyester fiberfill

Five 1$^{1}/_{4}$" joint sets

Two 9-mm eyes

Embroidery floss

INSTRUCTIONS

Note: All seam allowances are $^{1}/_{8}$" unless otherwise indicated.

1. Cut pattern per instructions in chapter 1.

2. Pin the two body fronts together along the center front seam. Stitch.

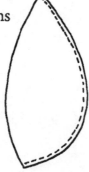

3. Pin the two body backs together along the center back seam. Stitch the seam to the first dot, backstitching at both ends to secure. Stitch the seam from the second dot to the bottom, backstitching at both ends to secure.

The gap left in the stitching between the two dots will provide access to the body cavity for joining and stuffing the bear.

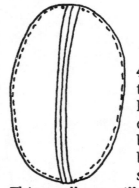

4. Pin the body sides together, matching front left side to back left side and front right side to back right side. Stitch between the dots, backstitching at both ends. This small gap will allow room for a cotter pin or bolt for the neck joint. Turn body right side out.

5. Pin the arms to the inner arms, right sides together, with the paw pads open. Stitch between the dots, all the way around the paw. Turn the arms right side out.

6. With right sides facing, pin the legs together. Stitch from the dot at the front of the thigh down the leg, around the toes, and ending at the bottom of the foot. Stitch from the dot at the back of the thigh down to the bottom of the back of the foot. Clip curves.

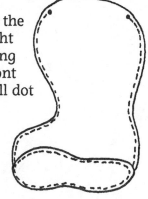

7. Pin the foot pads to the bottom of the foot, right sides together, matching the large dot to the front leg seam and the small dot to the back leg seam. Stitch. Turn the foot right side out.

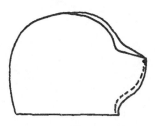

8. Pin the two side head pieces, right sides together, from the nose to the base of the neck. Stitch from the dot at the nose under the chin to the base of the neck.

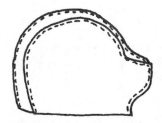

9. Pin the dot on the gusset to the seam where the two head pieces meet at the tip of the nose. Pin from the tip of the nose to the base of the neck at the back of the head, easing the gusset to fit as you go. Stitch. Repeat for the other side. Turn right side out. Stuff the head lightly.

10. Attach the eyes to the head as instructed in the general bearmaking instructions at the beginning of chapter 1.

11. Restuff the head firmly, beginning at the nose. Using a long running stitch and heavy duty thread, stitch along the neck opening. Insert a cotter pin and a washer or a bolt through a joint disk. Insert the disk into the head opening with the cotter pin or the threaded end of the bolt pointing out of the bottom of the head. Pull up the thread to tighten the neck opening around the joint post. Sew around the neck opening a few times, tightening up on the thread as you go, to secure the fabric around the disk.

12. Pin and sew the rounded part of the ears, right sides together, leaving the bottom edges open. Clip the curves. Turn. Turn the bottom edges under ¼" and handstitch closed.

13. With small scissors or an awl make holes for the joints in the arms, legs, and body as marked. Make sure you have a right and a left arm and leg. Put a washer and then a hardboard disk on a cotter pin or bolt. Insert the cotter pins or bolts through the holes you made for them in the arms and legs so that the post is sticking out.

14. To join the bear, begin with the head. Push the pin or bolt through the small gap in the stitching at the top of the body. Slip another disk over the pin or bolt, and then a washer. Bend the cotter pin as shown or tighten the bolt. Check to be sure that the disks are seated properly and that no fabric is caught between them.

15. Install the arms and legs to the body as you did the head, inserting the cotter pins or bolts through the holes on the body that you made for them with the awl. Double check the directions of the limbs.

16. Stuff the arms and legs tightly. Turn under ¼" at the top openings and sew them closed so that no raw edges show.

17. Decide where you want the ears. Pin them in place. Whipstitch.

18. Stitch the nose and mouth as instructed in the general bearmaking section at the beginning of chapter 1.

19. With a seam ripper or other pointed object, pick out any fur caught in the seams.

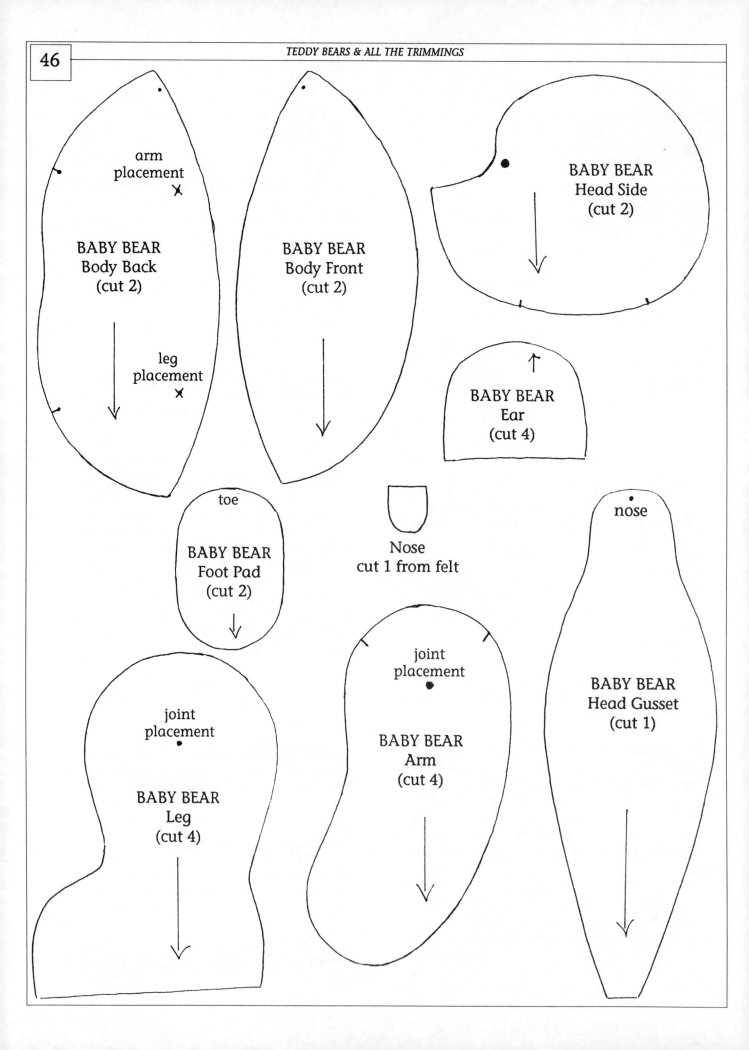

arm
placement
✗

BABY BEAR
Body Back
(cut 2)

leg
placement
✗

BABY BEAR
Body Front
(cut 2)

BABY BEAR
Head Side
(cut 2)

BABY BEAR
Ear
(cut 4)

toe

BABY BEAR
Foot Pad
(cut 2)

Nose
cut 1 from felt

nose

BABY BEAR
Head Gusset
(cut 1)

joint
placement

BABY BEAR
Leg
(cut 4)

joint
placement

BABY BEAR
Arm
(cut 4)

P O C K E T   B E A R

A mere five and one-half inches tall, this little bear will be your pal, traveling in your pocket wherever you go. And he'll make you giggle whenever you look at him. Though most of his seams are easy to stitch on the machine, you will end up with fewer handfuls of your own hair if you stitch the soles of the feet to the bottom of the legs by hand.

MATERIALS

12" x 12" piece of synthetic fur

Matching thread

Five ³/₄" joint sets

Polyester fiberfill

Two 7-mm eyes

Embroidery floss

I N S T R U C T I O N S

Note: All seam allowances are ¹/₈" unless otherwise indicated.

1. Cut pattern per instructions in chapter 1.

2. Pin the two body fronts together along the center front seam. Stitch.

3. Pin the two body backs together along the center back seam. Stitch the seam to the first dot, backstitching at both ends to secure. Stitch the seam from the second dot to the bottom, backstitching at both ends to secure.

The gap left in the stitching between the two dots will provide access to the body cavity for jointing and stuffing the bear.

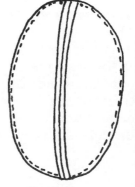

4. Pin the body sides together, matching front left side to back left side and front right side to back right side. Stitch between the dots, backstitching at both ends. This small gap will allow room for a cotter pin or bolt for the neck joint. Turn body right side out.

5. Pin the arms to the inner arms, right sides to-gether. Stitch between the dots, all the way around the paw. Turn the arms right side out.

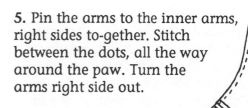

6. With right sides facing, pin the legs together. Stitch from the dot at the front of the thigh down the leg, around the toes, and ending at the bottom of the foot. Stitch from the dot at the back of the thigh down to the bottom of the back of the foot. Clip curves.

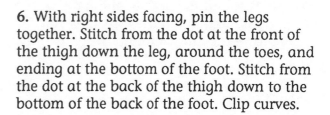

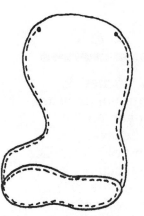

8. Pin the foot pads to the bottom of the foot, right sides together, matching the large dot to the front leg seam and the small dot to the back leg seam. Stitch. Turn the foot right side out.

8. Pin the two side head pieces, right sides together, from the nose to the base of the neck. Stitch from the dot at the nose under the mouth to the base of the neck.

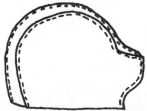

9. Pin the dot on the gusset to the seam where the two head pieces meet at the tip of the nose. Pin from the tip of the nose to the base of the neck at the back of the head, easing the gusset to fit as you go. Stitch. Repeat for the other side. Turn right side out. Stuff the head lightly.

10. Attach the eyes to the head as instructed in the general bearmaking instructions at the beginning of chapter 1.

11. Restuff the head firmly, beginning at the nose. Using a long running stitch and heavy duty thread, stitch along the neck opening. Insert a cotter pin and a washer or a bolt through a joint disk. Insert the disk into the head opening with the cotter pin or the threaded end of the bolt pointing out of the bottom of the head. Pull up the thread to tighten the neck opening around the joint post. Sew around the neck opening a few times, tightening up on the thread as you go, to secure the fabric around the disk.

12. Pin and sew the rounded part of the ears, right sides together, leaving the bottom edges open. Clip the curves. Turn. Turn the bottom edges under ¹/₄" and handstitch closed.

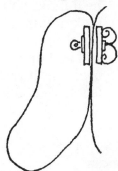

13. With small scissors or an awl make holes for the joints in the arms, legs, and body as marked. Make sure you have a right and a left arm and leg. Put a washer and then a hardboard disk on a cotter pin or bolt. Insert the cotter pins or bolts through the holes you made for them in the arms and legs so that the post is sticking out.

14. To join the bear, begin with the head. Push the pin or bolt through the small gap in the stitching at thetop of the body. Slip another disk over the pin or bolt, and then a washer. Bend the cotter pin as shown or tighten the bolt. Check to be sure that the disks are seated properly and that no fabric is caught between them.

15. Install the arms and legs to the body as you did the head, inserting the cotter pins or bolts through the holes on the body that you made for them with the awl. Double check the direction of the limbs.

16. Stuff the arms and legs tightly. Turn under ¹/₄" at the top openings and sew them closed so that no raw edges show.

17. Decide where you want the ears. Pin them in place. Whipstitch.

18. Stitch the nose and mouth as instructed in the general bearmaking section at the beginning of chapter 1.

19. With a seam ripper or other pointed object, pick out any fur caught in the seams.

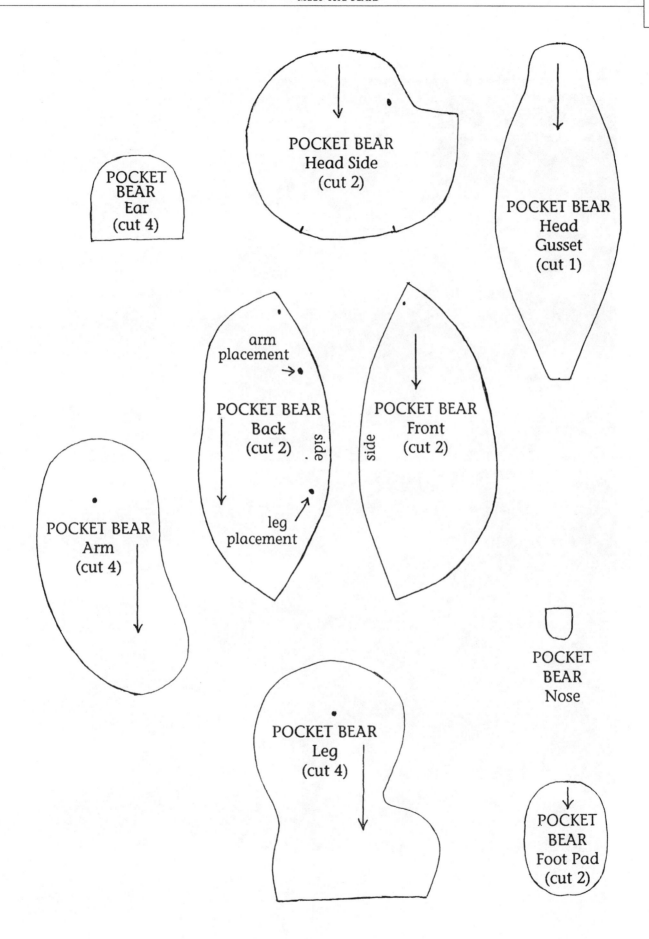

POCKET
BEAR
Ear
(cut 4)

POCKET BEAR
Head Side
(cut 2)

POCKET BEAR
Head
Gusset
(cut 1)

arm
placement

POCKET BEAR
Back
(cut 2)

side

side

POCKET BEAR
Front
(cut 2)

leg
placement

POCKET BEAR
Arm
(cut 4)

POCKET
BEAR
Nose

POCKET BEAR
Leg
(cut 4)

POCKET
BEAR
Foot Pad
(cut 2)

CHAPTER • 3

TEDDY'S TAILOR

♡　♡　♡

By following the step-by-step instructions in this chapter, you can create an entire wardrobe for your bear. To save time you might make two of each garment, one in a summer-weight fabric and the other in corduroy or wool for fall and winter. By choosing fabrics with the same color background you can make both garments at once, without having to change thread. Instead of completing one entire garment and then the other, simply complete each step for both garments in sequence. This assembly line process will save you a lot of time, and it's a nice way to make gifts for someone's favorite bear.

These patterns are sized to fit the two non-jointed bears in chapter 2. To size the clothes to another bear, first measure the bear and compare his measurements with those of the pattern. For instance, if you want to make pants, measure the bear's tummy. Measure him from your first measurement, where the waistband of the pants will be, down his leg to the bottom of the pants. (How about a pair of knickers or shorts?) Now measure the pants pattern across the top and subtract $\frac{1}{2}$ inch (that's

two $\frac{1}{4}$" seam allowances, one for each raw edge). Multiply by four. Calculate the difference between this measurement and that of your bear and divide this by four. Cut the pattern out of paper. Cut straight down the center of the pattern vertically. For a larger bear, separate the pieces at the cut by the measurement you just calculated. Tape across the gap to hold the pieces together. For a smaller bear, overlap the cut edges by the measurement you just calculated and tape in place. Measure the pants pattern from top to bottom. Subtract the amounts needed for the hem and the waistband casing (see instructions for the garment). Divide the difference in the length measurement of the adjusted pattern and the measurement from the bear. For a bear larger than the pattern, add half of this difference to the top of the pattern and half to the bottom, or cuff. For a smaller bear, subtract by cutting off the pattern.

More complicated patterns, such as the dress, will require a further step. Using your adjusted pattern, cut the garment out of scrap material. Pin it on the bear. Adjust where necessary. Adjust your new pattern.

GENERAL INSTRUCTIONS

Note: All seam allowances are $1/4$" unless otherwise indicated.

Prepare your paper patterns as instructed in chapter 1. Pin the patterns to the wrong side of your fabric and cut out the pieces. With dressmaker's tracing paper, transfer all markings to the wrong side of the fabric.

If you are uncomfortable making button-holes, you may choose to use snaps in place of buttons. You may still want to sew buttons over the snaps for decoration.

JUMPER & OVERALLS

Just the thing for everyday wear, your bear will love a jumper or overalls made of corduroy, denim, pillow ticking, calico, or cotton duck. Or choose velvet with lace trim for fancier occasions.

MATERIALS

$1/3$ yard of fabric for either size

$1/4$-inch wide elastic

Matching thread

2 buttons

2 snaps (if not making buttonholes)

INSTRUCTIONS

Note: All seam allowances are $1/4$" unless otherwise indicated.

1. As instructed in chapter 1, transfer the pattern to paper, pin and cut out the fabric. If making the jumper, cut skirt 6" x 20" for small bear or 8" x 24" for large bear.

2. Pin two bib fronts, right sides together, matching raw edges. Stitch, leaving bottom edge open. Clip into seam allowance to stitching at inward corners. Turn. Press. Turn under $1/2$" on bottom raw edges. Press. Repeat for bib backs.

3. JUMPER: Fold skirt right sides together, matching short, raw edges. Stitch center back seam. Press.

OVERALLS: Stitch inside leg seams. Press open. Pin long, curved crotch seams, right sides together, matching inside leg seams. Pin and stitch side seams.

4. Press under $1/4$" for hem. Press under another $3/8$". Top stitch $1/4$" from edge.

5. Press under $1/4$" at waist. Press under $3/4$" to form casing for elastic.

6. Pin bib to skirt or pants matching center back seam to the center of bib and having fold on lower bib even with fold on lower edge of casing. Repeat for bib front, matching center fronts. Topstitch $5/8$" from folded top edge of skirt or pants, leaving a $1/2$" gap in stitching to insert elastic. Topstitch $1/4$" from folded top edge.

7. Cut elastic; 14" for small bear, 16" for large bear. Insert elastic through casing by attaching a safety pin to one end and pushing the pin through the casing. Try on bear. Adjust elastic. Overlap raw edges of elastic and stitch back and forth to secure. Topstitch gap in casing closed.

8. Make buttonholes on long tabs of back bib. Sew on buttons. Or sew snaps on bib tabs, overlapping long tabs over front bib tabs. Sew buttons on top of long tabs.

STRAW HAT WITH DRIED FLOWERS

MATERIALS

Straw hat—available from craft shops, or The Teddy Works and Florida Supply (To size hat: Take your bear to the store with you or measure the circumference of his head at his ears.)

1 yard of $3/8$"-or $1/2$"-wide ribbon

Dried flowers such as baby's breath and statice

White craft glue or a glue gun

INSTRUCTIONS

1. On opposite sides of the hat, where the cap curves to the brim, use a seam ripper break a few of the stitches that hold the coils of the hat together. Insert the ribbon into one of the holes from the top. Take the other end of the ribbon and go all the way around the hat and halfway around again to the second hole. Insert the ribbon into the hole. Glue the ribbon in place along the hat.

2. Glue flowers over the ribbon on the two sides of the hat where you made the holes. Allow to dry.

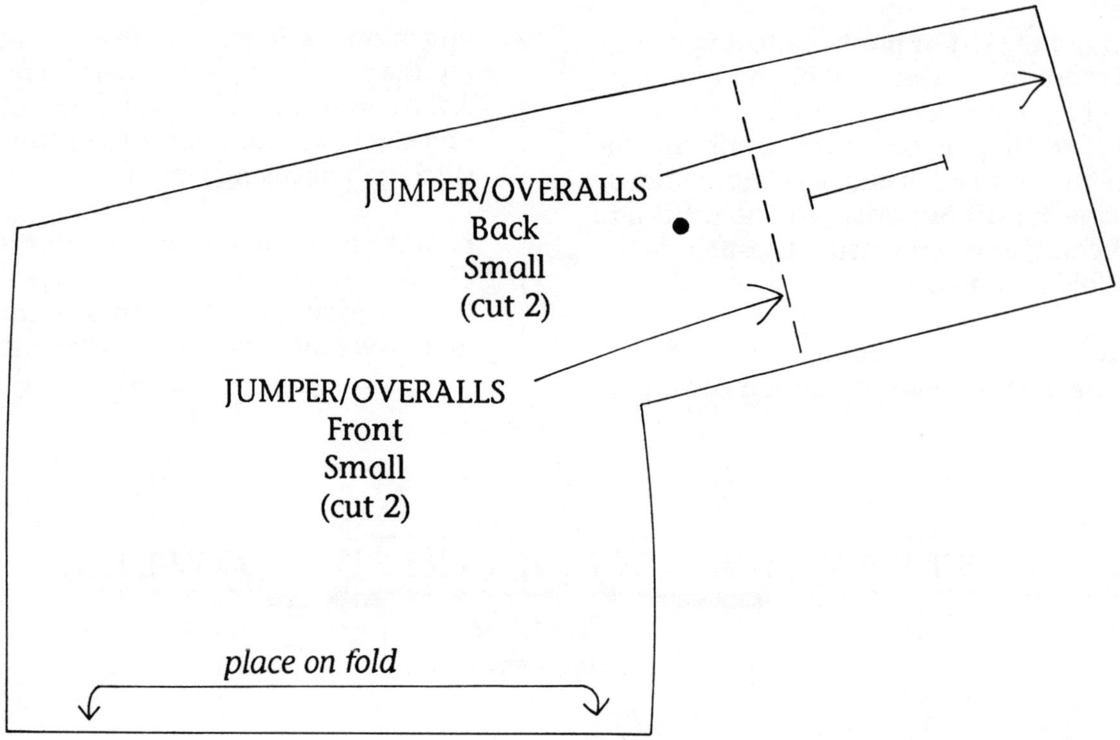

JUMPER/OVERALLS
Back
Small
(cut 2)

JUMPER/OVERALLS
Front
Small
(cut 2)

place on fold

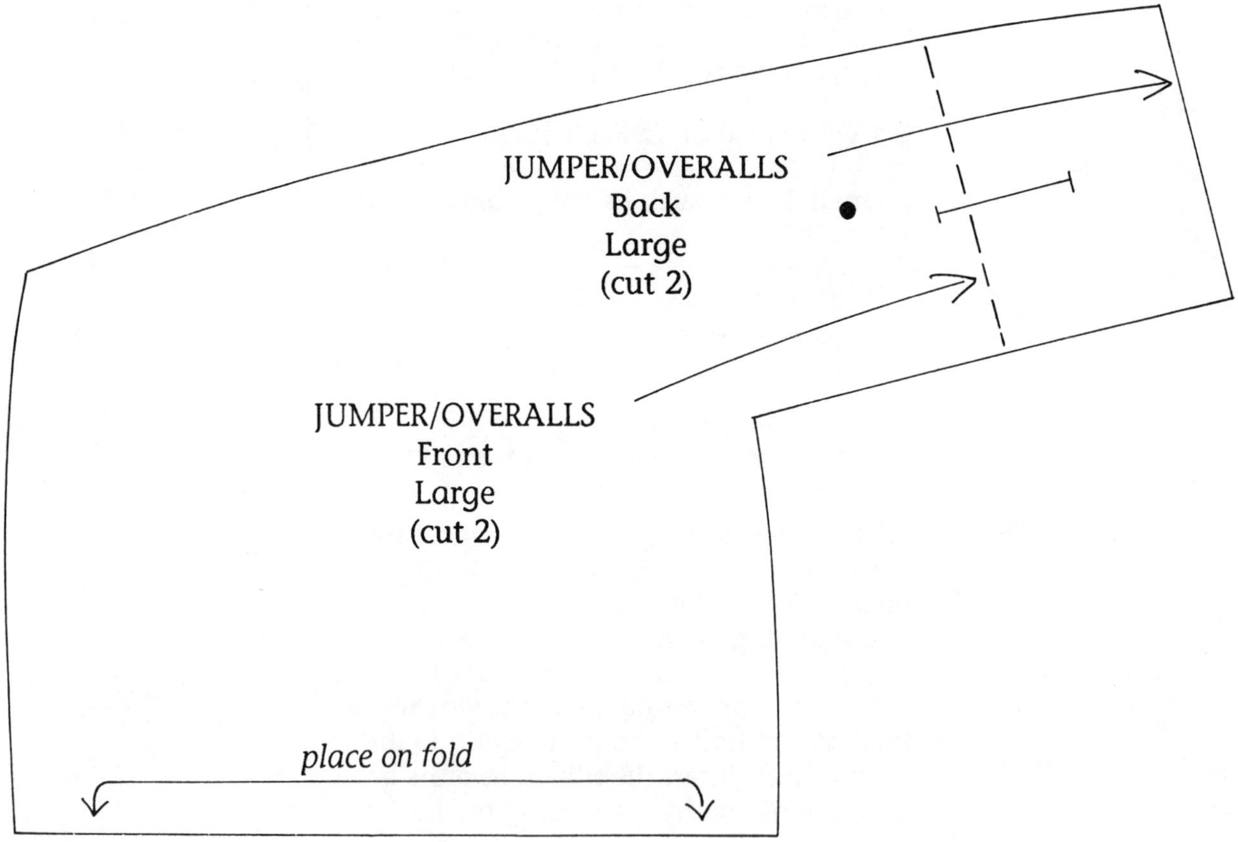

JUMPER/OVERALLS
Back
Large
(cut 2)

JUMPER/OVERALLS
Front
Large
(cut 2)

place on fold

BOY BEAR'S SUIT

Your bear will be quite a dapper fellow in this four-piece suit. Make the knickers, vest, and cap of corduroy for a casual fall picnic, wool for a day at the races (steeplechase, of course), or choose velveteen for an elegant holiday party. The vest might also be made of paisley, plaid, or stripe. Possibilities for the bow tie are endless. Bow ties require so little fabric that you may wish to make your bear a wardrobe of assorted, fun ties!

Knickers

MATERIALS

Fabric:

$\frac{1}{4}$ yard for small bear

$\frac{3}{8}$ yard for large bear

Matching thread

$\frac{1}{4}$"-wide elastic: 14: for small bear; 16" for large bear

Two small buttons

INSTRUCTIONS

1. As instructed in chapter 1, transfer the pattern to paper, pin to the wrong side of the fabric, and cut out the fabric.

2. Stitch inside leg seams. Press open. Pin long, curved crotch seams, right sides together, matching inside leg seams. Stitch center front and center back crotch seams together. Pin and stitch side seams, stopping two inches from the bottom of each leg. Starting at the bottom edge of each leg, topstitch $\frac{1}{8}$" from the edge of the opening, turning above the opening and continuing to stitch down the other side to the bottom of the leg. Repeat for the other leg.

3. Press under $\frac{1}{4}$" at waist. Press under $\frac{3}{4}$" to form a casing for elastic.

4. Topstitch $\frac{5}{8}$" from folded top edge, leaving a $\frac{1}{2}$" gap in stitching to insert elastic. Topstitch $\frac{1}{4}$" from folded top edge.

5. Insert elastic through casing by attaching a safety pin to one end. Try on bear. Adjust elastic. Overlap raw edges of elastic and stitch back and forth to secure. Topstitch gap in casing closed.

6. Using a long stitch, gather bottom edge of pant legs $\frac{1}{8}$" from edge.

7. Fold leg bands in half along fold line. Stitch across one short end. Stitch across other short end, pivot and continue up long side for one inch to form an extension for the buttonhole. Trim. Turn. Press.

8. Pin leg bands to bottom edge of pant legs, adjusting gathers evenly. Make sure that both tabs face in the same direction, which will be the back. Stitch. Trim.

9. Make buttonholes on leg band tabs. Sew buttons on other ends of tabs.

BowTie

MATERIALS

$3\frac{1}{2}$" x 8" piece of tie fabric for bow

$1\frac{1}{2}$" x 3" piece of tie fabric for knot

Matching thread

$\frac{1}{2}$"-wide black elastic

INSTRUCTIONS

1. Fold bow in half lengthwise. Starting at fold on one short end, stitch edge of bow, breaking stitching for one inch at the center of the long edge. Trim seams. Turn. Press.

2. Press under $\frac{1}{4}$" on long sides of knot. Turn under $\frac{1}{4}$" at short ends.

3. Overlap two ends of bow by about $\frac{1}{2}$". Handstitch one turned-under end of knot to middle of back of bow. Bring remainder of knot piece around front of bow. Pinch bow together at center and stitch remaining turned-under edge of knot piece securely.

4. Cut elastic to fit bear's neck, adding one inch. Overlap the raw ends of the elastic $\frac{1}{2}$" and sew to the back of the tie through both layers of the elastic.

Vest

MATERIALS

Fabric and lining:

12" x 12" piece of each for small bear

16" x 16" piece of each for large bear

Matching thread

Three buttons

INSTRUCTIONS

1. As instructed in chapter 1, transfer the pattern to paper, pin to the wrong side of the fabric, and cut out the fabric.

2. Stitch shoulder seams of both fabric and lining. Trim and press seams. Pin lining to fabric vest, right sides together. Starting about one inch from center back bottom of vest, stitch along edge of vest all the way around, ending about $1\frac{1}{2}$" from starting point.

3. Trim raw edges. Clip armhole and neck edge curves. Turn right side out. Press.

4. Handstitch opening at bottom back edge closed.

5. Butt and whipstitch side seams together.

6. Make buttonholes on left front of vest.

7. Try on bear. Mark button placement. Stitch buttons on right front of vest.

Cap

Fabric:

10" x 22" for small bear

12" x 30" for large bear

Matching thread

Interfacing

$\frac{1}{2}$"-wide twill tape or grosgrain ribbon

Fusible web

INSTRUCTIONS

1. As instructed in chapter 1, transfer the pattern to paper, pin to the wrong side of the fabric and cut out the fabric.

2. Stitch center front seam of cap sides, right sides together.

3. Stitch dart at center back of cap.

4. With long stitches $\frac{1}{8}$" from edge, gather around front of cap between dots on pattern.

5. Pin cap top to cap sides, matching center fronts and large dots. Stitch.

6. If using fusible interfacing, fuse to wrong side of cap brim bottom. Match cap brim pieces, right sides together. Pin, including non-fusible interfacing if that is what you're using. Stitch along round edge, leaving curved edge open. Trim and clip seam. Turn. Press.

7. Pin cap brim to front of cap sides, right sides together, matching center fronts. Stitch.

8. Starting at center back, pin twill tape to right side of bottom raw edge of cap. leaving about half the width of the twill tape extending over the edge. Stitch close to cap edge of twill tape. Turn under bottom edge of cap, so twill tape is not visible from right side. Press. Cut fusible web into $\frac{1}{2}$"-wide strips about one-inch long each. Fuse twill tape and edge of cap to inside of cap with these strips.

KNICKERS — Leg Band

Large and Small

foldline

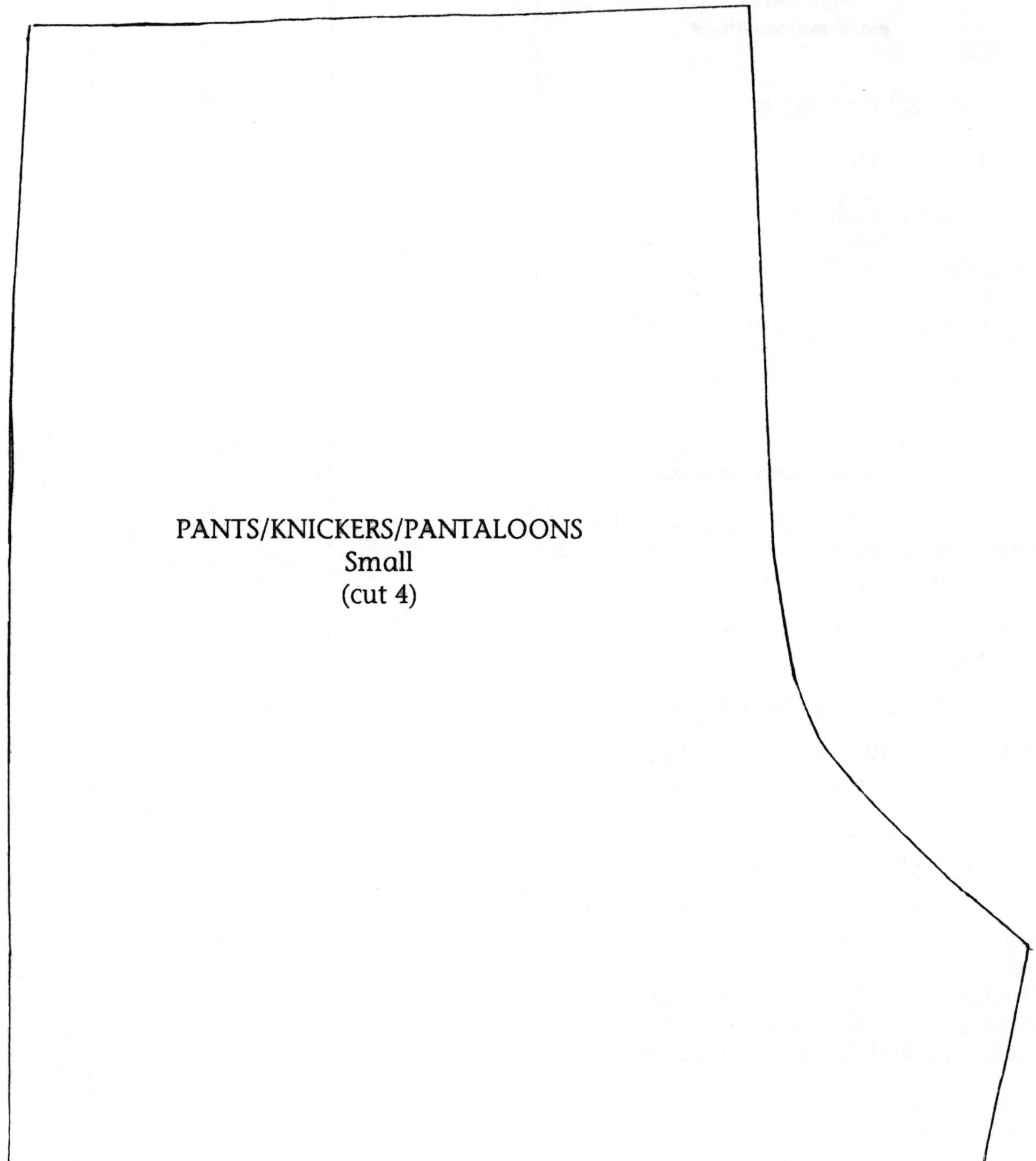

PANTS/KNICKERS/PANTALOONS
Small
(cut 4)

cut here for knickers

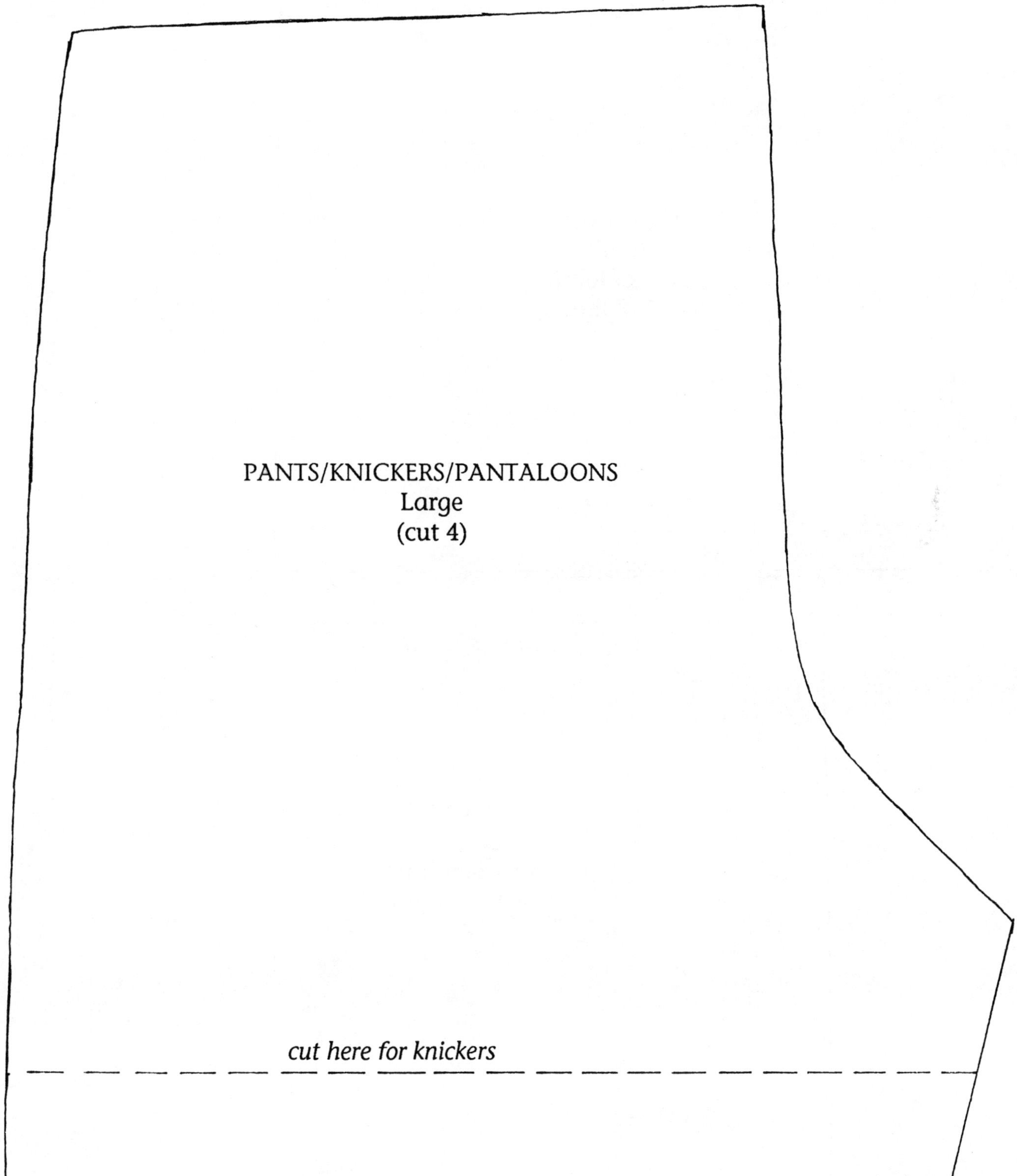

PANTS/KNICKERS/PANTALOONS
Large
(cut 4)

cut here for knickers

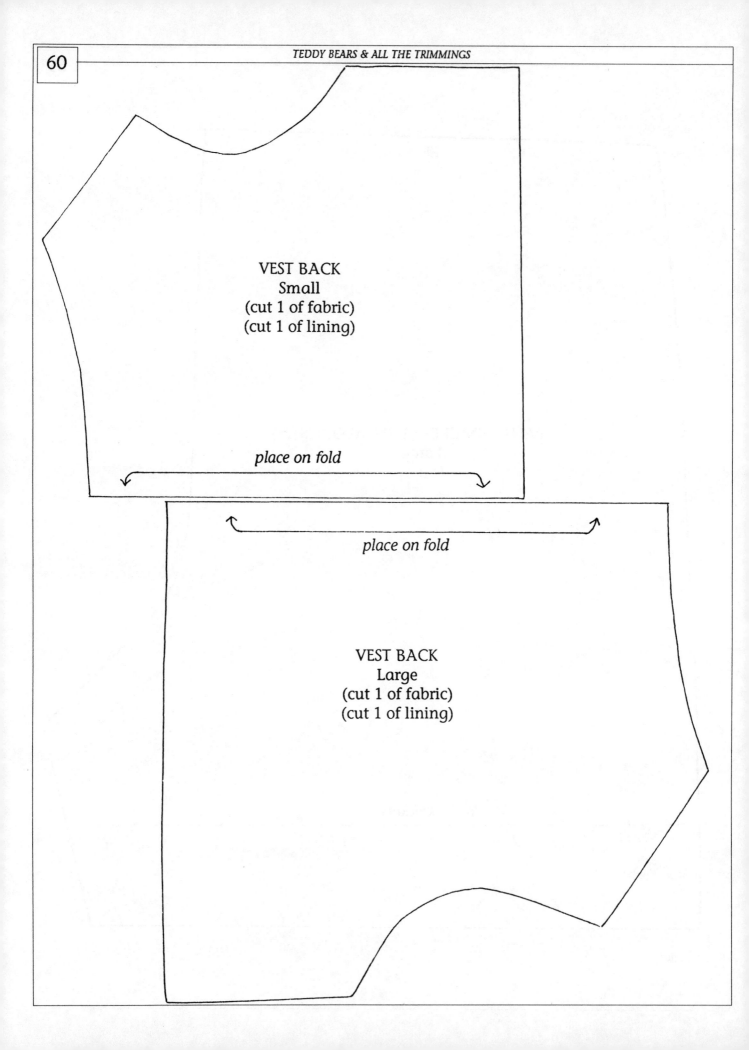

VEST BACK
Small
(cut 1 of fabric)
(cut 1 of lining)

place on fold

place on fold

VEST BACK
Large
(cut 1 of fabric)
(cut 1 of lining)

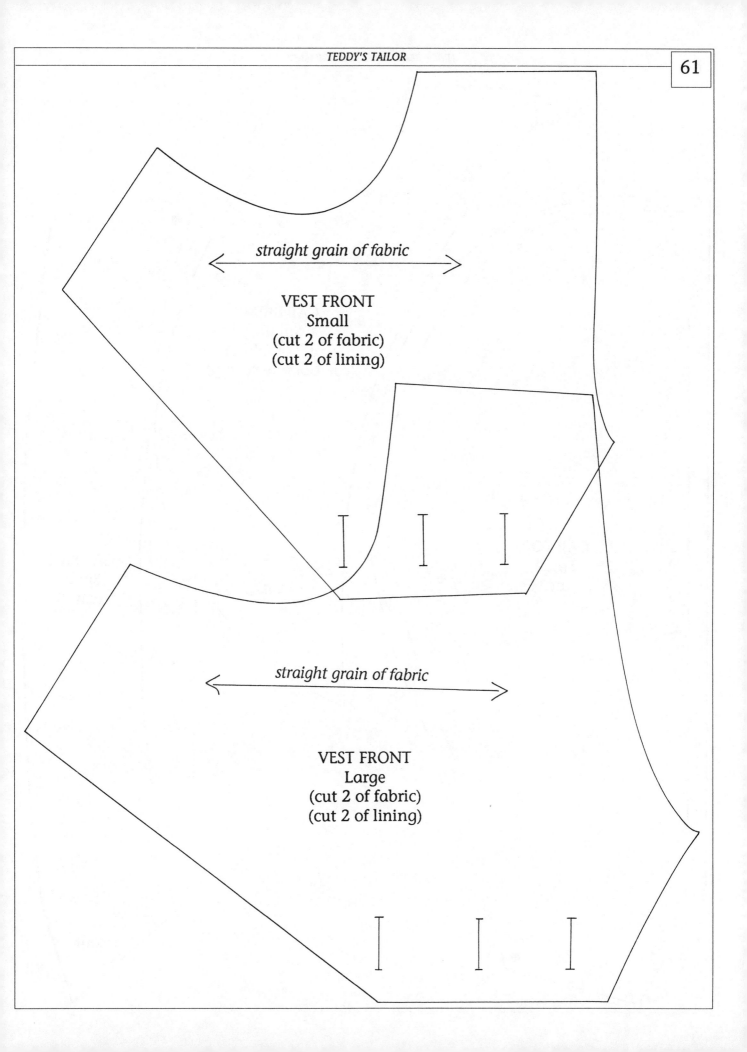

straight grain of fabric

VEST FRONT
Small
(cut 2 of fabric)
(cut 2 of lining)

straight grain of fabric

VEST FRONT
Large
(cut 2 of fabric)
(cut 2 of lining)

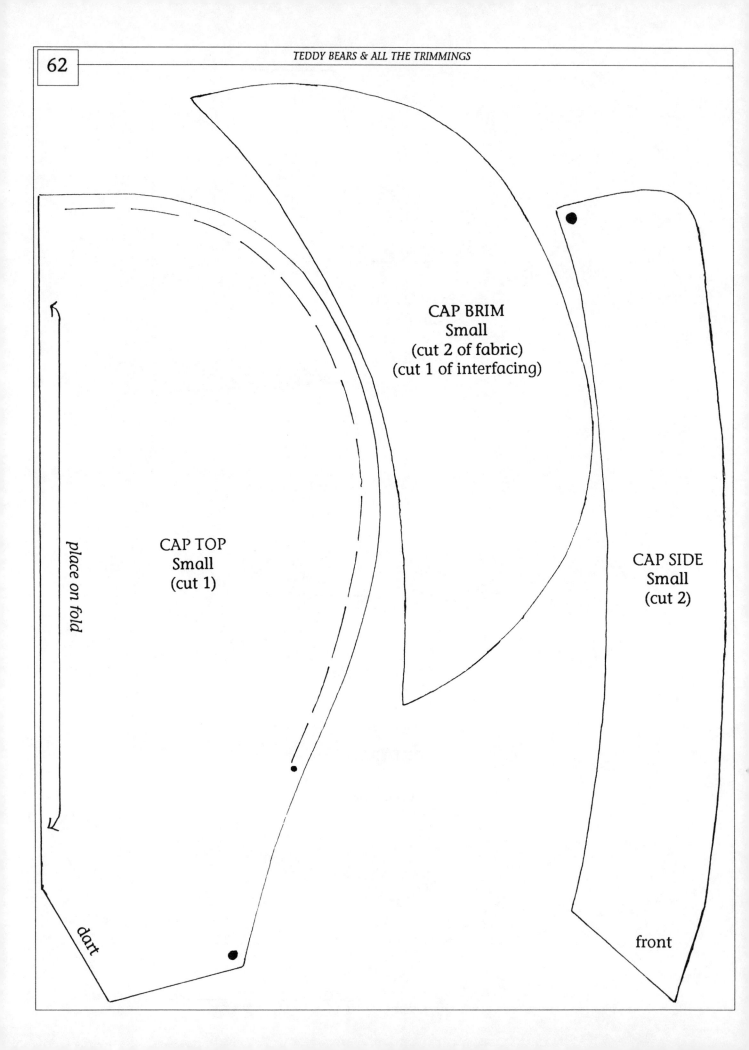

CAP BRIM
Small
(cut 2 of fabric)
(cut 1 of interfacing)

CAP TOP
Small
(cut 1)

place on fold

dart

CAP SIDE
Small
(cut 2)

front

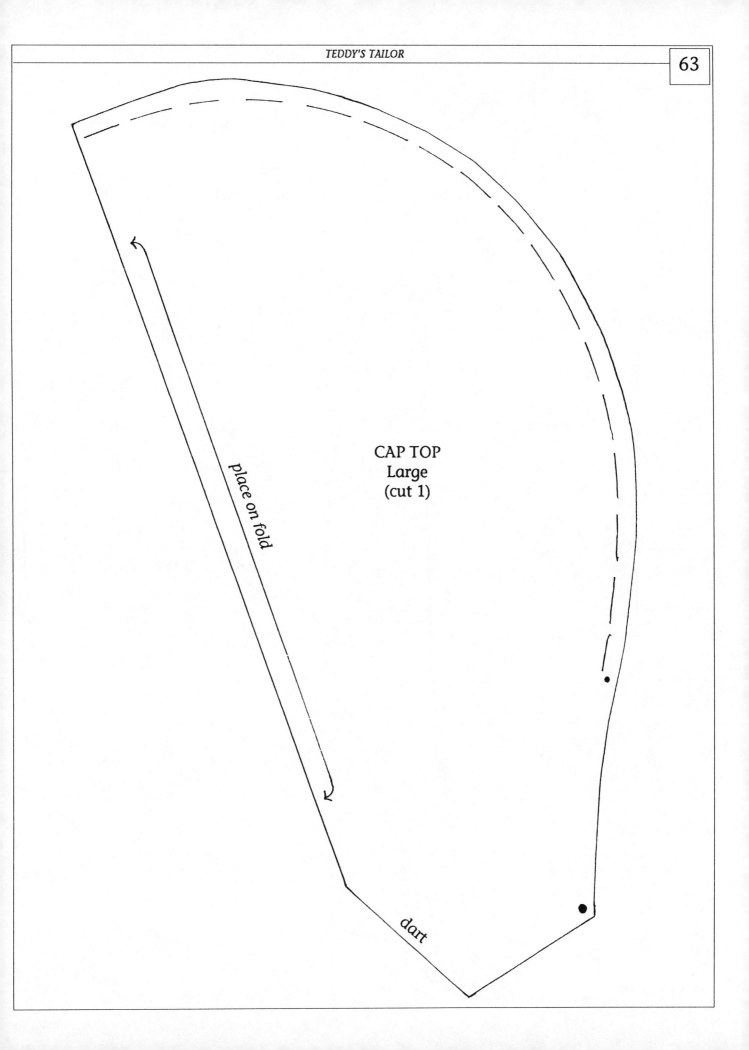

CAP TOP
Large
(cut 1)

place on fold

dart

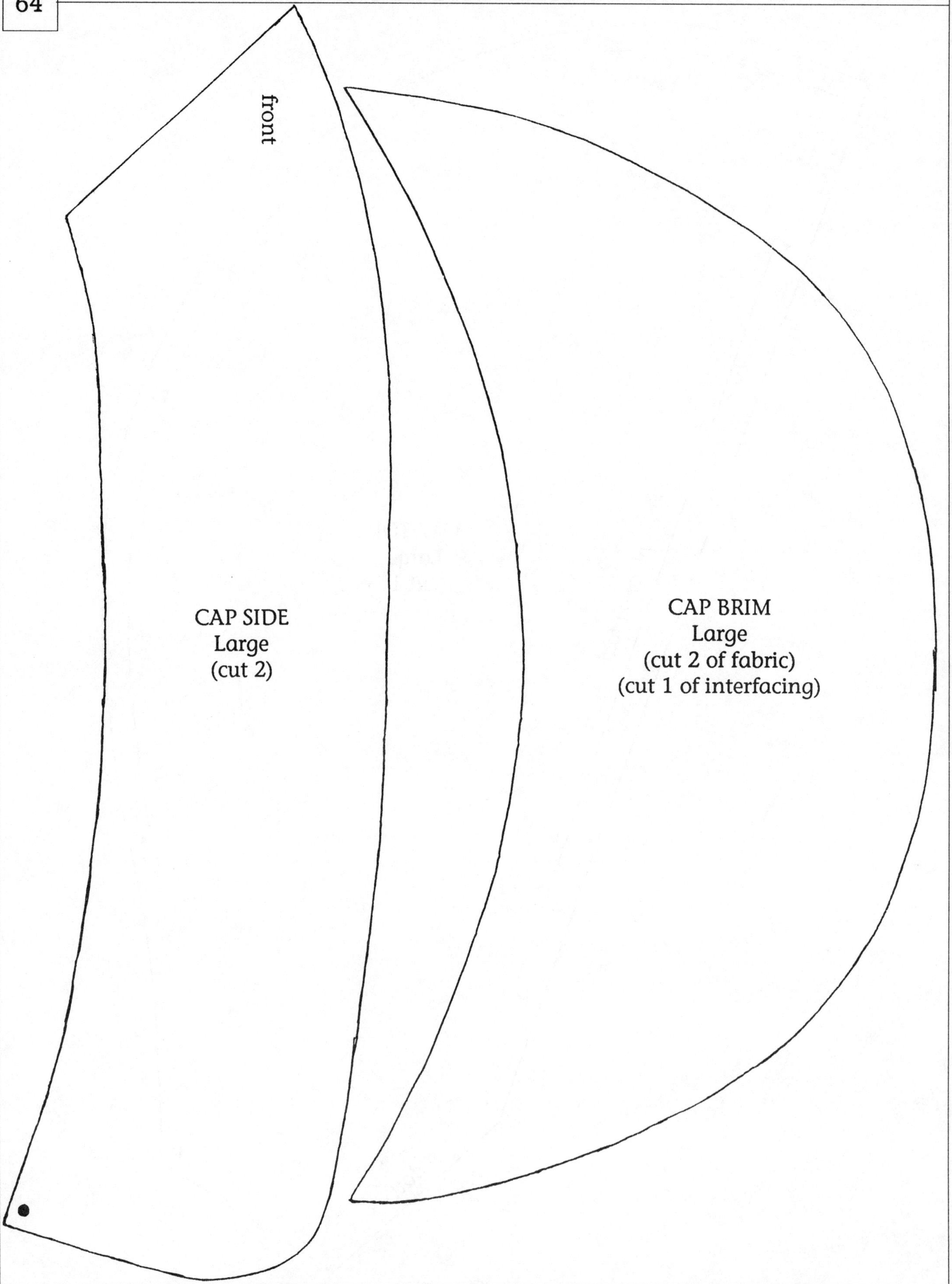

front

CAP SIDE
Large
(cut 2)

CAP BRIM
Large
(cut 2 of fabric)
(cut 1 of interfacing)

GIRL BEAR'S OUTFIT

What could be better than to while away a warm summer afternoon on a country porch dressed in this four-piece outfit, sipping honey-sweetened lemonade—the epitome of femininity?

Calico, corduroy (maybe to match your girl teddy's beau in his snappy knickers suit), velvet, and satin provide many variations in materials for this dress. Add a simple lace collar, a bow and ribbon rose at the neck, or a ribbon tied around the waist with the bow at the front or the back.

The pinafore, pantaloons, and bonnet can be worn by themselves as a set or over the dress. Made of natural or white muslin, they will be a very versatile addition to the well-dressed girl bear's wardrobe.

Dress

INSTRUCTIONS

1. As instructed in chapter 1, transfer the pattern to paper, pin to the wrong side of the fabric, and cut out the fabric. Cut the skirt piece: 6 ½" x 25" for small bear, 7" x 30" for large bear.

2. Stitch backs to fronts at shoulder seams for both dress and lining. Pin neck and back seams, right sides together, including the lace in the neck seam. Turn under raw edges at ends of lace and stitch so it won't peek out. Trim. You may wish to seal the loose threads of the lace with Fray Check™. Stitch back and neck as one continuous seam between the dots on the lower edges of the bodice backs. Trim seam. Clip neck curve. Turn. Press.

3. Press under ¼" at bottom edge of sleeve. Repeat. Top stitch. Cut a piece of elastic: 6" for the small bear, 7" for the large bear. Lay elastic about ⅝" from finished hem edge. Pin raw ends of elastic in place, even with raw sleeve edges. Hold the fabric and the elastic at both pinned ends and stretch the

MATERIALS

Fabric:

⅓ yard for small bear

½ yard for large bear

Matching thread

¼"-wide elastic

⅜ yard of lace for collar

Three buttons

elastic to lie flat. With a zigzag stitch, sew the elastic in place, beginning with a few backward and forward stitches to secure the elastic, stretching the elastic flat along the seam as you go.

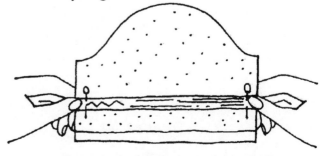

4. Using a long stitch, gather the sleeve heads between the dots, $\frac{1}{8}$" from the raw edge. Pin the sleeve to the dress. Adjust the gathers. Stitch in place.

5. Right sides together, sew the underarm and side seam.

6. With a $\frac{1}{2}$" seam allowance, sew the center back seam of the skirt from the bottom up, stopping three inches from the top of the skirt. Finish stitching the remainder of this seam with basting stitches. Press under $\frac{1}{4}$" of this seam allowance. Starting at the top of the skirt, topstitch $\frac{1}{8}$" from the turned under edge, pivoting below the opening and continuing to stitch up the other side back to the top of the skirt. Remove the basting stitches. This opening in the center back seam will allow room for your pleasingly plump bear to get in and out of her dress with ease.

7. Leaving two inches ungathered at each end of the skirt top, gather the skirt top with long stitches. Pin to bodice. Adjust gathers. Stitch.

8. Press under $\frac{1}{4}$" on bottom edge of dress for hem. Repeat. Topstitch.

9. Make buttonholes on bodice. Try on bear. Mark button placement. Sew buttons on.

Bonnet

MATERIALS

$\frac{1}{2}$ yard of fabric

Matching thread

Mid-to-heavy weight interfacing

$\frac{1}{4}$"-wide elastic

INSTRUCTIONS

1. As instructed in chapter 1, transfer the pattern to paper, pin to the wrong side of the fabric, and cut out the fabric. In addition, cut two 15" x 2" pieces for ties.

2. If using fusible interfacing, fuse to wrong side of one brim piece. Pin brim pieces, right sides together. If using non-fusible interfacing lay it on top of the two brim pieces before pinning. Stitch, starting at a short side, continuing along the long, straight edge and finishing with the second short side. Trim seam. Turn. Press.

3. Turn bonnet bottom flap extension under along fold line, right sides together. Stitch two short side seams. Trim. Turn. Press.

4. Cut a piece of elastic, 4-inches long for small and 6 inches for large. Lay elastic over raw edge of flap. Pin raw ends of elastic in place, $\frac{1}{4}$" from finished side edges of flap. Hold the fabric and the elastic at both pinned ends and stretch the elastic to lie flat. With a zigzag stitch, sew the elastic in place, centering it over the raw edge, beginning with a few backward and forward stitches to secure the elastic. Stretch the elastic flat along the seam as you go.

5. With long stitches, gather bonnet along lines marked on pattern, $\frac{1}{8}$" from raw edge. Pin to brim, matching large and small dots. Adjust gathers. Stitch.

6. Press ties in half lengthwise. Unfold. Press long raw edges to meet at center. Press again on the center fold. Topstitch close to open edge.

7. Stitch one end of each tie to bonnet at mark on pattern, raw edge even with raw edge of bonnet/brim seam. Tie will extend out from under bonnet brim. Tie a knot in the loose end of each tie.

Pinafore

MATERIALS

$1/3$ yard of fabric for either size bear

Matching thread

2 yards of $1 1/2$"-wide lace

Two buttons

INSTRUCTIONS

1. Cut skirt piece: $5 1/2$" x 28" for small bear, $5 1/2$" x 34" for large bear.

2. As instructed in chapter 1, transfer the pattern to paper, pin to the wrong side of the fabric, and cut out the fabric.

3. For bodice, stitch two backs to one front at shoulder seams. Stitch two side fronts to two side backs at shoulder seams so that you have a right and a left. Pin side fronts to front and side backs to backs, matching shoulder seams and including the lace in the seams. Stitch the seams.

4. For bodice lining, stitch the two remaining side fronts to the front. Stitch the two side backs to the two backs, being sure that you have a left and a right. Stitch the backs to the fronts at the shoulder seams, right sides together.

5. Pin the bodice to the bodice lining, right sides together, matching shoulder seams and armholes. Stitch entire neckline starting at one center back bottom dot and continuing around the neckline, finishing at the other center back bottom dot. Stitch armhole. Trim seams. Clip curves and trim corners. Turn. Press. Stitch side underarm seams together.

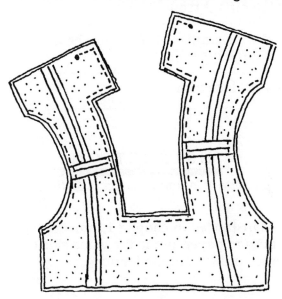

6. Using long stitches, gather skirt, starting and ending about one inch from each end. Pin skirt to bodice, adjusting gathers. Stitch. Be sure to include ends of lace in the seam.

7. Turn under $1/4$" on skirt bottom. Press under another $1/4$". Lay lace along underside of hem, turning under about $1/2$" of the raw end of the lace at each end. Topstitch. Apply Fray Check™ to the raw ends of the lace.

8. Make buttonholes on one bodice back.

9. Try on bear. Sew buttons in place to fit.

Pantaloons

MATERIALS

Muslin:

$1/4$ yard for small bear

$3/8$ yard for large bear

Matching thread

$1/4$"-wide elastic: 14" for small bear; 16" for large bear

1 yard lace trim

INSTRUCTIONS

Use patterns for knickers on pages 57 through 59.

1. As instructed in chapter 1, transfer the pattern to paper, pin to the wrong side of the fabric, and cut out the fabric.

2. Stitch inside leg seams. Press open. Pin long, curved crotch seams, right sides together, matching inside leg seams. Pin and stitch side seams.

3. Press under $1/4$" at waist. Press under $3/4$" to form casing for elastic.

4. Topstitch $5/8$" from folded top edge, leaving a $1/2$" gap in stitching to insert elastic. Topstitch $1/4$" from folded edge.

5. Insert elastic through casing by attaching a safety pin to one end and running it through the casing. Try on bear. Adjust elastic. Overlap raw edges of elastic and stitch back and forth to secure. Topstitch gap in casing closed.

6. Turn under $1/4$" for hem. Press under another $1/4$". Cut a piece of lace the measurement of the leg opening plus one inch. Fold lace, right sides together, and stitch a $1/2$" seam. Trim. Seal with Fray Check™. Matching lace seam with inside leg seam, stitch lace trim to underside of hem.

DRESS BACK
Small
(cut 4)

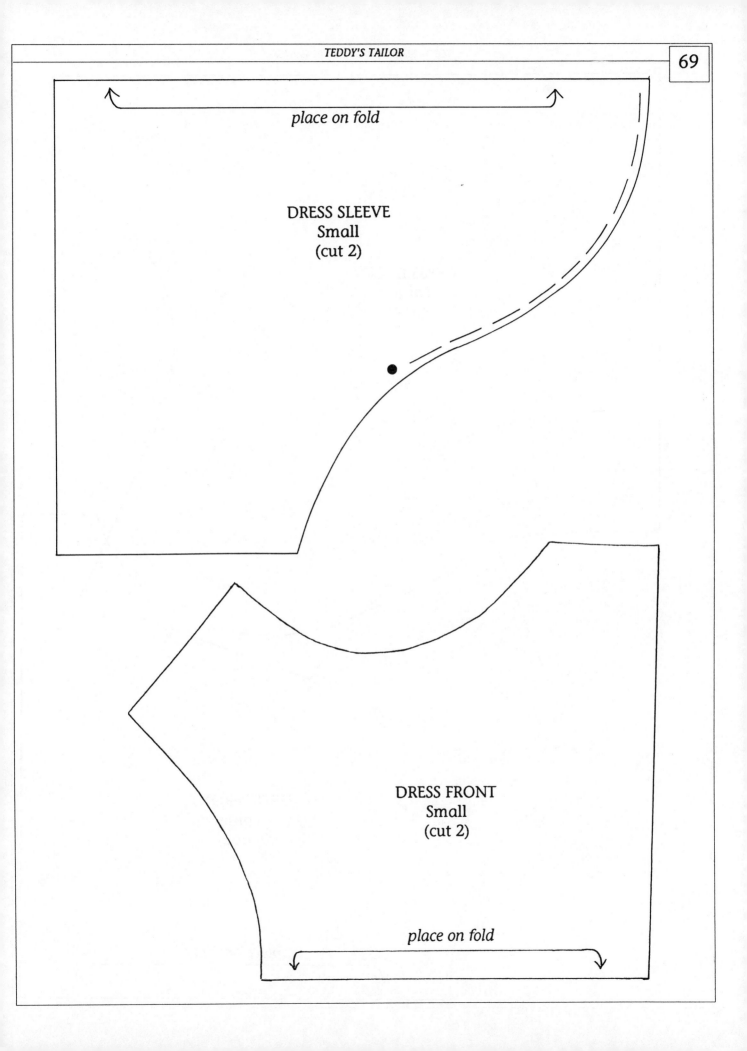

place on fold

DRESS SLEEVE
Small
(cut 2)

DRESS FRONT
Small
(cut 2)

place on fold

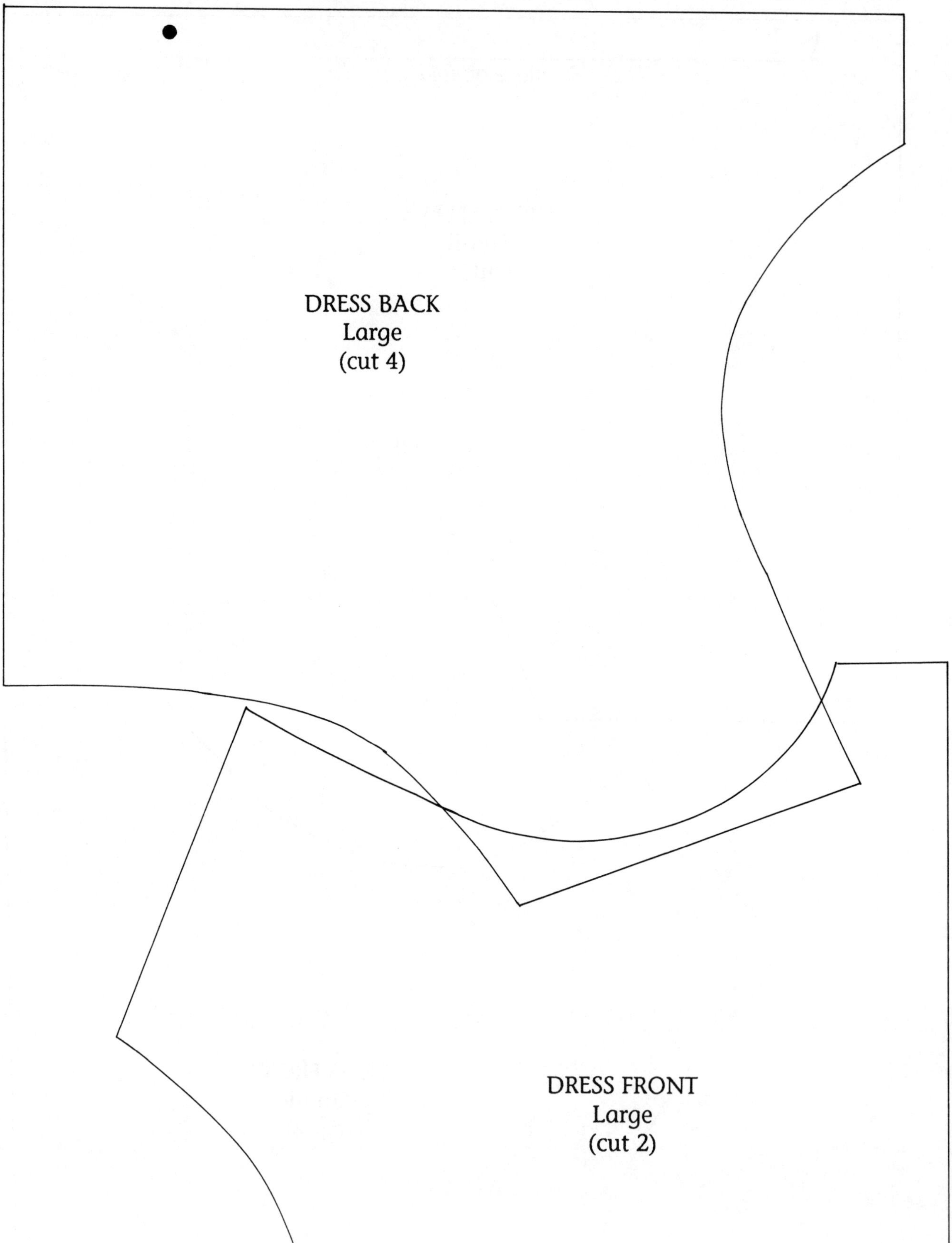

DRESS BACK
Large
(cut 4)

DRESS FRONT
Large
(cut 2)

place on fold

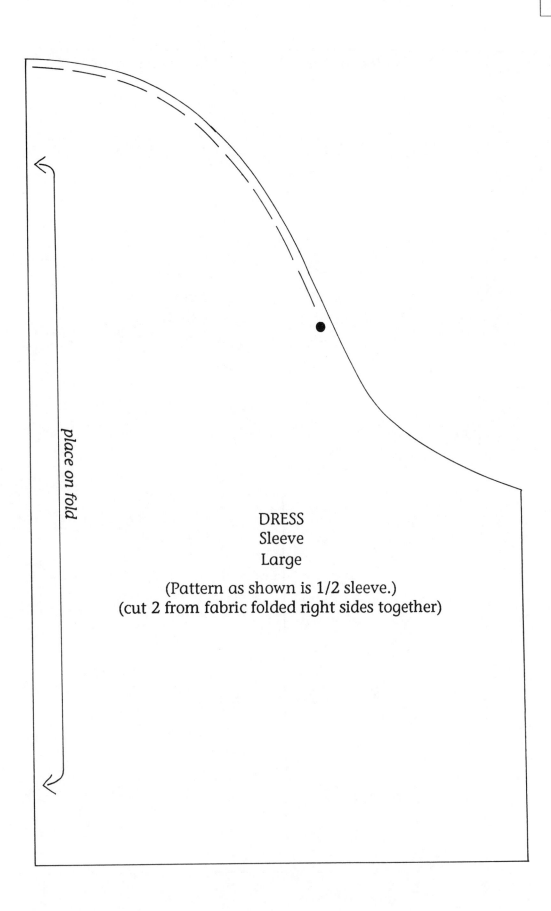

place on fold

DRESS
Sleeve
Large

(Pattern as shown is 1/2 sleeve.)
(cut 2 from fabric folded right sides together)

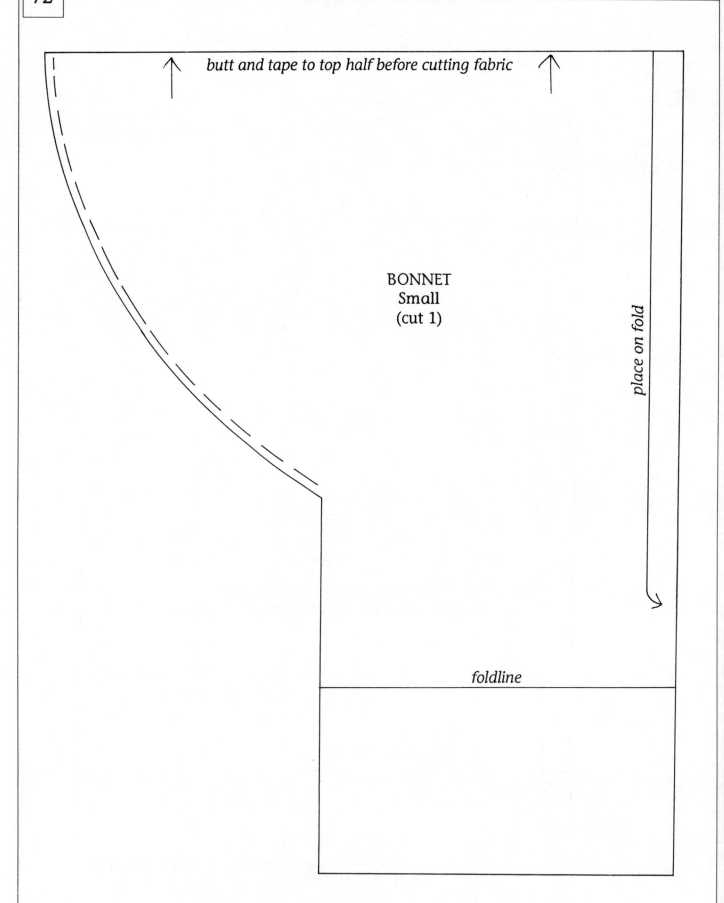

butt and tape to top half before cutting fabric

BONNET
Small
(cut 1)

place on fold

foldline

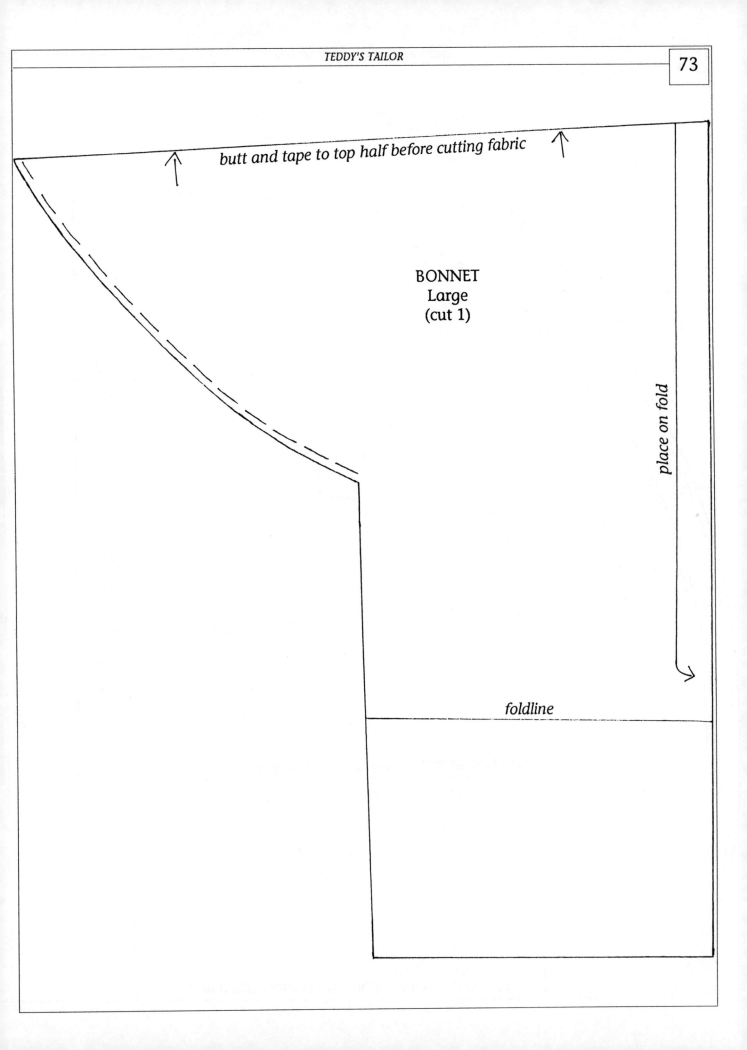

butt and tape to top half before cutting fabric

BONNET
Large
(cut 1)

place on fold

foldline

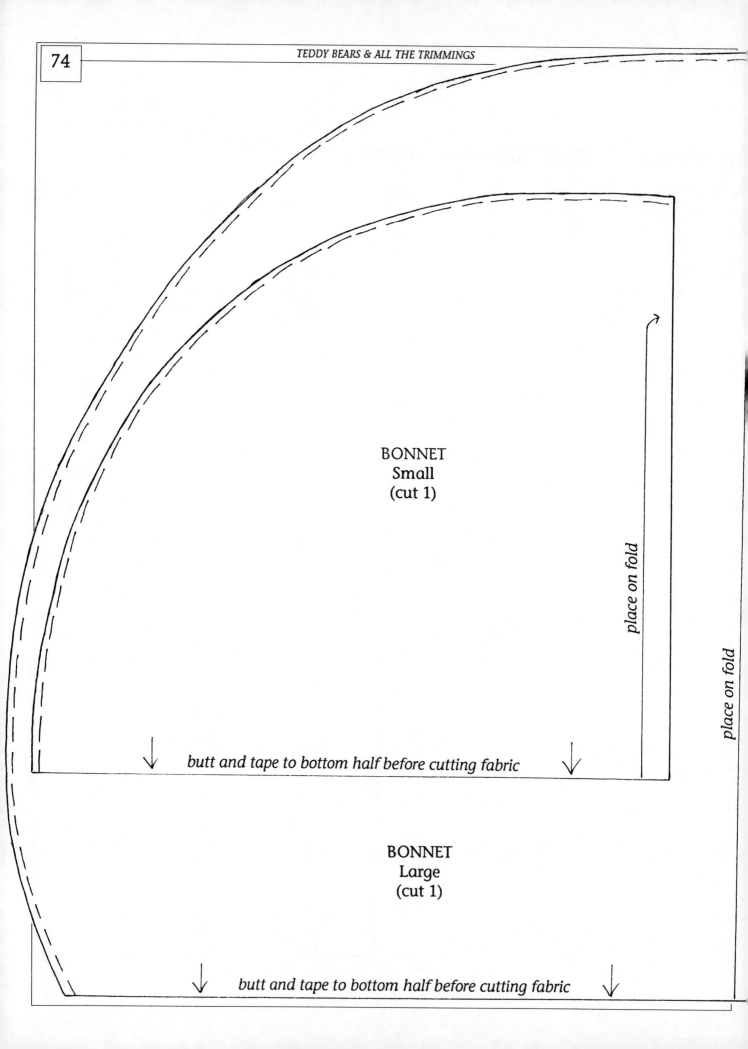

BONNET
Small
(cut 1)

place on fold

↓ *butt and tape to bottom half before cutting fabric* ↓

BONNET
Large
(cut 1)

place on fold

↓ *butt and tape to bottom half before cutting fabric* ↓

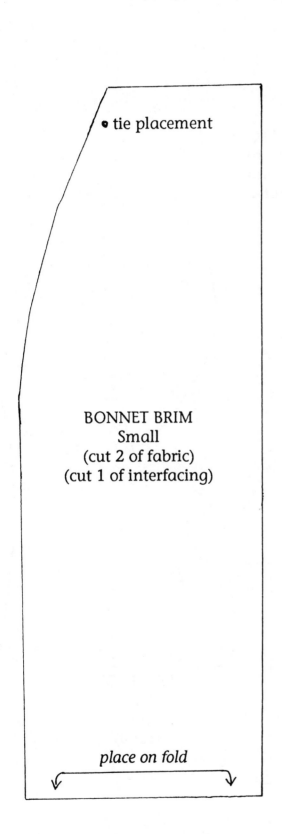

● tie placement

BONNET BRIM
Small
(cut 2 of fabric)
(cut 1 of interfacing)

place on fold

tie placement ●

BONNET BRIM
Large
(cut 2 of fabric)
(cut 1 of interfacing)

place on fold

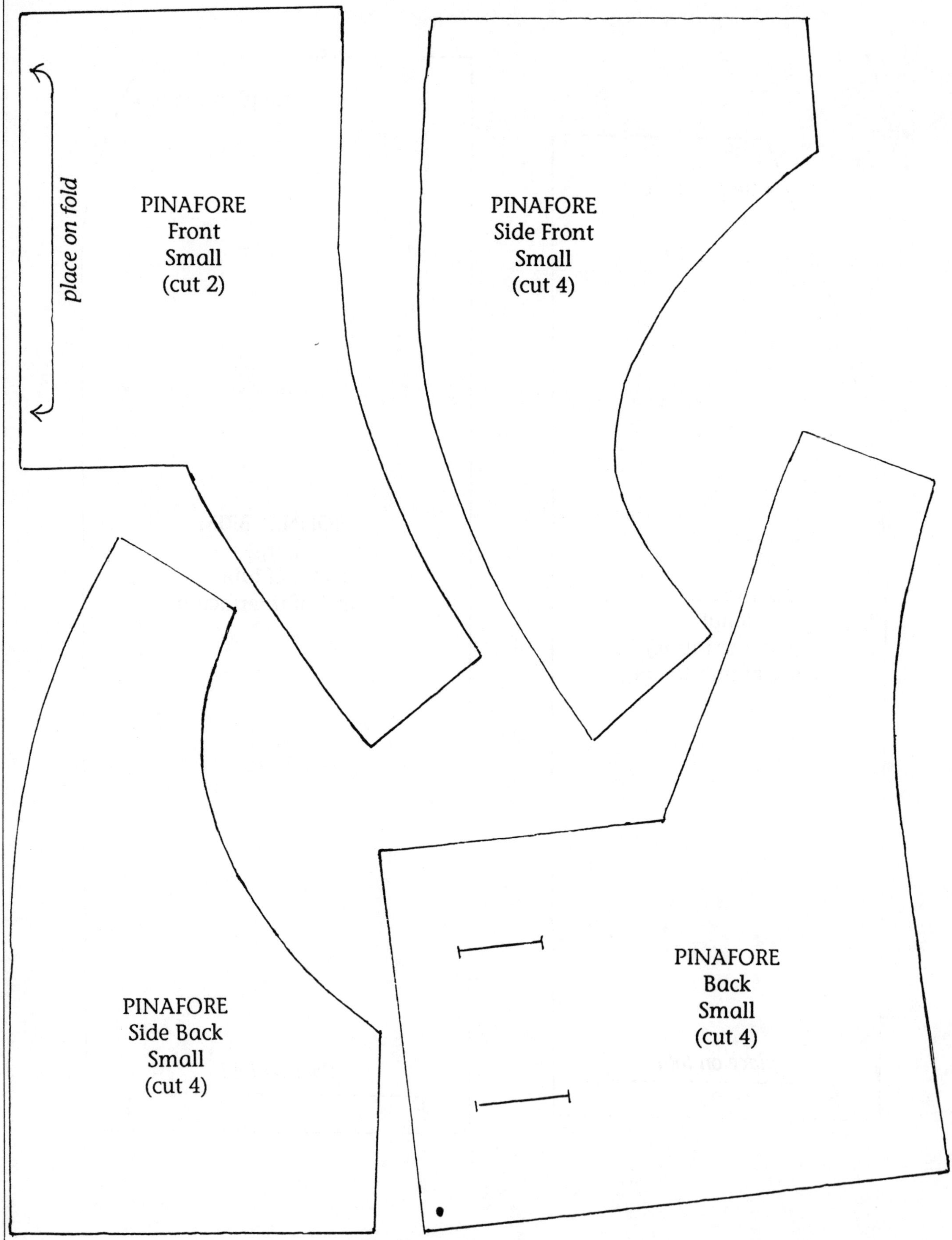

place on fold

PINAFORE
Front
Small
(cut 2)

PINAFORE
Side Front
Small
(cut 4)

PINAFORE
Side Back
Small
(cut 4)

PINAFORE
Back
Small
(cut 4)

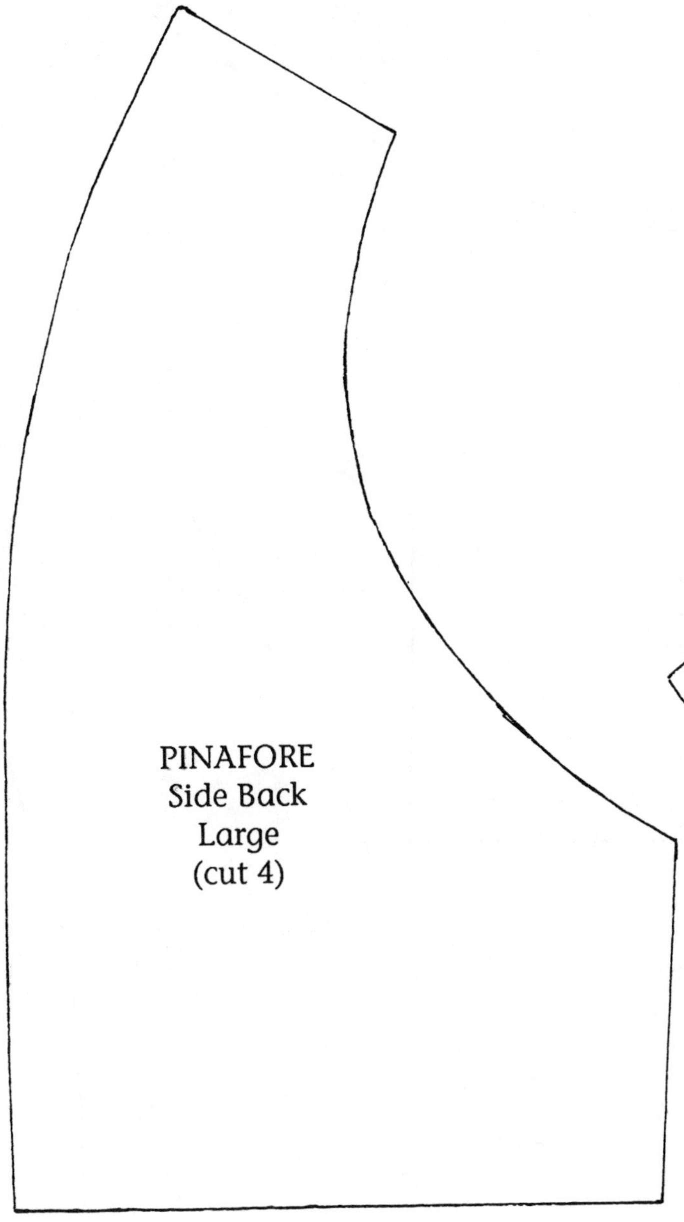

PINAFORE
Side Back
Large
(cut 4)

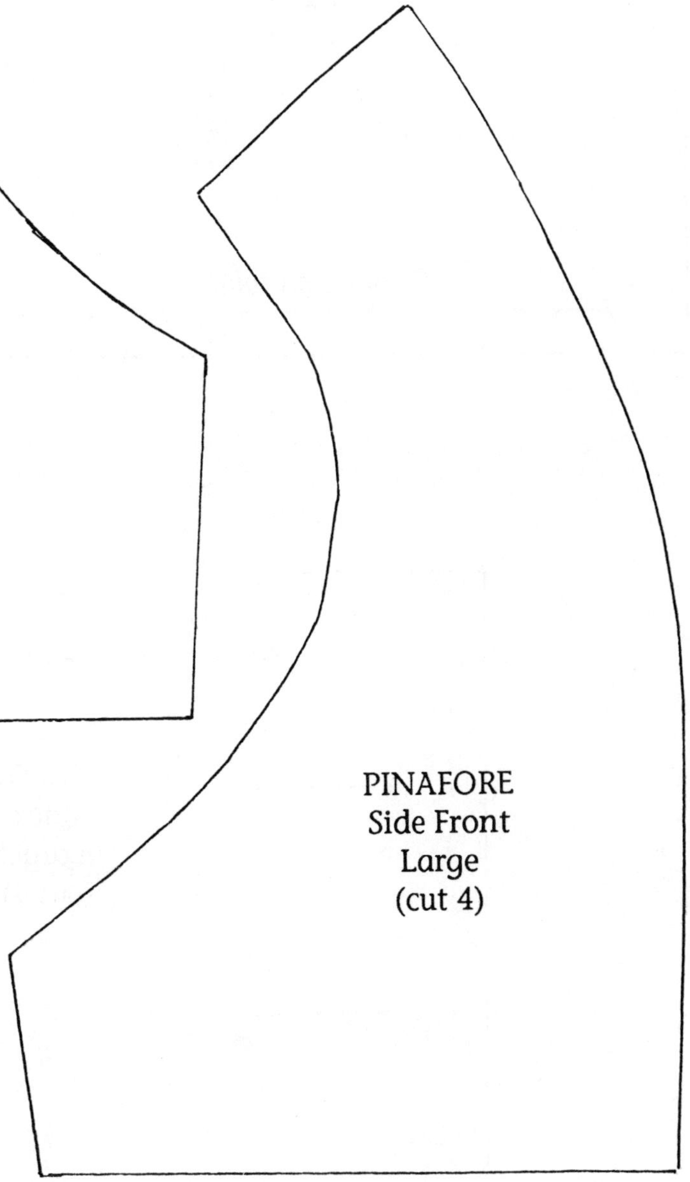

PINAFORE
Side Front
Large
(cut 4)

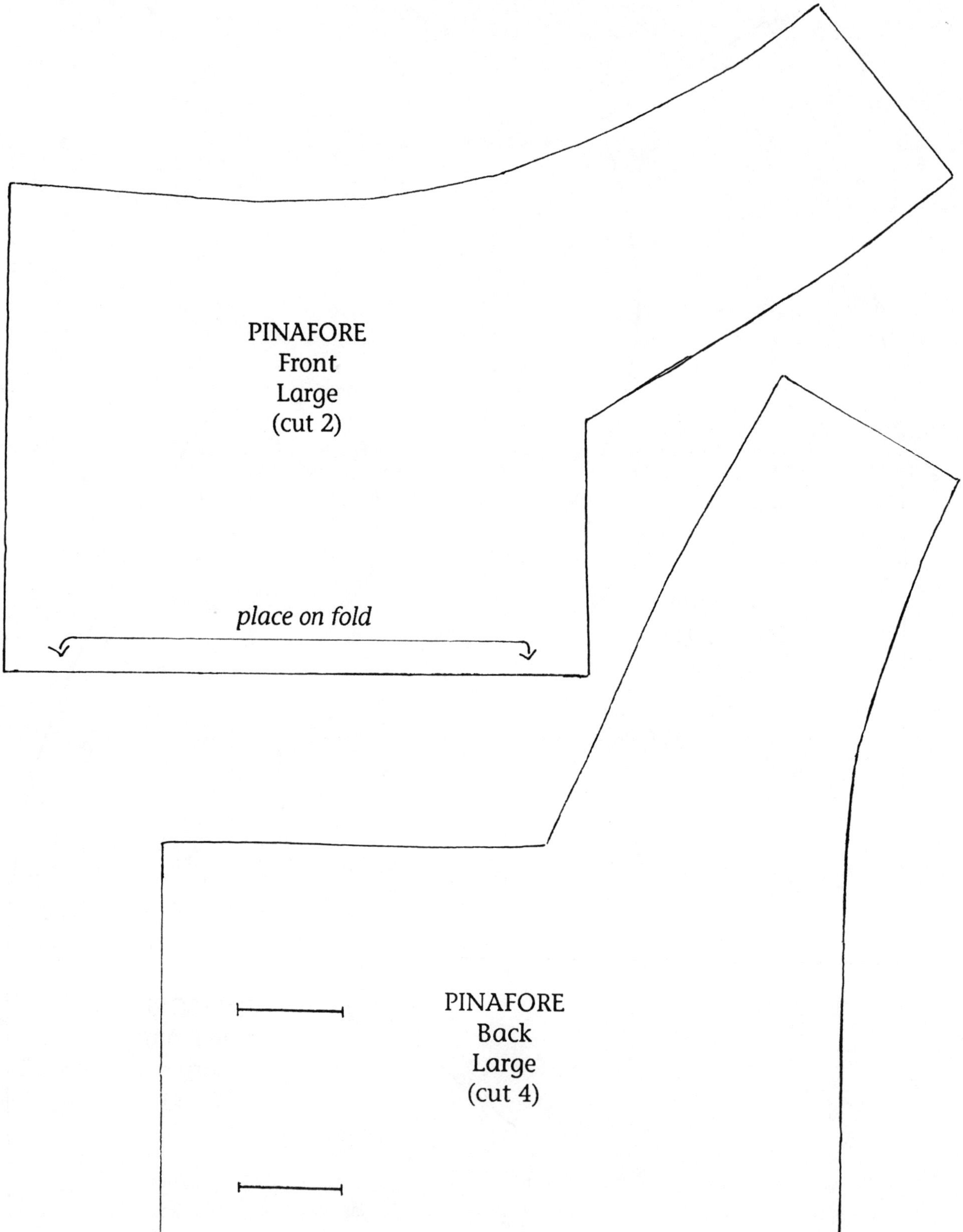

PINAFORE
Front
Large
(cut 2)

place on fold

PINAFORE
Back
Large
(cut 4)

NIGHTSHIRT & NIGHTCAP

Early to bed, early to rise...will be a pleasure for your bear when he wears this cozy duo. The old classic, red flannel, is sure to please your bear and ensure him many a sweet dream.

Nightshirt

MATERIALS

¹/₃ yard fabric for either small or large bear

Matching thread

Three buttons

INSTRUCTIONS

1. As instructed in chapter 1, transfer the pattern to paper, pin to the wrong side of the fabric, and cut out the fabric.

2. Fold front placket in half lengthwise. Pin to right side of front along slash, matching raw edges at top and along slash. Stitch. Repeat for other placket.

3. Clip diagonally from bottom of slit to dot through nightshirt front and both layers of placket.

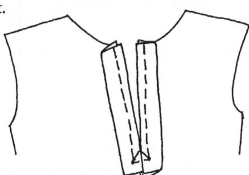

Turn right placket out flat, pushing bottom extension to wrong side of nightshirt front. Turn left placket out flat, with bottom

extension of placket on outside. Turn under bottom edge of top extension ³/₄". Topstitch a box with a "V" in it through all layers. Clip the excess inside placket extension close to stitching.

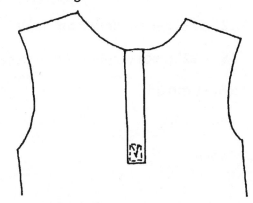

4. Stitch shoulder seams.

5. With right side of neck facing wrong side of nightshirt neck opening, pin neck facing to neckline, matching center backs and leaving ¹/₄" of neck facing extending past neckline edge in front. Stitch. Trim.

6. Turn facing to right side of neckline. Turn under ¹/₄" on raw edges of facing. Pin in place. Topstitch close to edge.

7. Pin sleeve to nightshirt matching large dot to shoulder seam. Stitch.

8. With right sides together, stitch front to back as one continuous seam, starting at sleeve opening and continuing along underarm and side seam to bottom of nightshirt, underarm seams and bottom edges.

9. Turn under $\frac{1}{4}$" at sleeve edge. Press under another $\frac{1}{4}$". Topstitch. Repeat for other sleeve.

10. Turn under $\frac{1}{4}$" at hem. Press under another $\frac{1}{4}$". Topstitch.

11. Make buttonholes on left front placket and neck facing.

12. Sew buttons in place.

Nightcap

MATERIALS

Fabric:

12" x 18" piece of fabric for small bear

15" x 22" piece of fabric for large bear

Matching thread

$\frac{1}{4}$"-wide elastic

Jingle bell

INSTRUCTIONS

1. As instructed in chapter 1, transfer the pattern to paper, pin to the wrong side of the fabric, and cut out the fabric.

2. Pin the two cap pieces together. Stitch long sides, leaving bottom edges open. Trim raw edges. Turn. Press.

3. Turn under $\frac{1}{4}$" on bottom edge. Turn under an additional $\frac{3}{4}$" to form casing for elastic.

4. Topstitch $\frac{5}{8}$" from folded edge, leaving a $\frac{1}{2}$" gap in stitching to insert elastic. Topstitch $\frac{1}{4}$" from folded edge.

5. Cut a piece of elastic to fit your bear's head plus 1". Insert elastic through casing by attaching a safety pin to one end and pushing it through the casing. Try on bear. Adjust elastic. Overlap raw edges of elastic and stitch back and forth to secure. Topstitch gap in stitching closed.

6. Sew the bell to the point of the cap.

top

NIGHTSHIRT PLACKET   Large and Small

foldline

(cut 2)

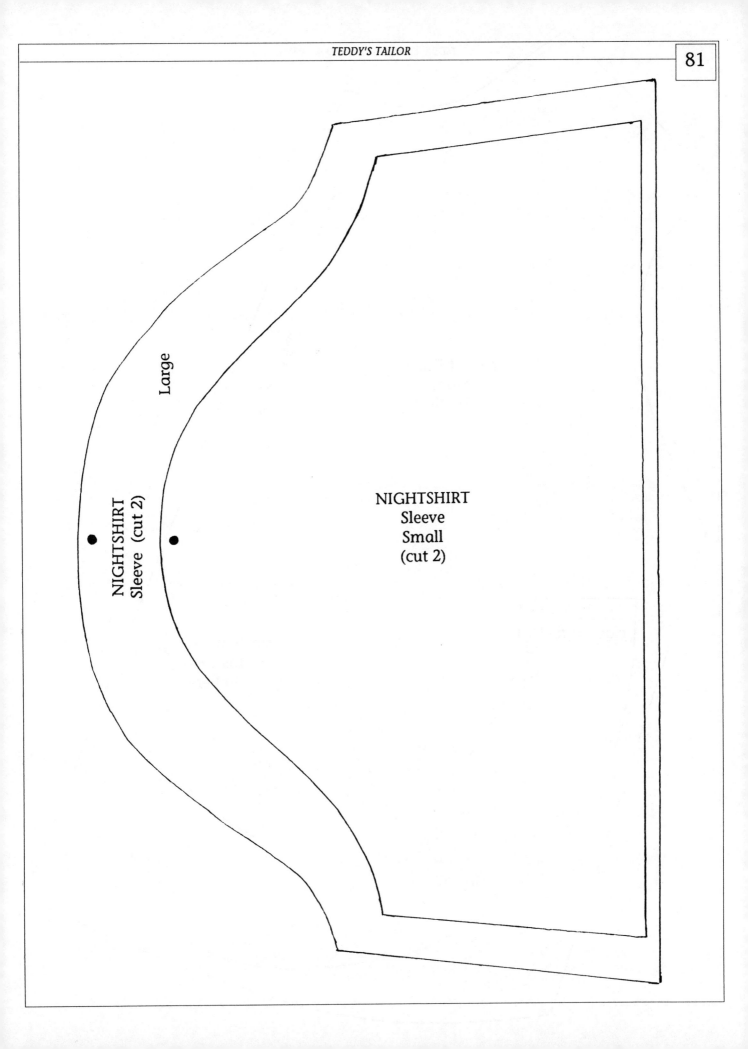

Large

NIGHTSHIRT
Sleeve (cut 2)

NIGHTSHIRT
Sleeve
Small
(cut 2)

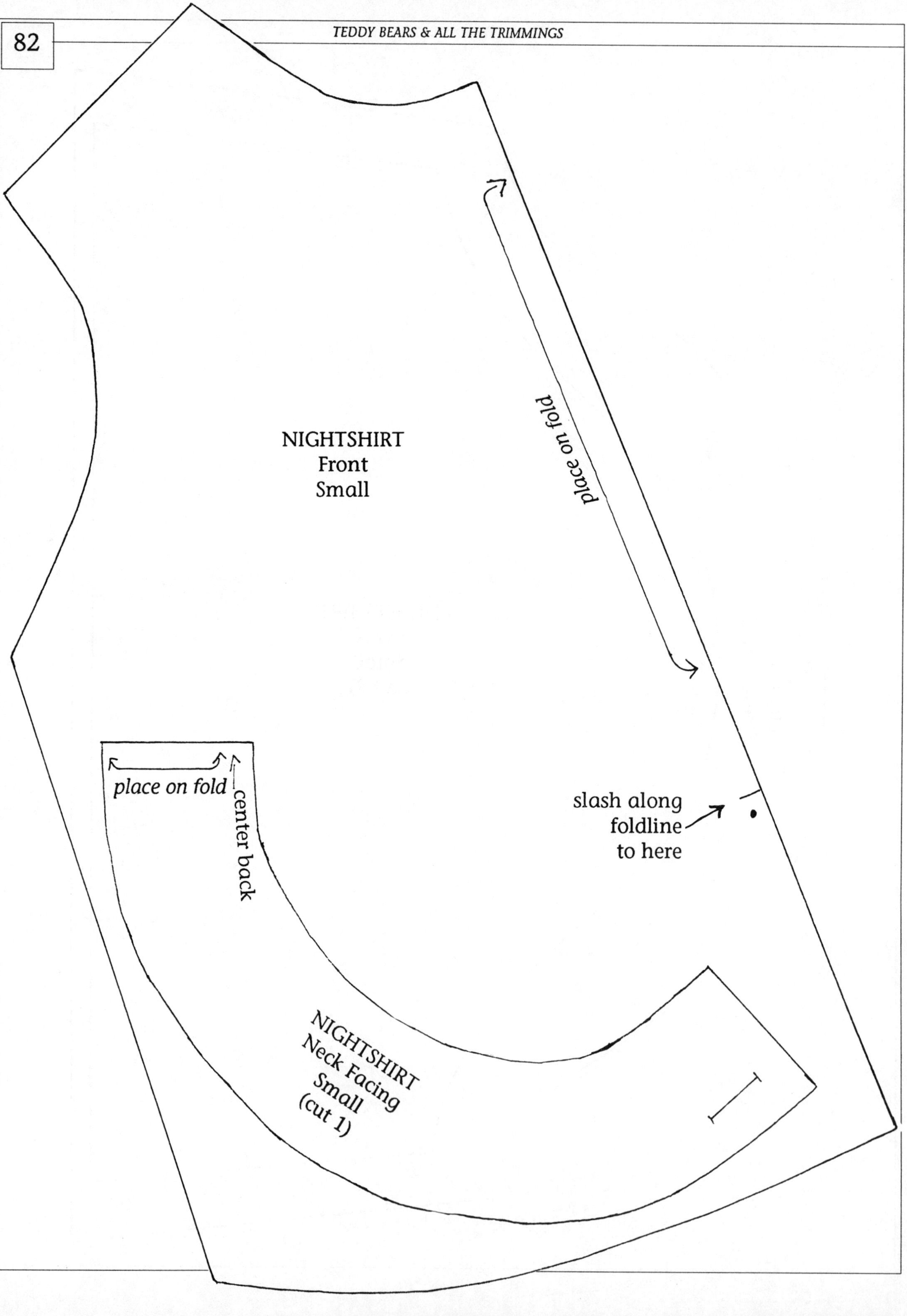

NIGHTSHIRT
Front
Small

place on fold

slash along
foldline
to here

place on fold

center back

NIGHTSHIRT
Neck Facing
Small
(cut 1)

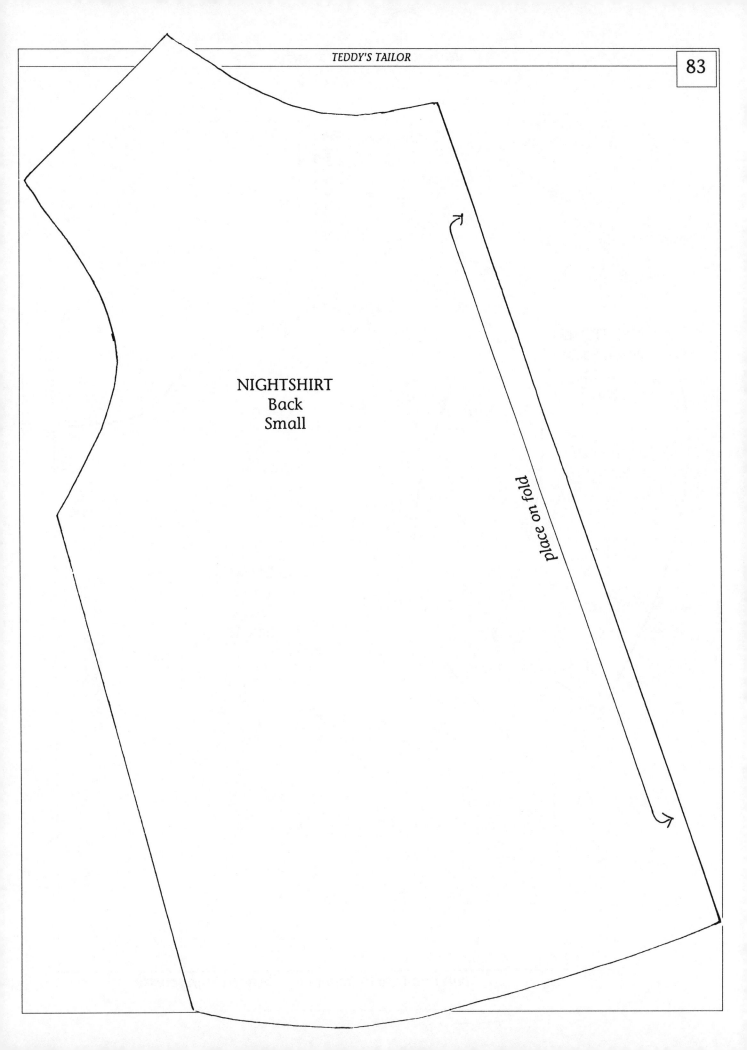

NIGHTSHIRT
Back
Small

place on fold

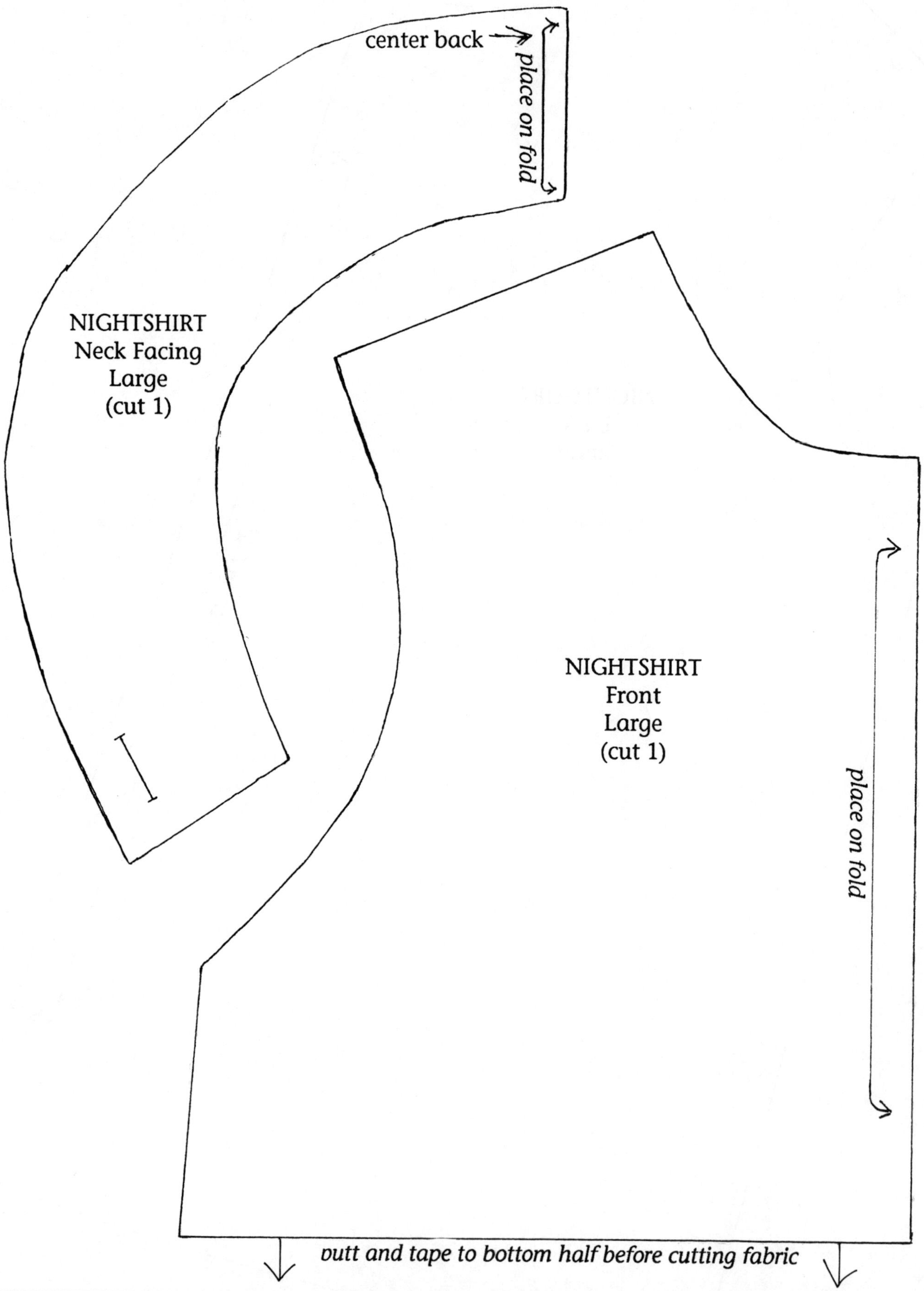

center back

place on fold

NIGHTSHIRT
Neck Facing
Large
(cut 1)

NIGHTSHIRT
Front
Large
(cut 1)

place on fold

butt and tape to bottom half before cutting fabric

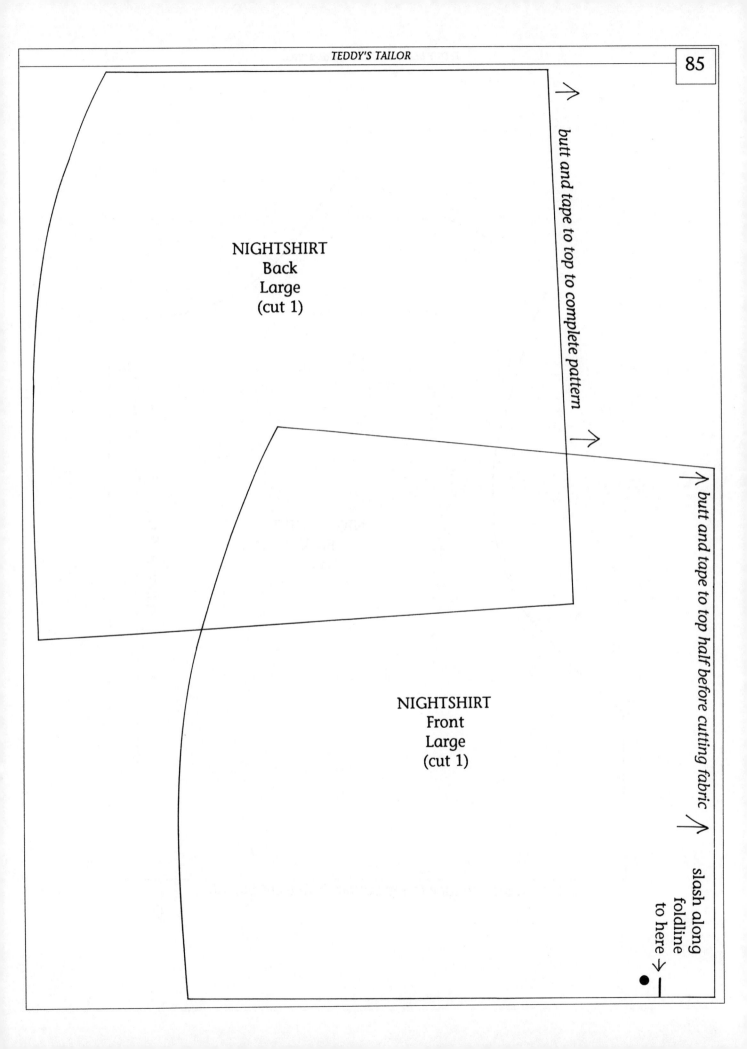

NIGHTSHIRT
Back
Large
(cut 1)

butt and tape to top to complete pattern

NIGHTSHIRT
Front
Large
(cut 1)

butt and tape to top half before cutting fabric

slash along
foldline
to here

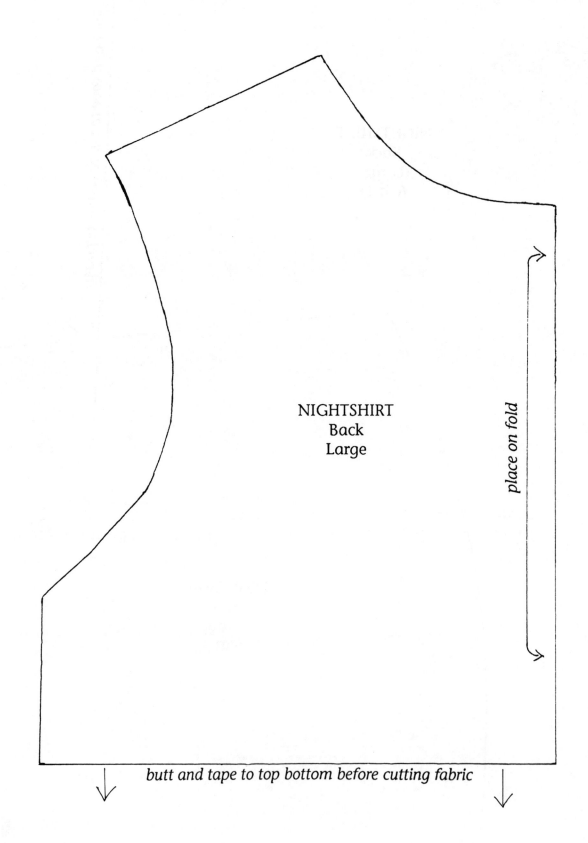

NIGHTSHIRT
Back
Large

place on fold

butt and tape to top bottom before cutting fabric

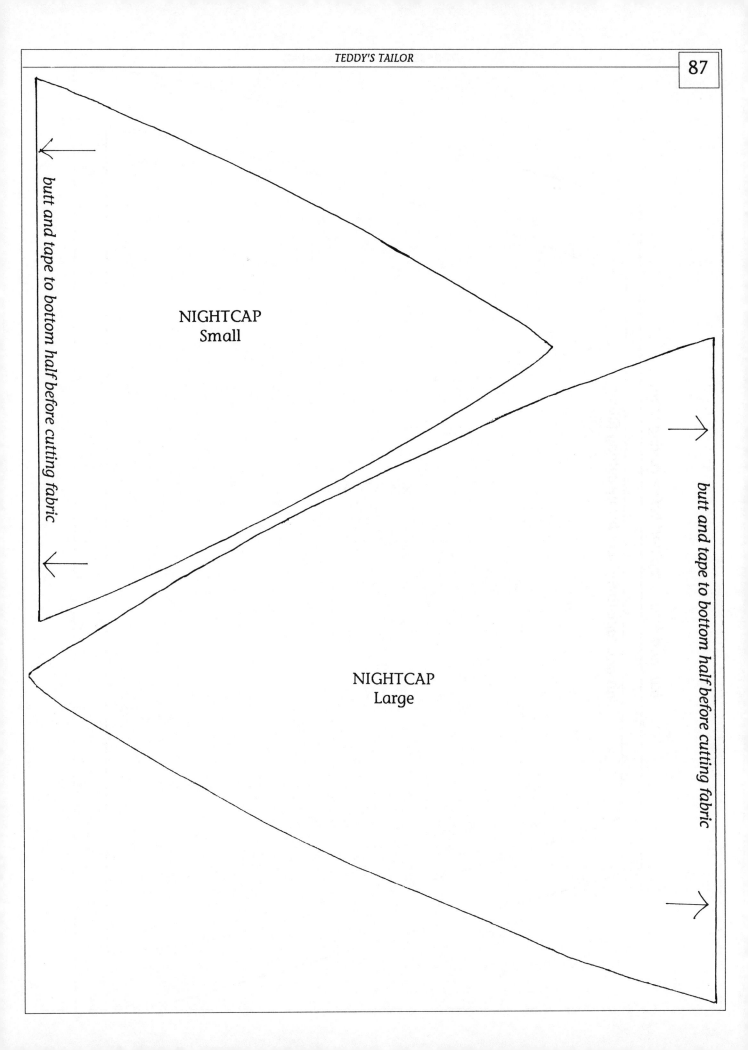

NIGHTCAP
Small

NIGHTCAP
Large

butt and tape to bottom half before cutting fabric

butt and tape to bottom half before cutting fabric

Large

Small

butt and tape to top half before cutting fabric

butt and tape to top half before cutting fabric

NIGHTCAP
(cut 2)

NIGHTIE & DUSTER

Sewn up in warm winter flannel or light lawn for summer, this dainty nightie will bring your bear many happy dreams. The lace-edged duster is a perfect complement in muslin or made of fabric to match the nightie.

Nightie

MATERIALS

Fabric:

$1/3$ yard for small bear

$3/8$ yard for large bear

Matching thread

$1/4$"-wide elastic

$1/4$"-wide ribbon

INSTRUCTIONS

1. As instructed in chapter 1, transfer the pattern to paper, pin to the wrong side of the fabric, and cut out the fabric.

2. Stitch sleeves to front of nightie, matching notches and large dots. Match front to back of nightie. Stitch one sleeve to respective back of nightie, matching notches and large dots.

3. Turn under $3/4$" on neck edge. Press. Cut a piece of elastic, 9" for small and 11" for large. Pin ends of the elastic to neck edge, raw edges of elastic even with the ends of the neck opening. With a zigzag stitch sew the elastic, centering it over the turned-under raw edge of the neck, taking a few stitches backwards and forwards at the beginning and end of the seam to secure the elastic. Stretch the elastic flat along the seam as you go. To do this, hold the fabric and the elastic at both pinned ends and stretch the elastic to lie flat.

4. Stitch the remaining sleeve edge to back of nightie.

5. Turn under $3/4$" on sleeve edges. Cut two pieces of elastic, 6" long for small and 7" for large. Lay the elastic along the raw edge. Pin the ends in place. Zigzag in place, holding the elastic and fabric together at each end, stretching it as you go.

6. Pin and stitch underarm/side seams.

7. Press under $1/4$" for hem. Press under another $1/4$". Topstitch.

8. Make a bow from the ribbon. Attach a small safety pin to the back of the bow. Pin to center front of nightie at neck.

Duster

MATERIALS

16"-square of muslin

Matching thread

Elastic thread

1"-wide or smaller lace

INSTRUCTIONS

1. Prepare the paper pattern as instructed in the first chapter of this book. Fold the square of fabric in half. Fold in half again. Place the corner of the paper pattern on the folded corner of the fabric, lining up the two straight sides. Pin to the wrong side of fabric. Cut out. Open the fabric into a circle.

2. Press under $1/4$" on duster edge for hem. Repeat. Topstitch lace to edge leaving an extra $1/2$" of lace at either end for a seam. Sew the seam in the lace. Trim the lace seam.

3. Zigzag over elastic thread in a circle 2" from finished edge, taking care not to stitch through the elastic. Backstitch at beginning and end. Tie a secure knot in the elastic. You may wish to pin a ribbon bow on the outside of the duster over the knot.

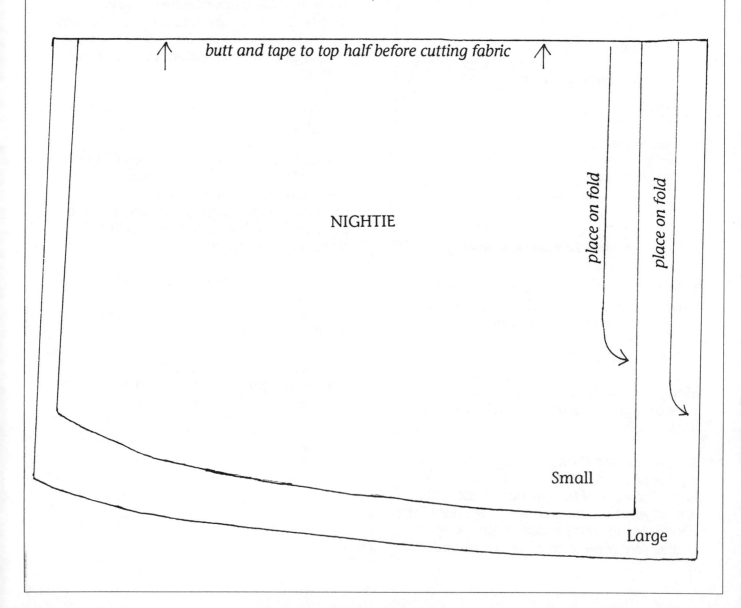

butt and tape to top half before cutting fabric

NIGHTIE

place on fold

place on fold

Small

Large

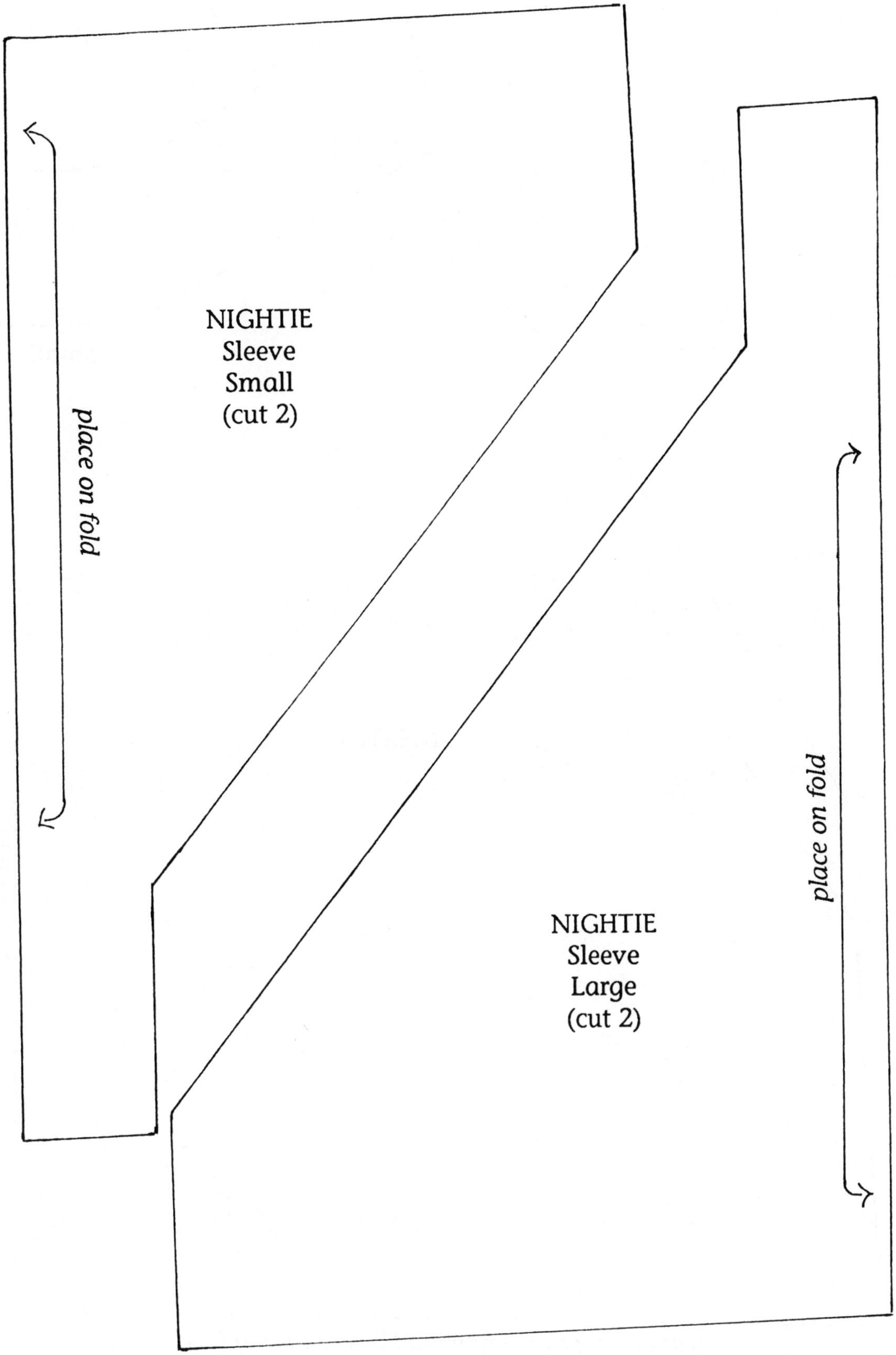

NIGHTIE
Sleeve
Small
(cut 2)

place on fold

NIGHTIE
Sleeve
Large
(cut 2)

place on fold

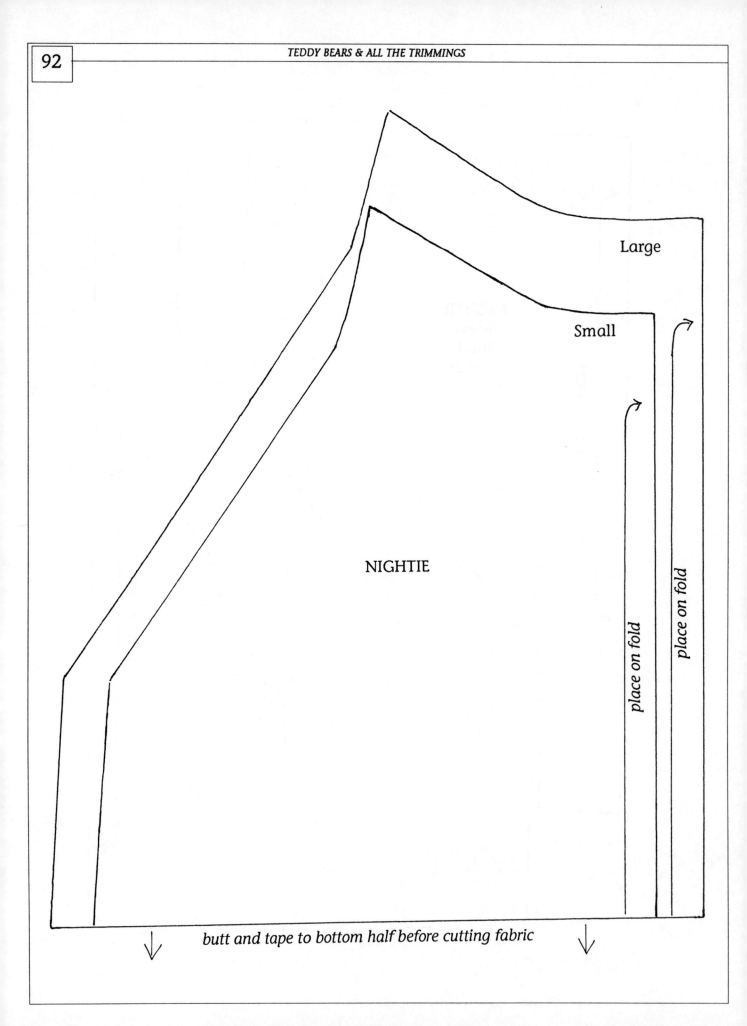

Large

Small

NIGHTIE

place on fold

place on fold

butt and tape to bottom half before cutting fabric

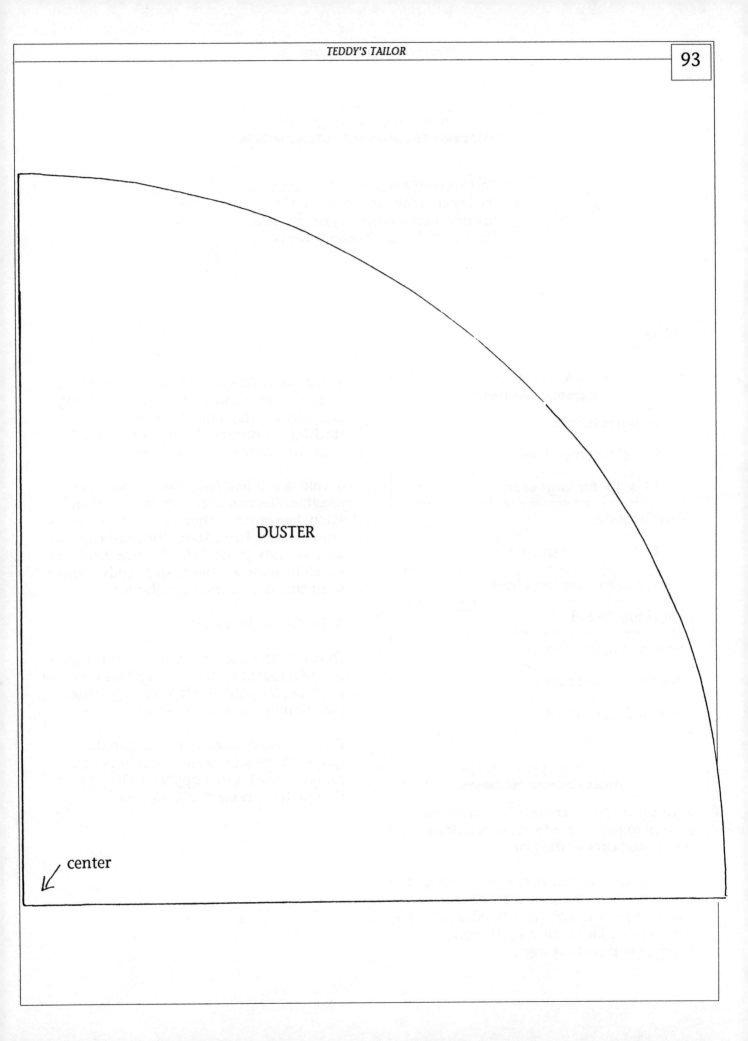

DUSTER

center

SAILOR SUIT

This ensemble is perfect for a picnic at the beach. Make the whole outfit for the soft stuffed bears or just the collar for a jointed bear. Anchors away!

Collar

MATERIALS

White collar fabric:

8" x 8" for small bear

10" x 10" for large bear

Red tie fabric:

$2^1/2$" x $6^1/2$" for small bear

$3^1/2$" x $7^1/2$" for large bear

Matching thread

$^2/_3$ yard red, braid trim

Two iron-on gold stars

Optional: fusible web

INSTRUCTIONS

1. As instructed in chapter 1, transfer the pattern to paper, pin to the wrong side of the fabric, and cut out the fabric.

2. Stitch, glue, or fuse trim to right side of one collar piece, $^3/_4$" from the three straight raw edges. Leave a tail of trim extending over the curved raw edge to catch in the neckline seam. Fuse stars in corners.

3. Pin two collar-pieces together, right sides together. Stitch, starting and ending along one side, leaving a one-inch gap in the stitching for turning. Trim seams. Turn. Press. Handsew openings closed.

4. Fold ties in half lengthwise, right sides together. Starting at fold on one short end, stitch, leaving the other end open for turning. Trim corners. Turn. Press. Turn raw edges of unsewn ends inside. Fold in thirds lengthwise. Carefully handsew ties to front ends of collar so stitches don't show on collar top.

5. Tie the ties in a knot.

DRESS: Follow instructions for dress (pages 65 and 66), making it out of navy blue cotton or wool. Don't apply lace to neck edge. (Use pattern on pages 68, 69, 70, 71.)

PANTS: Follow instructions for pantaloons (page 68), making them out of navy blue cotton or wool. Don't apply lace to leg hems. (Use pattern on pages 57, 58, 59.)

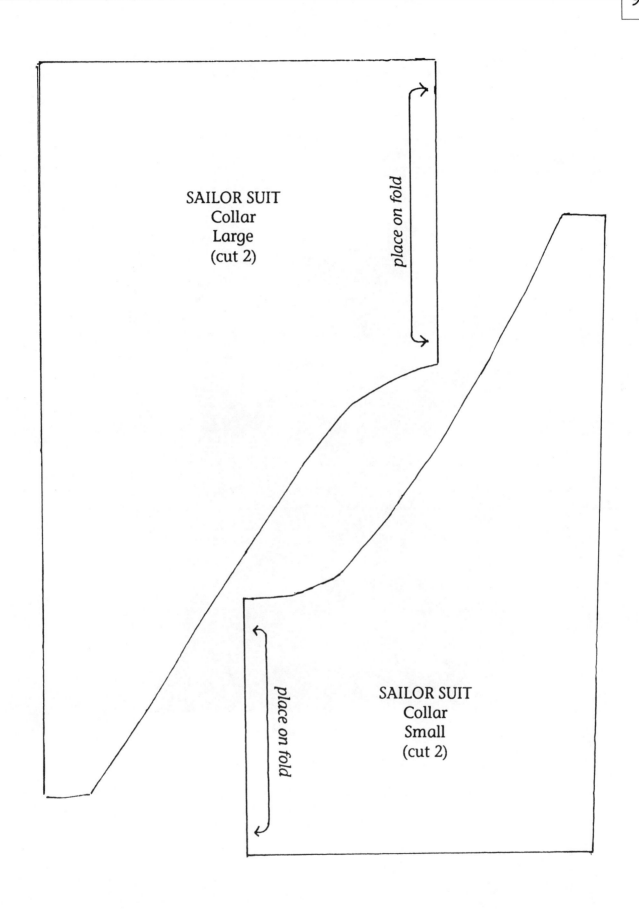

SAILOR SUIT
Collar
Large
(cut 2)

place on fold

SAILOR SUIT
Collar
Small
(cut 2)

place on fold

C H A P T E R • 4

DRESSED FOR THE HOLIDAYS

♡ ♡ ♡

Bears simply love to dress up for special occasions. Though they certainly don't need any help in getting in the spirit for any holiday, bears do seem to spread holiday cheer wherever they go.

In addition to holiday themes, you may wish to assemble a personalized outfit reflecting the recipient's occupation, favorite sport, or important event in life. Make a shortened version of the pants pattern out of white, match with a white shirt (perhaps with a red rugby stripe) made from the nightshirt pattern (crop just below the waist). Add a headband and there you have a beary important tennis player.

A pair of wire-rimmed glasses, a knitted muffler, and a stack of books (see Sources) will see a bear off to school, whether kindergarten or Harvard.

Let your imagination flow freely as you peruse your local crafts store. Holiday garb and personalized bear gifts can be enchanting or humorous, depending on the message you want to send. The possibilities are endless.

SANTA SUIT

Dressed in this Santa suit your teddy bear will become Christmas cheer personified. Choose either bright red or maroon flannel or wool for the suit. You will need ½ yard of fabric for all three pieces, either size.

Santa Cap

MATERIALS

Fabric:

12" x 18" piece of fabric for small bear

15" x 22" piece of fabric for large bear

Matching thread

¼"-wide elastic

2½" x 22" piece of synthetic shearling

Gold braid

Jingle bell

INSTRUCTIONS

Use pattern for cap on pages 87 and 88.

1. As instructed in chapter 1, transfer the pattern to paper, pin pattern to the wrong side of fabric, and cut out the fabric.

2. Pin the two cap pieces together. Stitch long sides leaving bottom edges open. Trim raw edges. Turn. Press.

3. Turn under ¼" on bottom edge. Turn under an additional ¾" to form casing for elastic.

4. Topstitch ⅝" from folded edge, leaving a ½" gap in stitching to insert elastic. Topstitch ¼" from folded edge.

5. Cut a piece of elastic to fit your bear's head, adding one inch. Insert elastic through casing by attaching a safety pin to one end and pushing it through the casing. Try on bear. Adjust elastic. Overlap raw edges of elastic and stitch back and forth to secure. Topstitch gap in stitching closed.

6. Sew the bell to the point of the cap.

7. Butt long raw edges of shearling together. Using a doubled thread, overcast stitch the raw edges together, using a long stitch.

8. Cut a piece of gold braid two inches longer than the length of the shearling. Leaving one inch extending past the raw edges on either end, stitch the braid along the center of the right side of the shearling. Catch just a single strand of the braid with each stitch so your sewing won't show on the right side.

9. Sew the shearling to the edge of the head opening of the cap, butting the raw edges and turning the gold braid under. Stitch the butted edges together.

Santa's Collar

MATERIALS

7" x 15" piece of fabric for large bear

Matching thread

2" x 15" shearling fleece

$^1/_2$ yard gold braid

INSTRUCTIONS

1. As instructed in chapter 1, transfer the collar pattern to paper, pin to the wrong side of the fabric, and cut out the fabric.

2. Pin two collar pieces together, right sides facing. Stitch, leaving an opening to turn the collar. Trim the seam. Clip neck curve. Turn. Handstitch the opening closed.

3. Handstitch gold braid to top of collar $^1/_4$" away from the edge, catching just one strand of the braid with each stitch.

4. With right sides together, fold the fleece in half lengthwise. Whipstitch the long raw edges together. Sew to the underside of the outside edge of the collar.

Santa's Bag

MATERIALS

10" x 20" piece of fabric

Matching thread

Gold cord for drawstring

INSTRUCTIONS

1. Transfer pattern from book onto heavy paper. Cut out. Lay pattern on folded fabric. Pin. Cut out.

2. Stitch sides and bottom of bag, right sides together, leaving the top of the bag open. Trim the seam.

3. Press under $^1/_4$" at the top opening of the bag. Press under $^3/_4$" to form casing. Topstitch $^5/_8$" from folded edge leaving a $^1/_2$" gap in stitching to insert the draw cord. Topstitch $^1/_4$" from folded edge.

4. Attach a safety pin to one end of the drawstring and insert the drawstring into the casing. Remove safety pin. Tie knots in the ends of the cord.

Fill Santa's bag with small ornaments, a little doll, wrapped candies, jewelry gift boxes wrapped in holiday paper and tied with ribbon, and small goodies from your local crafts shop.

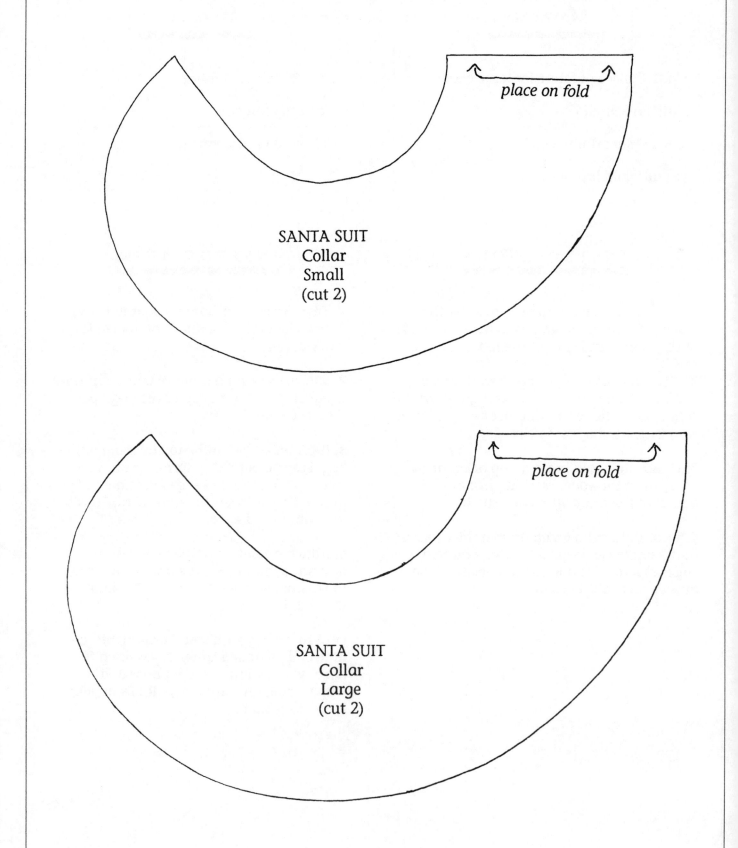

place on fold

SANTA SUIT
Collar
Small
(cut 2)

place on fold

SANTA SUIT
Collar
Large
(cut 2)

SANTA'S
SACK OF GOODIES
(cut 2)

place on fold

EASTER OUTFIT

To match the light-hearted cheer of this promising season, choose dotted swiss, a pink gingham check, or a pastel taffeta with the skirt and parasol overlaid in chantilly lace. Adorned with ribbons and roses, your bear's Easter outfit will make her the belle of your bear kingdom.

Easter Dress

MATERIALS

Fabric:

⅓ yard for small bear

½ yard for large bear

Matching thread

¼"-wide elastic

1½ yards of 3"-wide eyelet

½ yard ½"-wide lace trim

1 yard of ⅞"-wide ribbon

Three buttons

INSTRUCTIONS

Use pattern for dress on pages 68, 69, 70 and 71.

1. As instructed in chapter 1, transfer the pattern to paper, pin to wrong side of fabric, and cut out the fabric. Cut the skirt piece: 6½" x 25" for small bear, 7" x 30" for large bear.

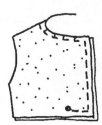

2. Stitch backs to fronts at shoulder seams for both dress and lining. Pin neck and back seams, right sides together, including the lace in the neck seam. Turn under raw edges at ends of lace and stitch so it won't peek out. Trim. You may wish to seal the loose threads of the lace with Fray Check™. Stitch back and neck as one continuous seam between the dots on the lower edges of the bodice backs. Trim seam. Clip neck curve. Turn. Press.

3. Press under ¼" at bottom edge of sleeve. Repeat. Topstitch. Cut a piece of elastic: 6" for the small bear, 7" for the large bear. Lay elastic about ⅝" from finished hem edge. Pin raw ends of elastic in place, even with raw sleeve edges. Hold the fabric and the elastic at both pinned ends and stretch the elastic to lie flat. With a zigzag stitch sew the elastic in place, beginning with a few backward and forward stitches to secure the elastic, stretching the elastic flat along the seam as you go.

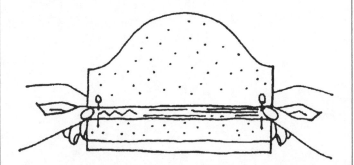

4. Using a long stitch, gather the sleeve heads between the dots, $1/8$" from the raw edge. Pin the sleeve to the dress. Adjust the gathers. Stitch in place.

5. Right sides together, sew the underarm and sides seam.

6. With a $1/2$" seam allowance, sew the center back seam of the skirt from the bottom up, stopping three inches from the top of the skirt. Finish stitching the remainder of this seam with basting stitches. Press under $1/4$" of this seam allowance. Starting at the top of the skirt, topstitch $1/8$" from the turned under edge, pivoting below the opening and continuing to stitch up the other side back to the top of the skirt. Remove the basting stitches. This opening in the center back seam will allow room for your pleasingly plump bear to get in and out of her dress with ease.

7. Leaving two inches ungathered at each end of the skirt top, gather the skirt top with long stitches. Pin to bodice. Adjust gathers. Stitch.

8. Press under $1/4$" on bottom edge of dress for hem. Turn under $1/4$". Stitch in place. Measure the circumference of the hem at this stitching. Cut a piece of eyelet this length plus $1/2$". Right sides together, sew the short ends of the eyelet together, using a $1/4$" seam allowance. Handstitch the eyelet to the underside of the hem, letting it show at the bottom of the dress. Handstitch the $1/2$"-wide lace on the outside of the hem over the stitching.

9. Handstitch the trim lace to the undersides of the sleeve edges, letting it peek out from under the sleeve edge.

10. Make buttonholes on bodice. Try on bear. Mark button placement. Sew buttons on.

Easter Bonnet

MATERIALS

Bonnet: available from craft shops, The Teddy Works and from Gailloraine Originals (see Sources)

$1 1/2$ yards of $7/8$"-wide ribbon to match the dress fabric

Six velvet leaves : available from craft shops and Florida Supply (see Sources)

One bunch of ribbon roses

Two hat pins

Glue

INSTRUCTIONS

1. Glue ribbon to hat brim leaving ends extending to tie around the bear's neck

2. Turn stem of ribbon roses back on itself. Entwine stems of leaves in the ribbon rose stem, hiding them.

3. With the hat pins, pin the roses/leaves to the hat on one side.

4. Put the hat on the bear and tie the bow under her chin or to one side.

Bear Parasol

MATERIALS

Parasol frame: available from craft shops and The Teddy Works (see Sources)

10" x 10" piece of fabric to match the Easter dress

$5/8$ yard of $1/2$"-wide lace trim to match dress

9 single ribbon roses

Glue

INSTRUCTIONS

1. Follow the instructions included with the parasol to cut the parasol fabric; pin, and sew it to the frame.

2. Glue a rose to the end of each arm of the parasol. Glue three roses around the peak of the parasol.

3. Handstitch lace trim to edge of parasol, just on top of the edge of the frame.

Bear Bunny Ears

MATERIALS

12" x 14" piece of fake-fur fabric

12" x 14" piece of satin-type fabric for lining the ears

Matching thread

Two pieces of wire, easily bent but strong enough to hold its shape, each 26" long

Wire cutters

1 yard of $1^1/2$"-wide ribbon

INSTRUCTIONS

1. Transfer the pattern for the ears from the book. Cut two out of fur and two out of lining.

2. Pin one fur ear to one lining ear, right sides together. Sew, leaving the bottom open. Repeat for the other ear.

3. Bend wire in half. Insert into ear, bent end first. Push all the way into the ear. Push and bend the wire into the shape of the ear until it fits smoothly along the inside edges of the ear. Fold the cut ends across the opening, inside the ear so that they won't poke out.

4. Turn under the bottom edges of the ears. Handstitch closed.

5. Lay the ears down side by side, touching. Whipstitch the adjacent sides of the ears together from the bottom up about four inches. Lay the middle of the ribbon over them on the fur side. Pin. Handstitch in place.

6. Tie snugly around the bear's neck.

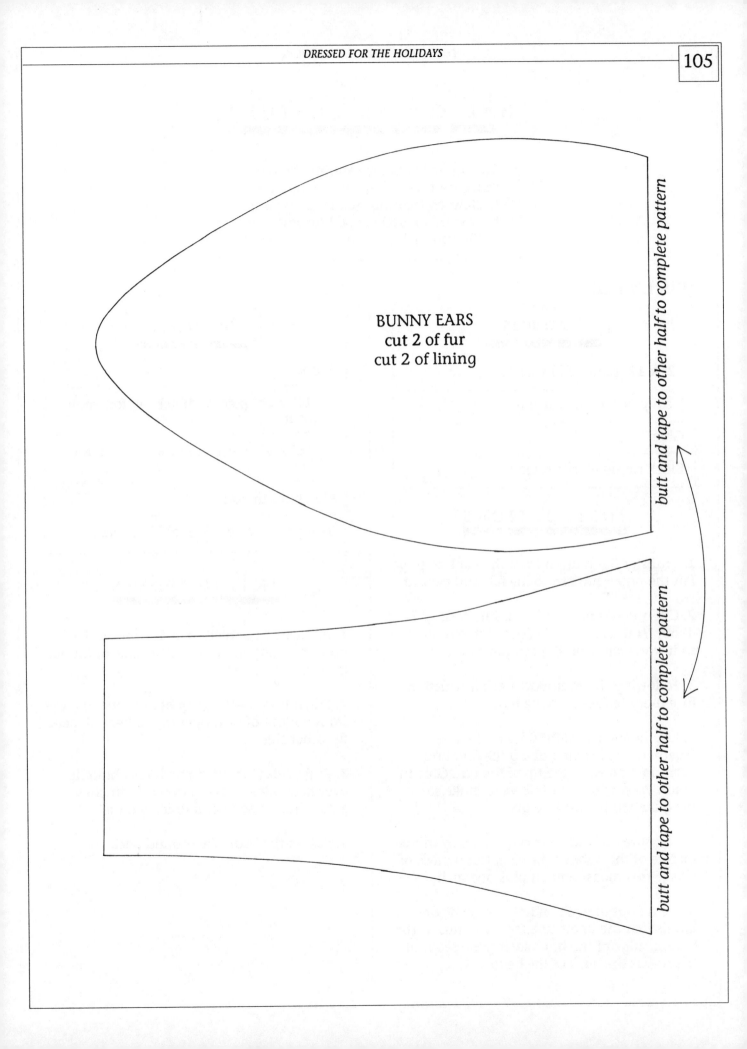

BUNNY EARS
cut 2 of fur
cut 2 of lining

butt and tape to other half to complete pattern

butt and tape to other half to complete pattern

HALLOWEEN COSTUME

Though teddy bears certainly aren't much on tricks, they love to join in on Halloween treating. So, dress up your bear with a simple cape/hat/broom outfit and trick or treat bag, and invite him to join in the fun!

Witch's Hat

MATERIALS

12" x 12" piece of black felt

Heavy fusible interfacing

Glue

Black round elastic thread

INSTRUCTIONS

1. Transfer the pattern from the book to paper. Pin the paper pattern to the felt and cut out.

2. Cut one hat pattern out of interfacing. Trim about $1/4$ inch from all edges of the interfacing so it won't show on the completed hat.

3. Following the manufacturer's instructions, fuse the interfacing to the hat.

4. Pin the long straight sides of the hat together, overlapping along the fold line, forming a point at the tip of the hat. Glue in place. Press with your fingers to make sure the glue bonds. Allow to dry.

5. Measure around your bear's chin from the middle of the back of the ears. Cut a piece of elastic this measurement plus one inch.

6. Tie a knot in each end of the elastic and handstitch the knots to opposite points at the bottom edge of the hat, placing the seam of the hat at the back of the head.

Cape

MATERIALS

Fabric:

14" x 28" piece of black felt for small bear

16" x 32" piece of black felt for large bear

Matching thread

$1/4$"-wide black double-fold bias tape

INSTRUCTIONS

1. As instructed in chapter 1, transfer the pattern to paper, pin to wrong side of fabric, and cut out fabric.

2. Stitch from neck to top of arm opening and from bottom of arm opening to hem. Repeat for other side.

3. Right sides together, stitch bias binding over neck edge, leaving about six inches extending on each end to form a tie.

4. Put on the bear. Tie around neck.

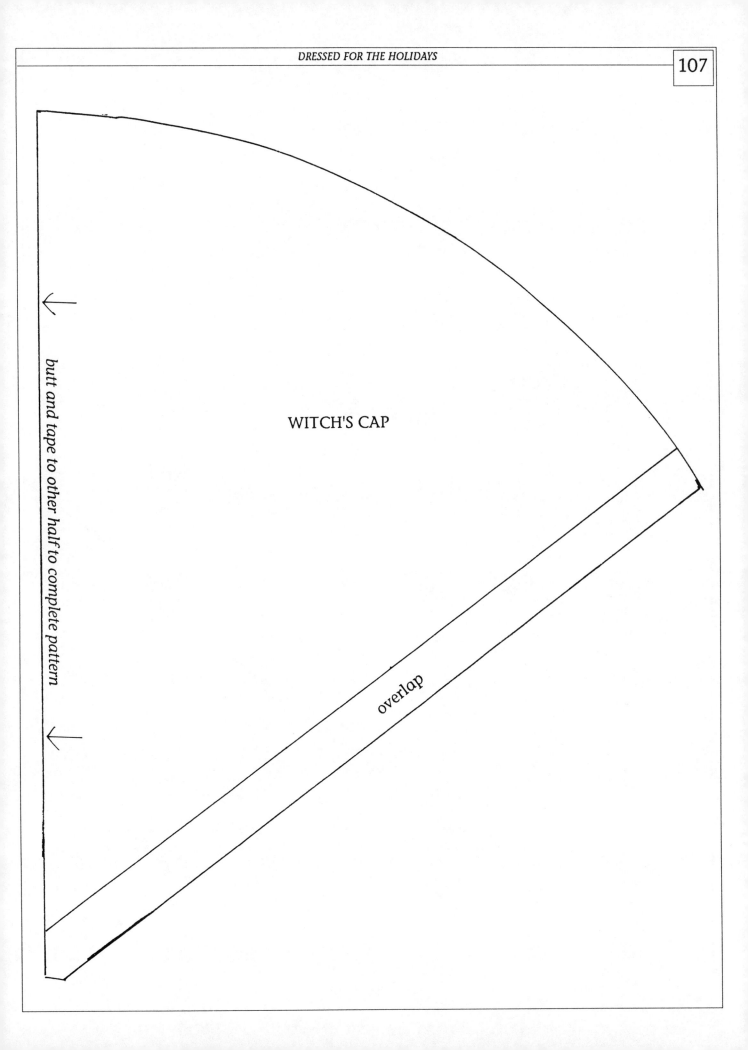

WITCH'S CAP

butt and tape to other half to complete pattern

overlap

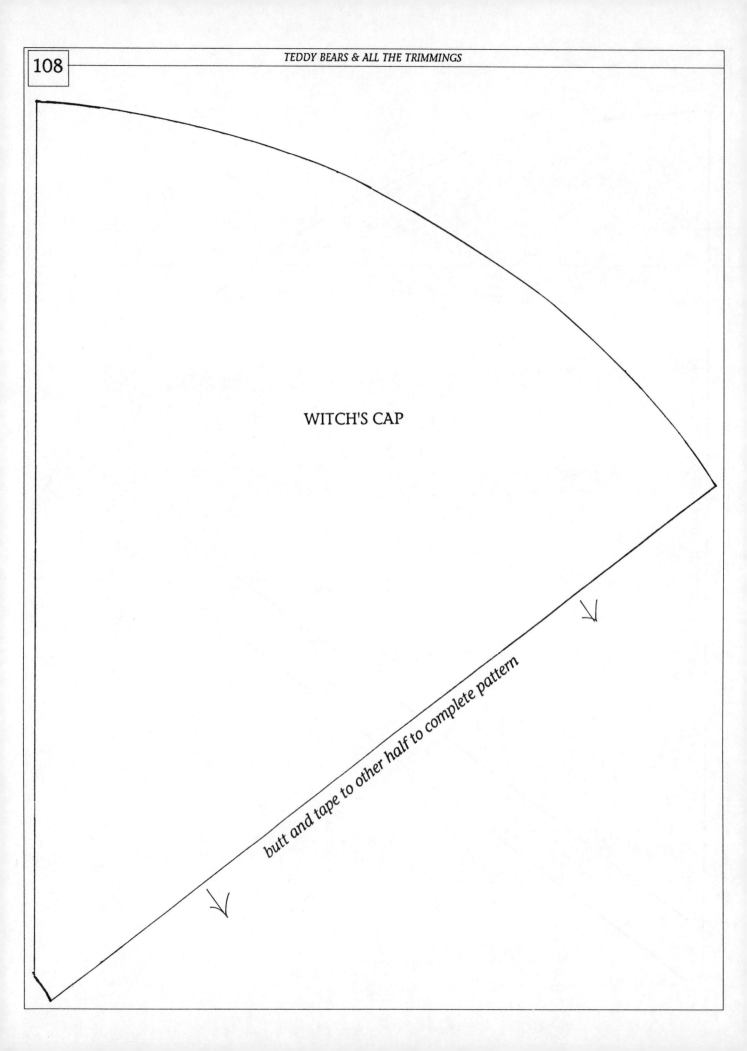

WITCH'S CAP

butt and tape to other half to complete pattern

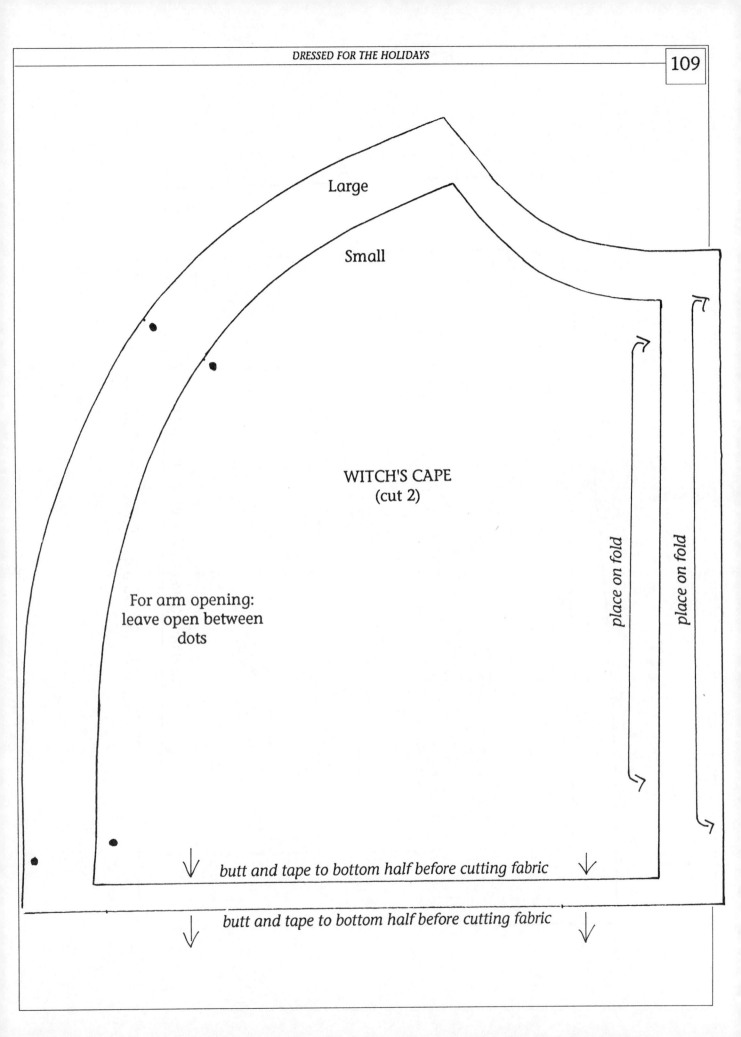

Large

Small

WITCH'S CAPE
(cut 2)

place on fold

place on fold

For arm opening:
leave open between
dots

butt and tape to bottom half before cutting fabric

butt and tape to bottom half before cutting fabric

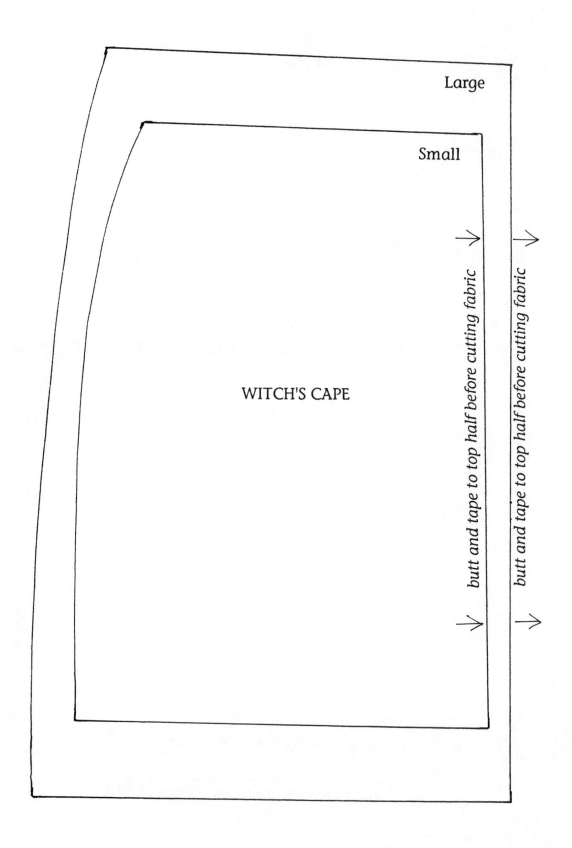

Large

Small

WITCH'S CAPE

butt and tape to top half before cutting fabric

butt and tape to top half before cutting fabric

INDEPENDENCE DAY

Teddy bears are patriotic too! And your teddy will enjoy showing his spirit in his Uncle Sam suit. Use blue cotton, wool, or a cotton/polyester blend fabric for the vest and a red and white striped cotton, wool, or flannel for the pants.

Top Hat

MATERIALS

Fabric:

One 9" x 12" piece of white felt, cut in half lengthwise

One 9" x 12" piece of red felt

One 9" x 12" piece of blue felt

Wonder Under™ or glue

Round elastic thread

Blue thread

White thread

One 12" x 12" piece of fusible interfacing or craft fuse

INSTRUCTIONS

1. Cut two top hat brim pieces of blue felt. Cut four $4^1/2$" x $1^1/2$" pieces and one hat top piece of red felt.

2. Cut one hat brim, one hat top, and one hat side ($4^1/2$" x 12") out of heavy weight fusible interfacing or craft fuse. Fuse to pieces as instructed on product directions.

3. Cut one hat brim, four strips $1^1/2$" x $4^1/2$", and one strip $1/2$" x $4^1/2$" of Wonder Under™. Fuse the first to the remaining hat brim, the second to the four red strips, and the third to one short end of the hat side.

4. With a disappearing marker, draw a line $1/2$" from one short edge of the hat side. Peel the paper off the red strips. Lay one red strip along the line. Space the remaining three strips evenly along the remaining white hat side. Fuse. Fuse the hat side into a cylinder.

5. Cut small pieces of fusible interfacing approximately $1/2$" wide and 1" long. Place them along the inside circle of the interfaced hat brim, having the pieces extend half way into the center of the circle with the fusible sides facing down. Use about sixteen pieces. Fuse the tabs in place, not letting the iron extend off the hat brim.

6. Peel the paper off the hat brim with the Wonder Under™. Fuse the two hat brims together.

7. Fuse the tabs on the hat brim to the hat sides. Running a rolled-up towel through the round hat sides may help give you a surface on which to press. Alternately, glue the strips in place.

8. Overcast stitch the hat top to the top edge of the hat side.

9. Overcast stitch the hat brim edges to give them a finished look.

10. Measure your bear's head from the middle of the back of his ear, under his chin, and to the opposite center back ear. Cut a piece of elastic this measurement plus one inch. Make a knot in each end. Handstitch the knots to the hat on opposite sides where the brim meets the sides.

Blue Vest

MATERIALS

Fabric and lining:

12" x 12" piece of each for small bear

16" x 16" piece of each for large bear

Matching thread

Three buttons

INSTRUCTIONS

Use pattern for vest on pages 60 and 61.

1. As instructed in chapter 1, transfer the pattern to paper, pin to the wrong side of the fabric, and cut out the fabric.

2. Stitch shoulder seams of both fabric and lining. Trim and press seams. Pin lining to fabric vest, right sides together. Starting about one inch from center back bottom of vest, stitch along edge of vest all the way around and ending about $1^1/2$" from starting point.

3. Trim raw edges. Clip armhole and neck edge curves. Turn right side out. Press.

4. Handstitch opening at bottom back edge closed.

5. Butt and whipstitch side seams together.

6. Make buttonholes on left front of vest.

7. Try on bear. Mark button placement. Stitch buttons on right front of vest.

Red & White Striped Pants

MATERIALS

Fabric:

$^1/4$ yard for small bear

$^3/8$ yard for large bear

Matching thread

$^1/4$"-wide elastic: 14" for small bear; 16" for large bear

INSTRUCTIONS

Use pattern for pants on pages 57, 58 and 59.

1. As instructed in chapter 1, transfer the pattern to paper, pin to the wrong side of the fabric, and cut out.

2. Stitch inside leg seams. Press open. Pin long, curved crotch seams, right sides together, matching inside leg seams. Pin and stitch side seams.

3. Press under $^1/4$" at waist. Press under $^3/4$" to form casing for elastic.

4. Topstitch $^5/8$" from folded inside edge, leaving a $^1/2$" gap in stitching to insert elastic. Topstitch $^1/4$" from folded top edge.

5. Insert elastic through casing by attaching a safety pin to one end and running it through the casing. Try on bear. Adjust elastic. Overlap raw edges of elastic and stitch back and forth to secure. Topstitch gap in casing closed.

6. Turn under $^1/4$" for hem. Press under another $^1/4$". Cut a piece of lace the measurement of the leg opening plus one inch. Fold lace, right sides together, and stitch a $^1/2$" seam. Trim. Seal with Fray Check™. Matching lace seam with inside leg seam, stitch lace trim to underside of hem.

All-American Bow Tie

MATERIALS

Fabric:

3½" x 8" piece of tie fabric for bow

1½" x 3" piece of tie fabric for knot

Matching thread

½"-wide black elastic

INSTRUCTIONS

1. Fold bow in half lengthwise. Starting at fold on one short end, stitch edge of bow, breaking stitching for one inch at the center of the long edge. Trim seams. Turn. Press.

2. Press under ¼" on long sides of knot. Turn under ¼" at short ends.

3. Overlap two ends of bow by about ½". Handstitch one turned under end of knot to middle of back of bow. Bring remainder of knot piece around front of bow. Pinch bow together at center and stitch remaining turned under edge of knot piece securely.

4. Cut elastic to fit bear's neck, adding one inch. Overlap the raw ends of the elastic ½" and sew to the back of the tie through both layers of the elastic.

Flag

MATERIALS

Fabric:

White felt

Red felt

Blue felt

Glue

7"-long piece of ¼"-wide dowel

INSTRUCTIONS

1. Cut one piece of white felt 9" x 4½", one piece of blue felt 5" x 1½", four pieces of red felt 9" x ¼", and six pieces of red felt 2" x ¼". Trace the star pattern from the book to paper. Cut eight stars from white felt.

2. Apply glue to one side of the white felt. Fold in half around the dowel, placing the dowel in the middle, making sure the edges of the felt are even. Press with your fingers.

3. Apply glue to the blue felt piece and place it on the flag. Glue the short stripes to the side of the blue patch. Glue the long stripes evenly on the bottom half of the flag. Glue the stars on the blue felt, four on each side.

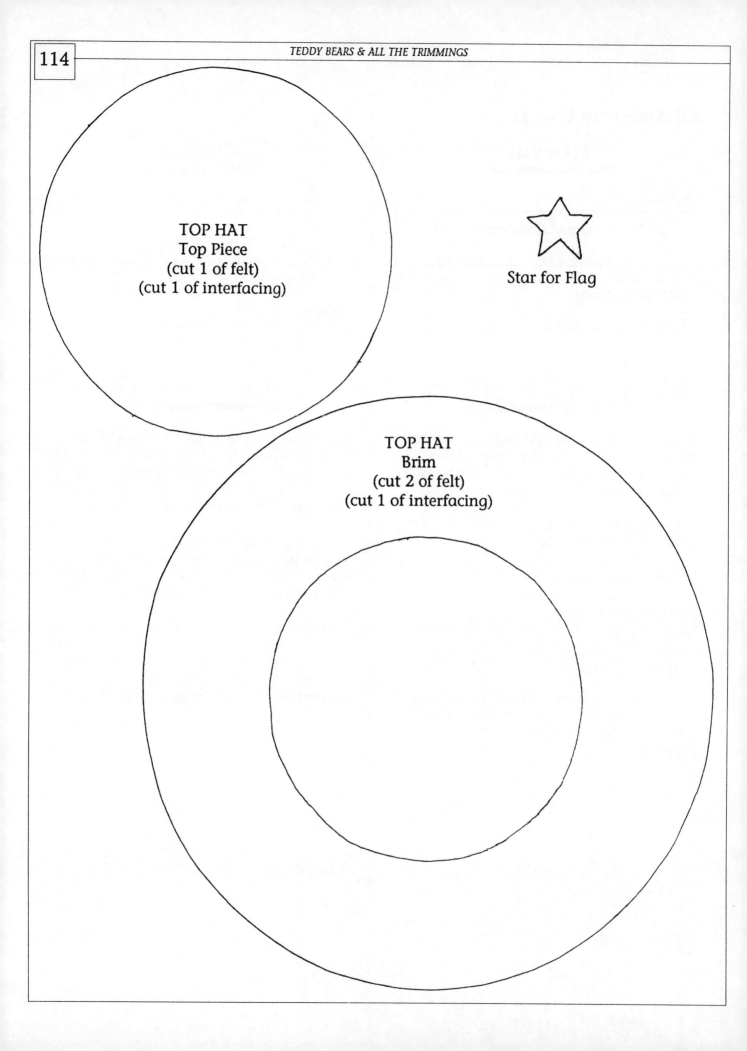

TOP HAT
Top Piece
(cut 1 of felt)
(cut 1 of interfacing)

Star for Flag

TOP HAT
Brim
(cut 2 of felt)
(cut 1 of interfacing)

TUX & GOWN

Your bears will look forward to the most formal occasions as opportunities to show off their most luxurious attire. Make the tux out of wool, choosing basic black for both jacket and pants or maybe gray pin stripe for a slightly different flair. The gown will elicit many an "Ah" when made of velvet, satin, silk, chantilly lace, or dotted swiss. The limo is waiting!

Tuxedo

MATERIALS

Fabric:

$1/3$ yard fabric for small bear

$1/4$ yard fabric for lining, tie, and cummerbund for small bear

$1/2$ yard fabric for large bear

$1/3$ yard fabric for lining, tie, and cummerbund for large bear

Matching thread

$1 1/4$"-wide elastic

$1/2$"-wide elastic: 14" for small bear; 16" for large bear

$3/4$ yard $1/2$"-wide black satin ribbon

Two buttons

INSTRUCTIONS

1. As instructed in chapter 1, transfer the patterns to paper, pin to the wrong side of the fabric, and cut out. Cut one $3 1/2$" x 8" piece of lining fabric for bow and one $1 1/2$" x 3" piece of lining fabric for knot of the bow tie.

JACKET:
2. Stitch the center back seams of the jacket and the jacket lining from the top to the dot, right sides together. Press seams open.

3. Stitch the shoulder and side seams of the jacket and the jacket lining, right sides together. Press seams open.

4. Pin the jacket lining to the jacket, right sides together. Starting at the bottom of the center back seam, stitch down one tail, up the other side of the tail, all the way around the outside edge of the jacket, down the outside edge of the second tail, and up the inside edge of the second tail, ending at the stitching at the bottom of the center back seam. Trim the seam allowances. Leave the armholes open. Turn. Press.

5. Stitch the underarm seam of the sleeve. Pin the sleeve to the armhole of the jacket, right sides together, including the jacket lining and the jacket fabric in the seam as one. Stitch. Trim.

6. Turn under $1/4$" on the bottom of the sleeves. Turn under another $1/4$". Topstitch.

7. Make hand or machine buttonholes on the tuxedo front. Try the jacket on the bear. Sew buttons in place.

PANTS:

8. Use pattern for pants on pages 57, 58 and 59. Stitch inside leg seams, right sides together. Press open. Pin long, curved crotch seams, right sides together, matching inside leg seams. Stitch. Pin and stitch side seams.

9. Cut two pieces of ribbon the length of the pants side seam. Glue on top of the seam on the outside of the pant legs.

10. Press under $1/4$" at waist. Press under $3/4$" to form casing for elastic.

11. Topstitch $5/8$" from folded top edge, leaving a $1/2$" gap in stitching to insert elastic. Topstitch $1/4$" from folded inside edge, leaving a $1/2$" gap in stitching to insert elastic. Topstitch $1/4$" from folded top edge.

12. Insert elastic through casing by attaching a safety pin to one end and running it through the casing. Try on bear. Adjust elastic. Overlap raw edges of elastic and stitch back and forth to secure. Topstitch gap in casing closed.

13. Turn under $1/4$" for hem. Press under another $1/4$". Topstitch.

BOW TIE:

14. Fold bow in half lengthwise. Starting at fold on one short end, stitch edge of bow, breaking stitching for one inch at the center of the long edge. Trim seams. Turn. Press.

15. Press under $1/4$" on long sides of knot. Turn under $1/4$" at short ends.

16. Overlap two ends of bow by about $1/2$". Handstitch one turned under end of knot to middle of back of bow. Bring remainder of knot piece around front of bow. Pinch bow together at center and stitch remaining turned under edge of knot piece securely.

17. Cut elastic to fit bear's neck, adding one inch. Overlap the raw ends of the elastic $1/2$" and sew to the back of the tie through both layers of the elastic.

CUMMERBUND:

18. Fold and press the cummerbund $2 1/4$" from one long edge, wrong sides together. This $2 1/4$" wide section will be the back of the cummerbund. Open flat. Measure $3/4$" into the remainder of the cummerbund. Fold and press, wrong sides together. Measure another $1 1/2$". Fold and press, wrong sides together.

19. Turn and pin the cummerbund, right sides together, along the first fold line. Stitch all around the three raw edges, using a $1/4$" seam allowance, and leaving a $1 1/2$" gap in the stitching for turning. Trim the seam allowances. Turn. Press. Stitch the gap closed.

20. Place the cummerbund around the bear's tummy. Measure the gap in the cummerbund. Cut a piece of elastic that measurement plus 1". Turn under each end $1/2$", center the doubled $1/2$" ends of the elastic on the wrong sides of the two short ends of the cummerbund. Whipstitch in place.

Gown

MATERIALS

Fabric:

$\frac{1}{3}$ yard for small bear

$\frac{1}{2}$ yard for large bear

Matching thread

$\frac{1}{4}$"-wide elastic

$\frac{3}{8}$ yard of lace for collar

$\frac{1}{2}$"-wide ribbon for bow at neck

Ribbon roses

Small safety pin

1"-wide ribbon to tie at waist

Three buttons

INSTRUCTIONS

Use pattern for dress on pages 68, 69, 70, and 71.

1. As instructed in chapter 1, transfer the patterns to paper, pin to wrong side of fabric, and cut out the fabric. Cut the skirt piece: $6\frac{1}{2}$" x 27" for small bear, 7" x 32" for large bear.

2. Stitch backs to fronts at shoulder seams for both dress and lining. Pin neck and back seams, right sides together, including the lace in the neck seam. Turn under raw edges at ends of lace and stitch so it won't peek out. Trim. You may wish to seal the loose threads of the lace with Fray Check™. Stitch back and neck as one continuous seam, between the dots on the lower edges of the bodice backs. Trim seam. Clip neck curve. Turn. Press.

3. Press under $\frac{1}{4}$" at bottom edge of sleeve. Repeat. Topstitch. Cut a piece of elastic: 6" for the small bear, 7" for the large bear. Lay elastic about $\frac{5}{8}$" from finished hem edge. Pin raw ends of elastic in place, even with raw sleeve edges. Hold the fabric and the elastic at both pinned ends and stretch the elastic to lie flat. With a zigzag stitch sew the elastic in place, beginning with a few backward and forward stitches to secure the elastic, stretching the elastic flat along the seam as you go.

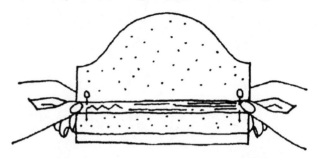

4. With a long stitch, gather the sleeve heads between the dots, $\frac{1}{8}$" from the raw edge. Pin the sleeve to the dress. Adjust the gathers. Stitch in place.

5. Right sides together, sew the underarm and the side seam.

6. With a $\frac{1}{2}$" seam allowance, sew the center back seam of the skirt. Press open continuing to press over $\frac{1}{2}$" to the top of the skirt. Press under $\frac{1}{4}$" of this seam allowance. Starting at the top of the skirt, topstitch $\frac{1}{8}$" from the edge, turning below the opening and continuing to stitch up the other side to the top of the skirt.

7. Leaving two inches ungathered at each end of the skirt top, gather the skirt top with long stitches. Pin to bodice. Adjust gathers. Stitch.

8. Press under $\frac{1}{4}$" on bottom edge of dress for hem. Repeat. Topstitch.

9. Make buttonholes on bodice. Try on bear. Mark button placement. Sew buttons on.

10. Make a bow out of the narrow ribbon. With a small safety pin attach it and the ribbon roses to the front neckline. Tie the wide ribbon at the bear's waist, tying the bow in back.

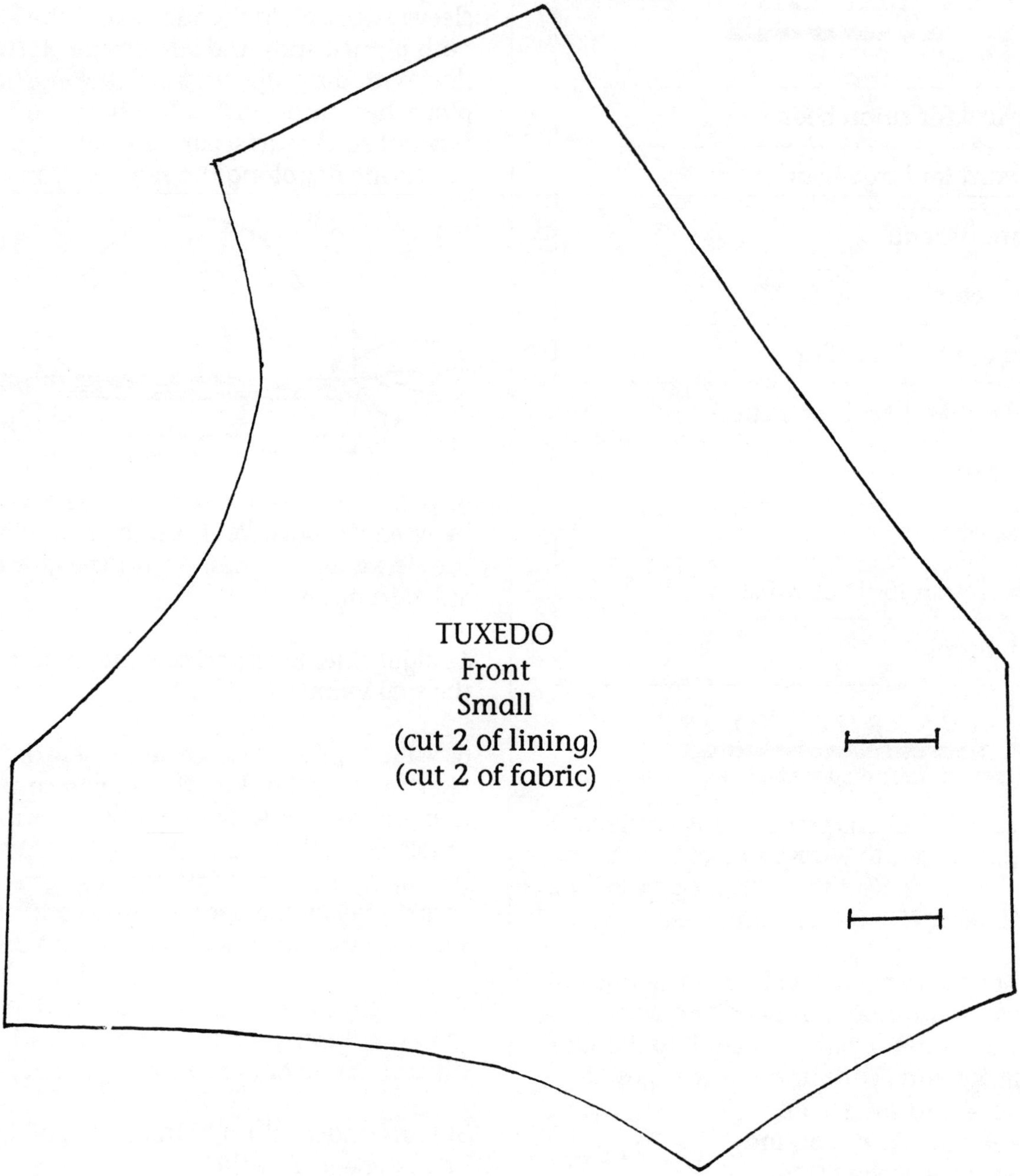

TUXEDO
Front
Small
(cut 2 of lining)
(cut 2 of fabric)

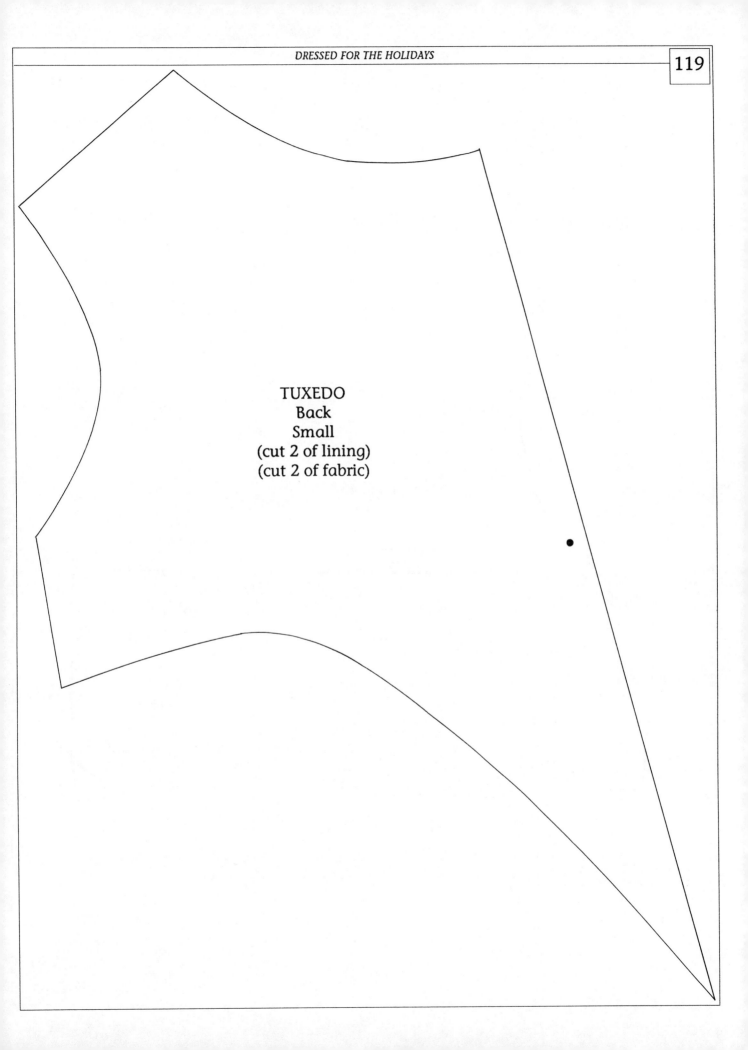

TUXEDO
Back
Small
(cut 2 of lining)
(cut 2 of fabric)

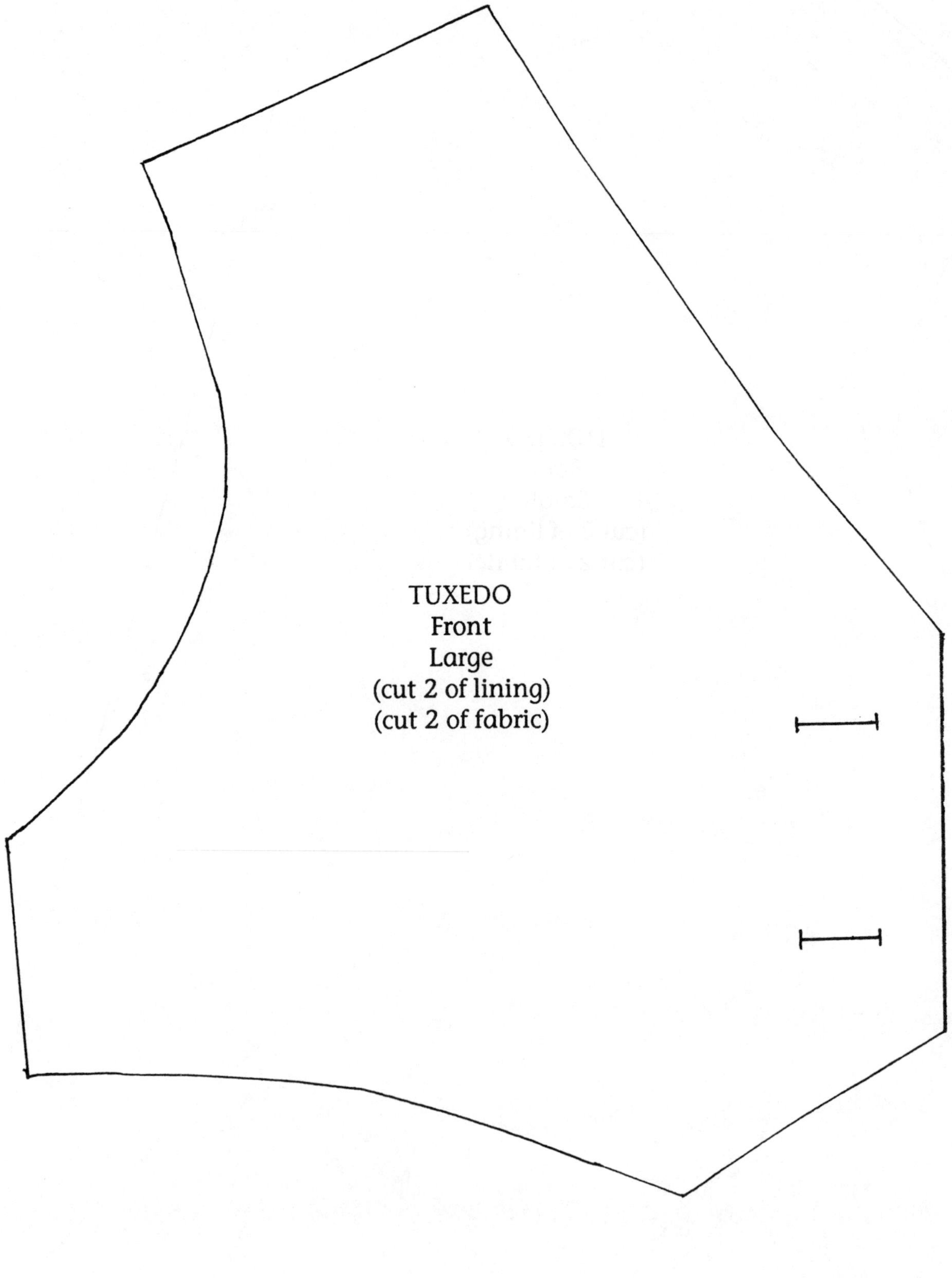

TUXEDO
Front
Large
(cut 2 of lining)
(cut 2 of fabric)

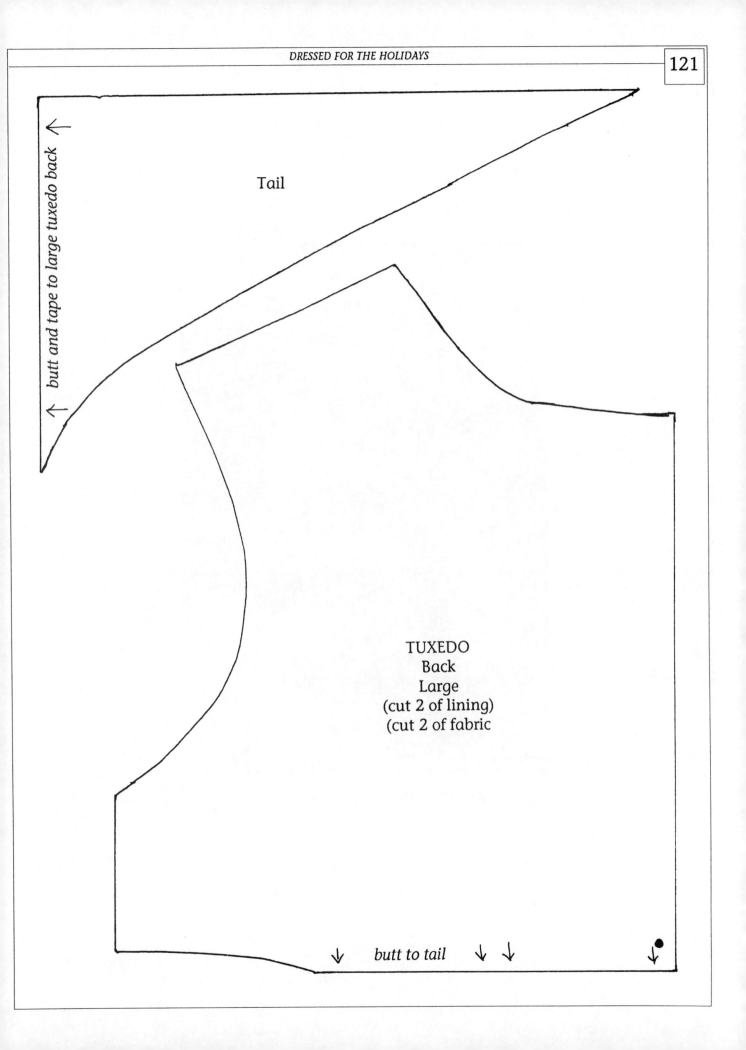

Tail

butt and tape to large tuxedo back

TUXEDO
Back
Large
(cut 2 of lining)
(cut 2 of fabric

↓ *butt to tail* ↓ ↓ ↓

CHAPTER • 5

A TEDDY BEAR CHRISTMAS

Start with a country home's cozy living room. Build a crackling fire in the old brick fireplace. Hang hand-decorated stockings on the oak mantel. Move some furniture out of the way and stand a fragrant spruce, fresh from the snowy woods, in a place of honor. Adorn it with old-fashioned, handmade ornaments, strings of popcorn and cranberries, and tiny white lights. Cover the braided rug under the tree with gaily wrapped boxes, beribboned with every imaginable color. Sit a sweet rag doll in her own little chair. Lean a new wooden sled in the corner to one side. Set a hobby horse galloping among the packages.

Now...What's missing?

A teddy bear! How can any Christmas be complete without at least one teddy bear? Teddy bears are synonymous with Christmas, their hearts are full of that indescribable feeling that is Christmas. And one can never have enough of either.

So why not make this Christmas a teddy bear Christmas. Follow the instructions in this chapter for your own teddy bear Christmas cheer. Decorate your front door wreath with the felt teddy bear tree ornaments, maybe adding some tiny wooden toys and a plaid fabric bow. Make a center piece for your holiday table with your teddy bear in his Santa suit, his bag filled with little toys and packages, seated in a wicker sleigh. Some people have even made an entire Christmas tree of teddy bears! One of the prettiest had scotch plaid bear ornaments and red and green grosgrain bows covering the tree with tiny white lights twinkling from behind. What a warm-hearted and strikingly beautiful tree it was!

○ CHRISTMAS TREE ORNAMENTS ○

FELT CHRISTMAS TREE ORNAMENTS

Felt certainly has a lot of things going for it. Not only does it come in a variety of colors, is soft and has a warm look, but, the biggest plus, felt has non-fraying edges which need no finishing. All of these attributes make felt perfect for Christmas tree ornaments, stockings, and even a Christmas tree skirt.

The ornaments described throughout this chapter can be made in bear colors—tans, browns, whites with splashes of red and green—or they are great in holiday colors or winter ice blue. These are easy enough to make extras for gift toppers, stocking stuffers, or to adorn a package of Christmas cookies.

Standing Teddy Bear Ornament

MATERIALS

Brown or other color felt for bear

Matching thread

Embroidery floss

Ribbon for bow

Small amount of polyester fiberfill

INSTRUCTIONS

1. Transfer patterns from book to cardboard or heavy paper as instructed in chapter 1. Lay patterns on felt and trace. Cut out.

2. Using an overstitch, sew the head pieces together, stitching the ears into the seam. Stuff the head lightly once you have sewn to about one inch from the beginning of your stitching. Finish stitching.

3. Overstitch the arms together leaving the body edges open. Stuff the arms lightly.

4. Stitch the inside and outside leg seams. Stitch the sole of the foot to the bottom opening of the leg. Stuff the leg lightly.

5. Overstitch the body, starting at one shoulder, including the arms and legs as indicated on the patterns. When you reach the second shoulder, stuff the body lightly and finish stitching.

6. From the back of the bear, tack the head to the body.

7. Embroider the face.

8. Tie a bow out of ribbon and tack it to the bear, under his chin.

9. If the bear is to be hung, double thread a needle with embroidery floss, run it through the back side of the head at the top. Tie a knot to make the hanger about two inches long, and clip the thread.

Teddy Bear-in-a-Stocking Ornament

MATERIALS

Felt:

brown or other color for the bear

beige for the stocking

red for the heel and toe of the stocking

Matching thread

Embroidery floss

Ribbon

Small amount of polyester fiberfill

INSTRUCTIONS

1. Transfer patterns from book to cardboard or heavy paper as instructed in chapter 1. Lay patterns on felt and trace. Cut out.

2. Using an overstitch, sew the head pieces together, stitching the ears into the seam. Stuff the head lightly once you have sewn to about one inch from the beginning of your stitching. Finish stitching.

3. Overstitch the arms together leaving the body edges open. Stuff the arm lightly.

4. Overstitch the body, starting at one shoulder, including the arms in the seam. When you reach the second shoulder, stuff the body lightly and finish stitching.

5. From the back of the bear, tack the head to the body.

6. Embroider the face.

7. Tie a bow out of ribbon and tack it to the bear, under his chin.

8. Overstitch the stocking together, leaving the top opening of the stocking unstitched.

9. Stitch the heel and toe to the stocking.

10. Lightly stuff the stocking. Position the bear in the stocking opening and stitch the opening closed, making sure the bottom of the bear is sewn securely into the seam.

11. If the bear is to be hung, double thread a needle with embroidery floss, run it through the back side of the head at the top, tie a knot to make the hanger about two inches long, and clip the thread.

Gift Bear Ornament

MATERIALS

Felt:

brown or other color for the bear

red or other color for the package

Matching thread

Embroidery floss

Ribbon

Ribbon or braid to trim the package

Small amount of polyester fiberfill

INSTRUCTIONS

1. Transfer patterns from book to cardboard or heavy paper as instructed in chapter 1. Lay patterns on felt and trace. Cut out.

2. Using an overstitch, sew the head pieces together, stitching the ears into the seam. Stuff the head lightly once you have sewn to about one inch from the beginning of your stitching. Finish stitching.

3. Overstitch the arms together, leaving the body edges open. Stuff the arm lightly.

4. Overstitch the body, starting at one shoulder, sewing the arms into the seam. When you reach the second shoulder, stuff the body lightly and finish stitching.

5. From the back of the bear, tack the head to the body.

6. Embroider the face.

7. Tie a bow out of ribbon and tack to the bear.

8. Cut a piece of ribbon the width of the felt box plus about an inch. Glue it vertically or horizontally to the front center of the box. Turn under the ends to the back side of the box and glue down.

9. Overstitch the two box pieces together, leaving the top open. Stuff lightly. Stitch the top opening closed making sure the bear is sewn securely into the seam.

10. If the bear is to be hung, double thread a needle with embroidery floss, run it through the back side of the head at the top, tie a knot to make the hanger about two inches long, and clip the thread.

Sled Bear Ornament

MATERIALS

Felt:

brown or other color for the bear

gold for the sled

red for the bear's cap

Matching thread

Embroidery floss

Small amount of polyester fiberfill

Small jingle bell

INSTRUCTIONS

1. Transfer patterns from book to cardboard or heavy paper as instructed in chapter 1. Lay patterns on felt and trace. Cut out.

2. Using an overstitch, sew the head pieces together, stitching the ears in the seam. Stuff the head lightly once you have stitched to about one inch from the beginning of your stitching. Finish stitching.

3. Overstitch the arm together, leaving the body edges open. Stuff the arm lightly.

4. Stitch the leg together. Stuff the leg lightly once you are about one inch from the beginning of your stitching. Finish stitching the leg.

5. Overstitch the body. When you are about one inch from the beginning of your stitching, stuff the body lightly and finish stitching.

6. Tack the head to the body from the back of the bear. Tack the arm and leg in place.

7. Embroider the face.

8. Glue the cap to the bear's head. Tack the jingle bell to the tip of the cap.

9. Overstitch the sled edges, stuffing lightly before closing the seam. Tack the sled to the bear.

10. If the bear is to be hung, double thread a needle with embroidery floss, run it through the back side of the head at the top, tie a knot to make the hanger about two inches long, and clip the thread.

Rocking Horse Bear Ornament

MATERIALS

Felt:

brown or other color for bear and horse

Matching thread

Embroidery floss

Yarn

Ribbon

Small amount of polyester fiberfill

INSTRUCTIONS

1. Transfer patterns from book to cardboard or heavy paper as instructed in chapter 1. Lay patterns on felt and trace. Cut out.

2. Using an overstitch, sew the head pieces together, stitching the ears into the seam. Stuff the head lightly when you have sewn to about one inch from the beginning of your stitching. Finish stitching.

3. Overstitch the arm together leaving the body edges open. Stuff the arm lightly.

4. Stitch the leg together, stuffing the leg lightly once you are about one inch from the beginning of your stitching. Finish stitching the leg.

5. Overstitch the body. When you are about one inch from the beginning of your stitching, stuff the body lightly and finish stitching.

6. Tack the head to the body from the back of the bear. Tack the arm and leg in place.

7. Embroider the face.

8. Tie a bow out of ribbon and tack it to the bear, under his chin.

9. Overstitch the hole in the rocking horse.

10. Starting on the bottom of one leg just above the rocker, overstitch around the bottom of the rocker to the bottom of the other leg. Stuff the rocker lightly, pushing the stuffing in with the eraser end of a pencil, a pen, or a short length of dowel.

11. Continue stitching around the rocking horse until you are about one inch from the beginning of your stitching. Stuff. Finish stitching.

12. Sew on the yarn mane and tail.

13. Embroider the eye.

14. Tie a bow out of ribbon and tack it to the top of the tail.

15. If the bear is to be hung, double thread a needle with embroidery floss, run it through the back side of the head at the top, tie a knot to make the hanger about two inches long, and clip the thread.

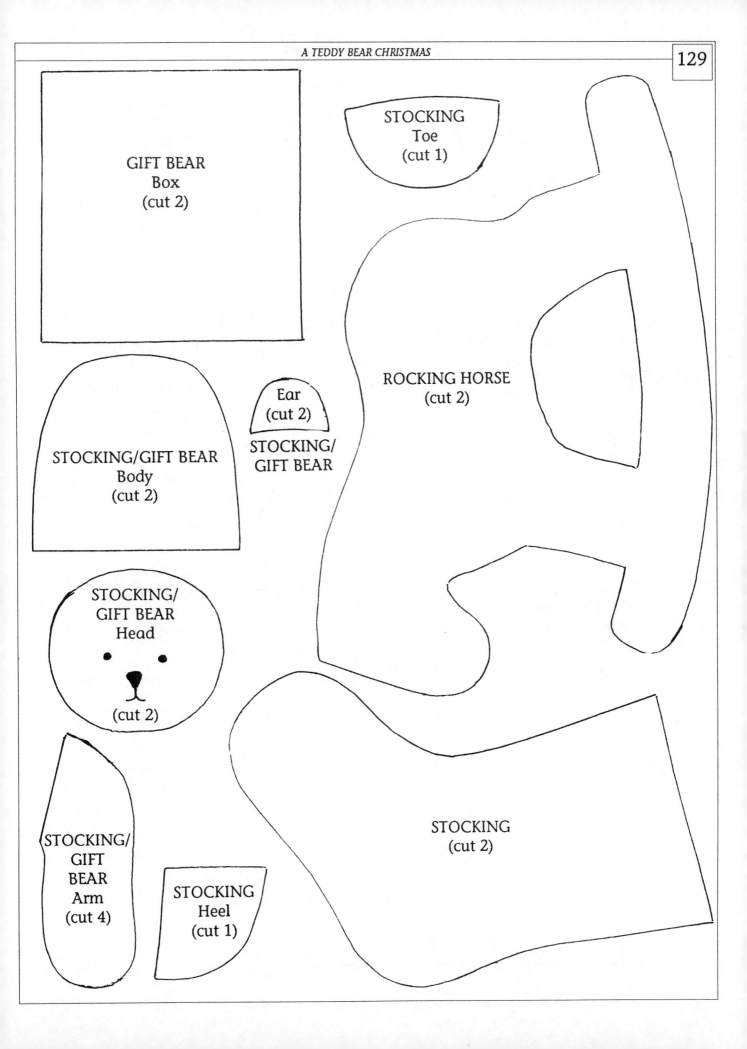

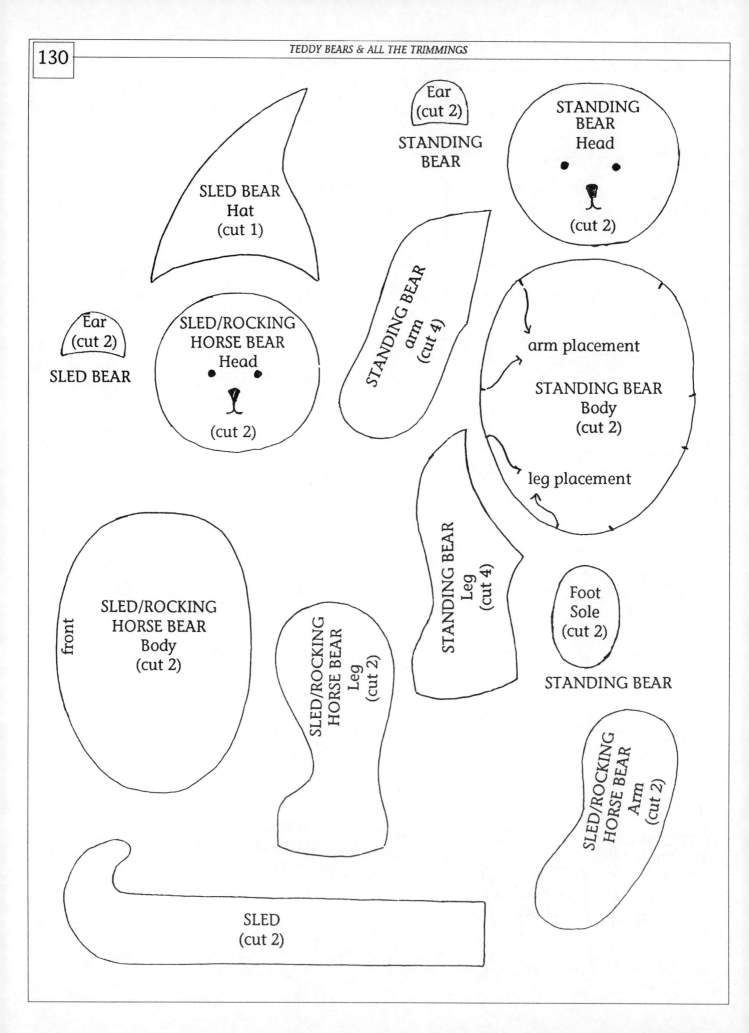

SLED BEAR
Hat
(cut 1)

Ear
(cut 2)
STANDING
BEAR

STANDING
BEAR
Head

(cut 2)

Ear
(cut 2)

SLED BEAR

SLED/ROCKING
HORSE BEAR
Head

(cut 2)

STANDING BEAR
arm
(cut 4)

arm placement

STANDING BEAR
Body
(cut 2)

leg placement

STANDING BEAR
Leg
(cut 4)

Foot
Sole
(cut 2)

STANDING BEAR

front

SLED/ROCKING
HORSE BEAR
Body
(cut 2)

SLED/ROCKING
HORSE BEAR
Leg
(cut 2)

SLED/ROCKING
HORSE BEAR
Arm
(cut 2)

SLED
(cut 2)

FABRIC TEDDY BEAR ORNAMENTS

These little bears are such a snap to make that you can stitch them up in batches to decorate an entire tree, give them freely as gifts, or decorate packages with them and, perhaps, a basket filled with an assortment of fun things.

For a lacey Victorian flavor, turn to chapter 6 and make lace sachet teddy bears for your Christmas decorating.

MATERIALS

7" x 14" piece of cotton or other fabric: solid or print

Matching thread

Ribbon

Small amount of polyester fiberfill

INSTRUCTIONS

1. Transfer the pattern to heavy paper or cereal box cardboard as instructed in the first chapter.

2. Cut two fabric pattern pieces for each ornament.

3. With right sides together stitch the two pieces, starting and ending at the dots indicated on the pattern, leaving an opening for stuffing.

4. Turn the ornament right sides out.

5. Stuff.

6. Sew the opening closed.

7. Tie a ribbon in a bow around the bear's neck. You may also wish to embroider a face on the bear or include ribbon roses on the bow.

8. Double thread a needle with embroidery floss, run it through the back of the head at the top, tie a knot to make the hanger about two inches long, and clip the thread.

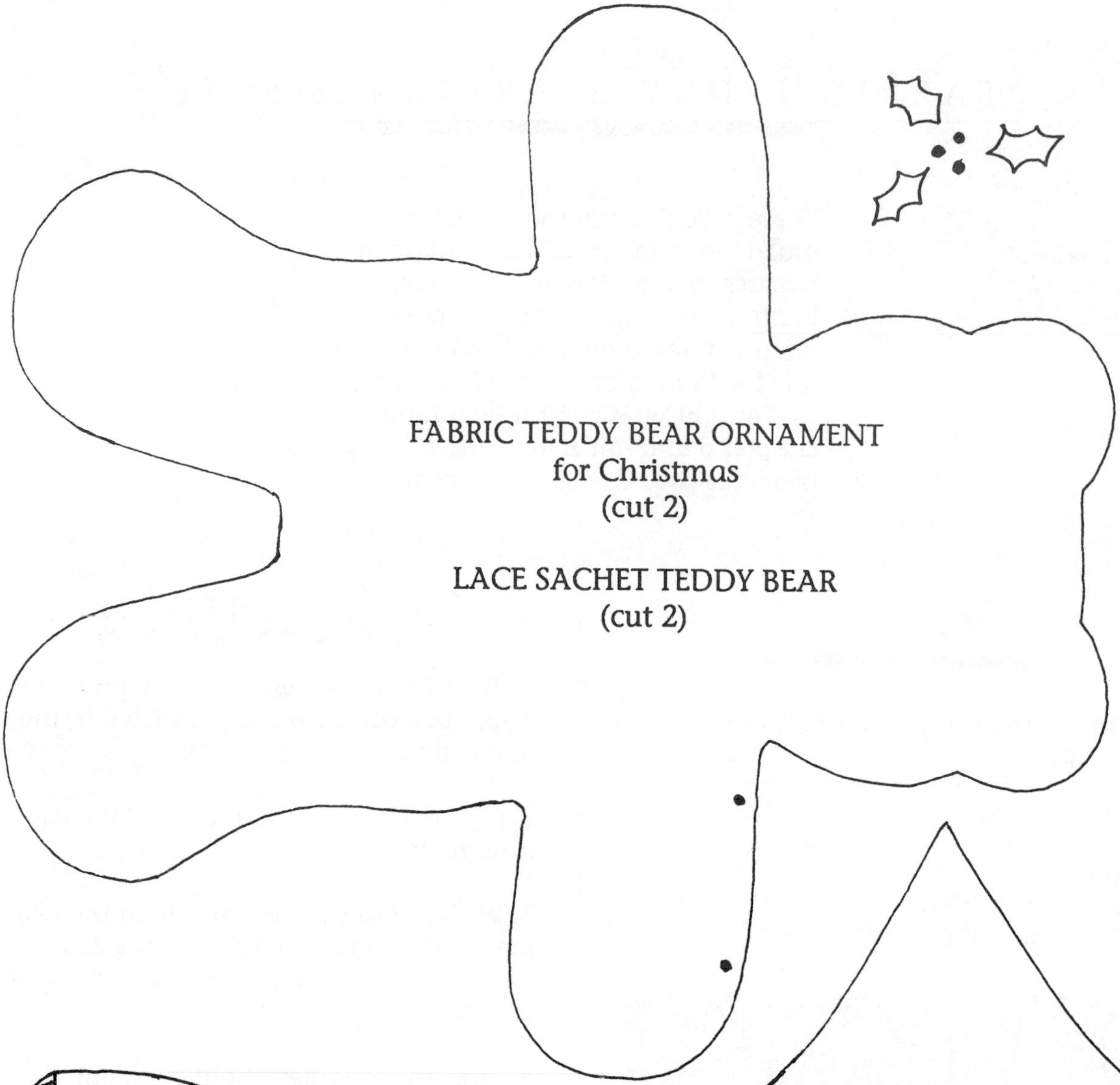

FABRIC TEDDY BEAR ORNAMENT
for Christmas
(cut 2)

LACE SACHET TEDDY BEAR
(cut 2)

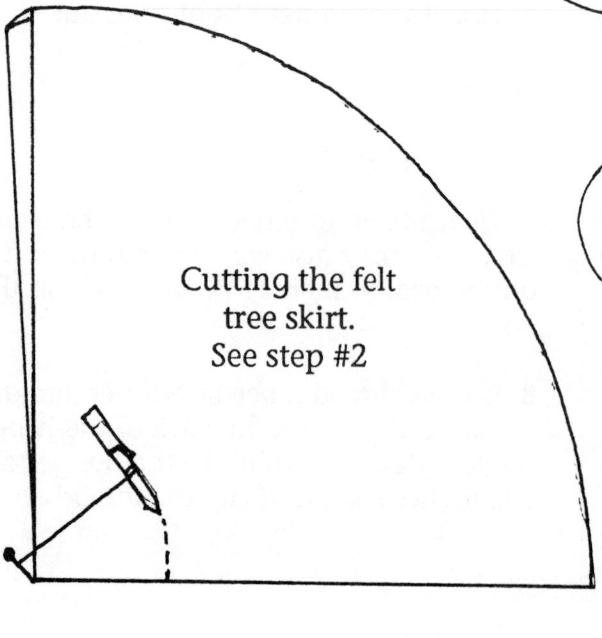

Cutting the felt
tree skirt.
See step #2

Holly
Berry

FELT TREE
SKIRT
&
STOCKING
Holly Leaf

FELT TREE SKIRT

MATERIALS

1^1/$_3$ yards white felt

Scraps or purchase 9" x 12" piece of felt for bears, holly leaves, etc.

^{1}/$_2$ yard Wonder Under™

3 packages gold double-fold bias binding

Green and red ribbon for bows for bears' necks

Plaid ribbon for gift bear

Small jingle bell

INSTRUCTIONS

1. Make paper patterns for each of the five bear ornaments, the holly leaf and berry. Trace only one of each pattern piece (not a front and a back) on felt and on Wonder Under™ and cut out. Trace and cut out 16 holly leaves and 18 holly berries of both felt and Wonder Under™.

2. Fold the white felt in half and in half again. Tie a string to a pencil at one end and a pin at the other making the string 22" between the two. Place the pin at the center of the folded point (which will become the center of the tree skirt). Holding the pin, place the pencil point at the edge of the fabric 22" from the pin. Draw an arc. Cut. Repeatwith a string 2^1/$_2$" long for the center hole. Cut out the hole. Cut along one fold to make an opening.

3. Apply the Wonder Under™ to the wrong sides of the felt pieces, following package instructions. Remove the paper from the back of the pieces. Lay the skirt out flat and position the felt pieces. Pin them in place.

4. At the ironing board, remove the pins and fuse the pieces in place as in the Wonder Under™ instructions, working on one bear or holly section at a time. When you get to the gift bear, fuse or glue a piece of ribbon vertically to the front of the package, turning the ends at top and bottom under the package, before fusing the package to the tree skirt.

5. Stitch the bias binding to all raw edges of the tree skirt.

6. Embroider faces on the bears and an eye on the rocking horse.

7. Stitch loops of yarn to the horse for his mane and tail.

8. Make six bows and tack them to the bears' necks and to the horse's tail.

9. Tack the jingle bell to the tip of the sled bear's cap.

FELT CHRISTMAS STOCKING

MATERIALS

³/₈ yard red felt

Matching thread

12" x 24" piece of white felt

Matching thread

One 9" x 12" piece of green felt

Scraps or purchase 9" x 12" pieces of felt for bear applique

Gold embroidery floss

15" of 1"-wide plaid ribbon

Three large gold jingle bells

Wonder Under™ (if fusing design rather than stitching)

INSTRUCTIONS

1. Transfer patterns for the stocking, holly, berries, and the bear ornament you wish to place on your stocking from the book to heavy paper as instructed in chapter 1. Lay patterns on felt and trace. Cut out.

2. Overstitch or fuse the bear ornament to the stocking front. If you stitch it, stuff lightly as you go.

3. Embroider the face.

4. Stitch the side seams of the white stocking tops together. Place the narrower end (which will be the top) of the white stocking top between the top opening of the stocking, having the stocking edges overlap the stocking top's bottom edge ¹/₂" on the inside of the stocking. Stitch the edges of the stocking and stocking top together.

5. Overstitch the stocking edges together with the gold embroidery floss, starting at the top of one side of the stocking and sewing down around the foot and up the other side, ending at the top of the stocking again, leaving the top open.

6. Overstitch the bottom, wider, edge of the stocking top with gold embroidery floss. Turn down the stocking top on the fold line.

7. Pin two holly leaves together. Overstitch the edges, stuffing the leaf lightly when almost finished stitching. Stitch a line of straight stitches down the center of the leaf through all thicknesses. Repeat for other leaf. Tack to stocking top.

8. Position the holly berries on the stocking top. Overstitch them in place, stuffing lightly as you go.

9. Fold the hanger in half lengthwise. Overstitch the edges. Fold it in half and tack it in place at the top of the stocking.

10. Make a bow for the bear. Tack it in place.

11. Cut three pieces of ribbon five inches long each. Fold them in half and stitch them to the underside of the stocking top. Stitch the jingle bells to the bottom folds of the ribbon.

butt and tape to bottom (toe) 1/3 of pattern

CHRISTMAS STOCKING
Middle 1/3 of pattern

(cut 2 for felt stocking)

(cut 2 of muslin and 1 of batting for
crayon-painted stocking)

butt and tape to top 1/3 of pattern

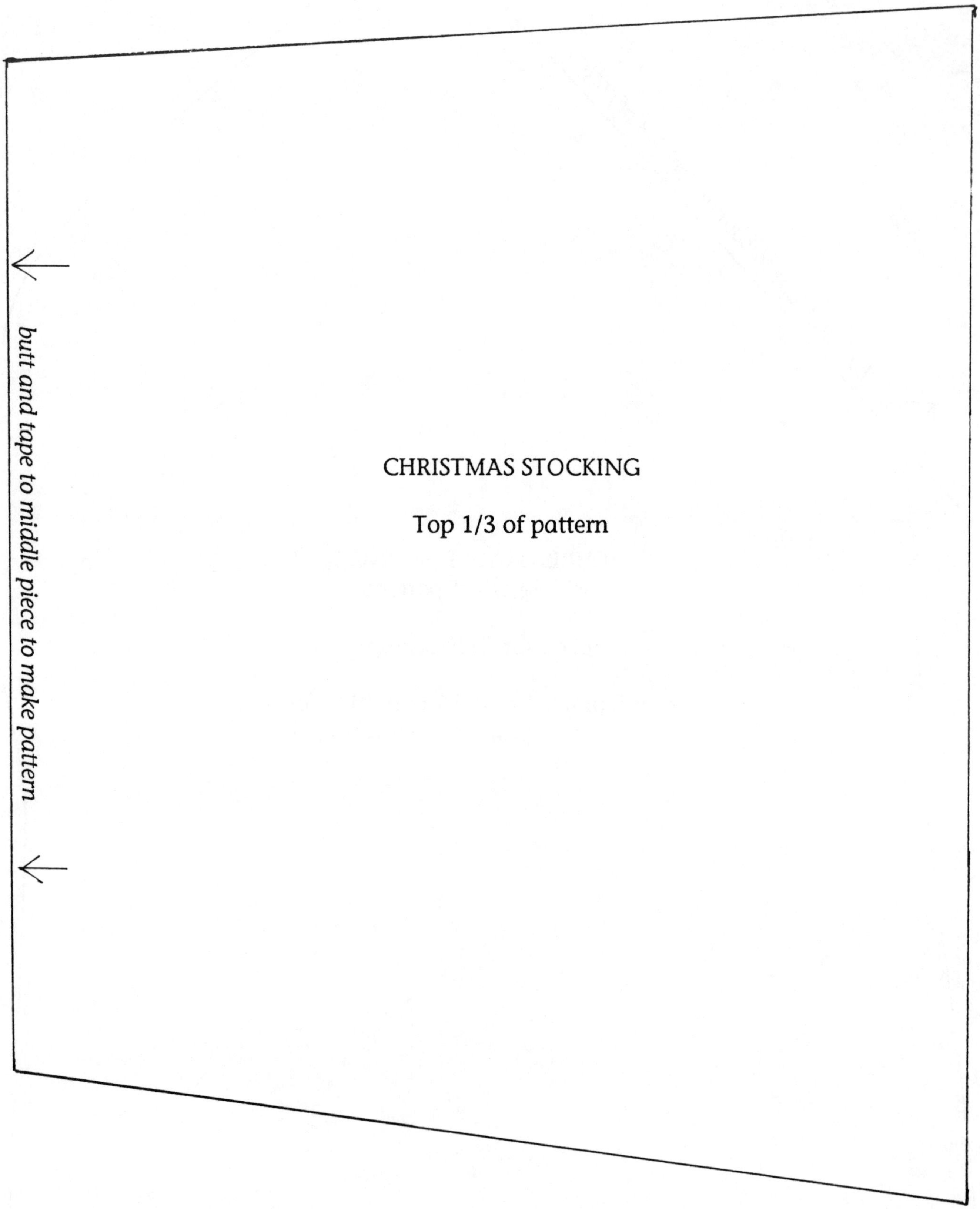

butt and tape to middle piece to make pattern

CHRISTMAS STOCKING

Top 1/3 of pattern

STOCKING HANGER   (cut 1)

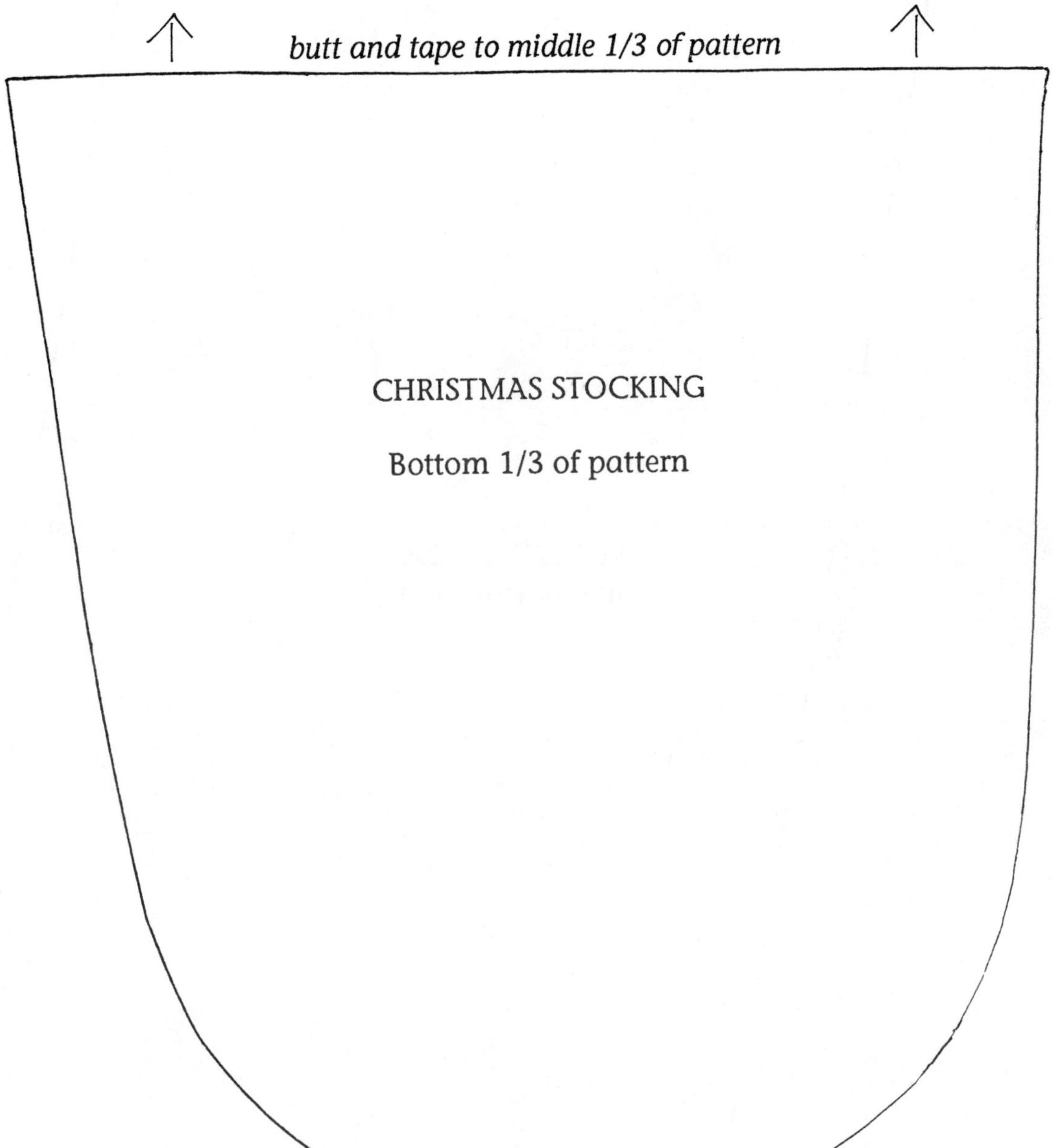

butt and tape to middle 1/3 of pattern

CHRISTMAS STOCKING

Bottom 1/3 of pattern

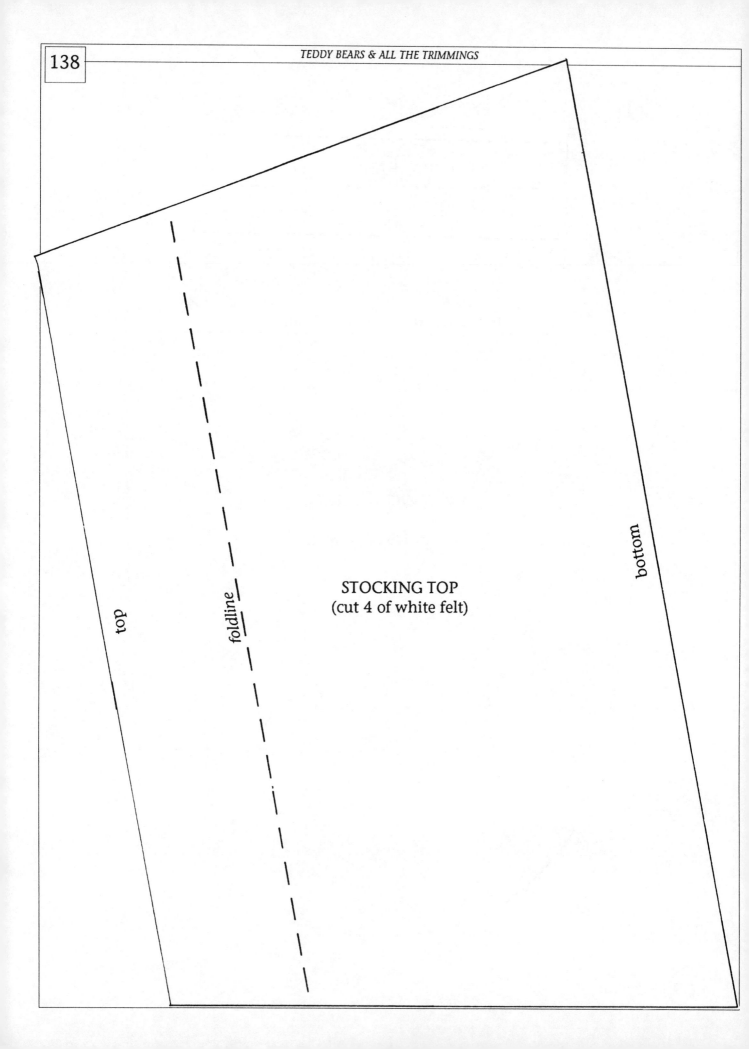

top

foldline

STOCKING TOP
(cut 4 of white felt)

bottom

TEDDY BEAR HEART WREATH

This cheerful soft sculpture wreath will greet your guests as they remove their hats and mittens in your foyer, grace your kitchen filled with those memory-laced aromas which convince your nose that yes, this is finally Christmas, or bestow the holiday spirit to a child's bedroom. This wreath was made of bright red and green microdot calico for the hearts and a red, green, and cream stripe for the bears. A trip to your local fabric shop will provide you with many other possibilities for fabrics. For a Victorian Christmas theme choose velvet hearts and lace bears stuffed with potpourri. Satin fabrics will add a shimmer. Once you have chosen your fabrics rummage through the enticing trim selection, considering some of those lovely braids and ribbons you've been eyeing.

For the Bears:

MATERIALS

½ yard fabric

Matching thread

2 yards ¼"-wide ribbon

Polyester fiberfill

INSTRUCTIONS

1. Transfer the pattern to heavy paper or cereal box cardboard as instructed in the first chapter.

2. Cut two fabric pattern pieces for each ornament.

3. With right sides together stitch the two pieces, starting and ending at the dots indicated on the pattern, leaving an opening for stuffing.

4. Turn the ornament right sides out.

5. Stuff.

6. Sew the opening closed.

7. Tie a ribbon in a bow around the bear's neck. You may also wish to embroider a face on the bear.

For the Hearts:

MATERIALS

¼ yard each of two fabrics

Matching thread

Polyester fiberfill

2 yards gold braid or ribbon

White craft glue

INSTRUCTIONS

1. Transfer the pattern from book to cardboard or heavy paper as instructed in chapter 1. Lay patterns on the wrong side of one of the fabrics and trace three hearts. Cut out. Repeat for the other fabric.

2. Glue two parallel pieces of braid to the right sides of six of the hearts, three of each of the two fabrics, as if the braid were the ribbon wrapping a package. On one heart the braid might run diagonally and on another the two sets of braid might run horizontally and vertically, crossing off-center on the heart.

3. With a ¼" seam allowance, stitch the hearts together, right sides facing. Leave a ¾" gap in the stitching for turning the hearts.

4. Turn the hearts right side out. Stuff. Stitch the opening closed.

Assembling the wreath:

MATERIALS

1 clothes hanger

1½ yards matching cord

1 round plastic ring (used for crochet)

INSTRUCTIONS

1. Lay the hearts in a circle with their tops facing the center of the circle and their sides touching. Whipstitch the edges of the hearts together where they touch.

2. Place the bears on top of the hearts where the hearts touch one another. Stitch the backs of the bears to the hearts.

3. Turn the wreath over. Bend the hanger into a circle, overlapping the ends about 4", and twisting them together. Lay the hanger on the back of the wreath. Stitch it in place.

4. Turn the wreath right side up. Tie knots in the ends of the cording. Run the cording behind and under the bears. Tie a bow in the cording over one of the hearts. Whipstitch it in place.

5. Stitch the ring to the back of the top heart.

CHRISTMAS WREATH
Heart
(cut 2 for each heart)

Teddy bear pattern is the same one used for
Fabric Teddy Bear Ornaments

C H A P T E R • 6

BEAR GIFTS
&
WHAT NOT'S

Just stand quietly by and watch an elderly person light up when given a teddy bear-related gift. This is proof of what we all know—teddy bears are not just for children. In fact, teddy bear items are perfect shower gifts and make wonderful Christmas, Chanukah, Valentine, and birthday presents. Anyone who is convalescing can't help but cheer up at the sight of a homemade teddy bear gift.

Any day is a great day to receive a teddy bear.

SHADOW APPLIQUE TEDDY BEAR HEART PILLOW

This lovely pillow or quilt is sure to delight any one, any age, any time. You may wish to use a heart-shaped pillow form, centering the design evenly.

MATERIALS

½ yard red cotton fabric, cut into one 16" x 16" square and two 11" x 16" pieces

Matching thread

Solid pink cotton fabric

Solid colored and calico scraps

Embroidery floss

16" x 16" piece of white voile or organza

16" x 16" piece of muslin or other fabric, for lining for quilted pillow front

16" x 16" piece of batting

16" x 16" pillow form

Glue stick

Water-soluble fabric marker

1⅞ yards of 4"-wide gathered white lace with holes for running ribbon

1⅞ yards of 3½"-wide gathered white lace to match above

1⅞ yards of 1½"-wide gathered wine-colored lace

1⅞ yards of ⅛"-wide wine-colored ribbon

1½ yards of ⅜"-wide wine-colored ribbon

White thread

INSTRUCTIONS

1. Transfer the designs from the book to paper as instructed in chapter 1. Mark and cut out the heart from the pink fabric. Do the same for the bear, ribbon, flowers, and remaining pattern pieces. Cut the edges very cleanly, leaving no frayed threads. Handle these pieces as little as possible.

2. Position the pink heart in the center of one red square of foundation fabric. Dab small amounts of glue stick on the back of the heart. Press it in place. Pin the pieces in place over the pink heart, overlapping the flowers over the leaves as in the pattern, adjusting the positions until you are happy with the placement. Dab a small dot of glue stick to the back of each pattern piece and press in place.

3. Lay the voile over the glued design. Pin in place. With long stitches, baste through the two layers about one inch from the design.

4. Using a single strand of embroidery floss, stitch around each cut out piece of the design, just catching the very edge threads of the pieces with each stitch, with as short a stitch as possible on the underside and a long (about ¼") stitch on the front. Use a double strand of embroidery floss for the edges of the pink heart to give it greater definition. You may choose embroidery floss colors to match or contrast with the fabric pieces.

5. Embroider the face of the bear, and the fold lines on the ribbon.

6. Place your work in a sink or basin of cool water and let it soak for a few minutes to soften the glue. Rinse under cool water. Roll in a towel. Air dry or press with your iron.

7. With a ruler and a water-soluble marker draw quilting lines on the pink heart. Lay the muslin square on your work surface, place the batting over it, and lay the pillow front on top, right side up. Pin the three layers together all around the edges and around the pink heart. Using two strands of embroidery floss, quilt along these lines. Quilt around the heart, about $\frac{1}{8}$-inch away from it, including design pieces which extend out of the heart and onto the red foundation fabric.

8. Pin the $3\frac{1}{2}$"-wide lace to the edge of the pillow, right sides together and having the lace extend into the center of the pillow, with the top edge of the lace $\frac{1}{4}$" from the raw edges of the pillow. Make a small pleat at each corner. Adjust the length of the lace to fit. Stitch a seam in the short ends of the lace. Trim.

9. Turn under $\frac{1}{4}$" on one long side of each of the two remaining red pillow backing pieces. Turn under another $\frac{1}{4}$". Topstitch. Lay these pieces over the lace and pillow front, right sides down, overlapping the stitched edges to form a pocket for inserting the pillow form. Pin. Stitch the pillow edge seam, $\frac{1}{2}$" wide. Trim corners. Turn.

10. Pin the red $1\frac{1}{2}$"-wide lace to the pillow, even with the 4"-wide lace, extending it into the pillow front. Adjust the length of the lace to fit. Stitch a seam across the short ends of the lace. Trim. Handstitch the lace in place.

11. Run the $\frac{1}{8}$"-wide ribbon through the holes in the 4"-wide lace. Pin the lace to the pillow top over the other two laces, having the ribbon cover the bottom of the red lace and the lace extending away from the center of the pillow. Adjust the length of the lace to fit. Stitch a seam across the short ends of the lace. Trim. Handstitch the lace in place.

12. Divide the $\frac{3}{8}$"-wide ribbon into four pieces. Tie them into bows. Tack them onto the four corners of the pillow.

13. Insert the pillow form. You may stitch the back opening closed, if desired.

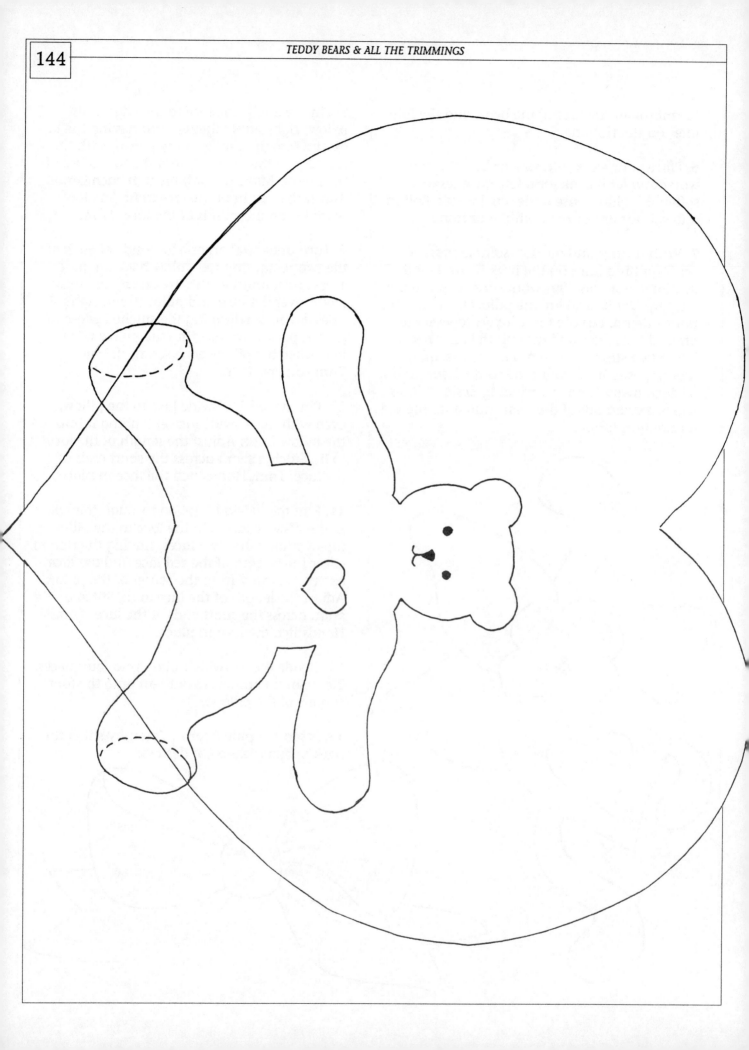

BEAR-IN-THE-SKY
SOFT SCULPTURE WALL HANGING

Perfect for a child's room, this cheery bear floats from a handful of balloons, landing right in your child's imagination. Made from tan micro-dot calico or a print, velour, or even synthetic fur, the bear is lined with batting to give him just a little poof. For a chubbier bear, add another layer of batting or stuff him with polyester fiberfill.

MATERIALS

2 yards of 45"-wide fabric

Polyester batting, one small batt or craft batt

Matching thread

Embroidery floss

Black felt

Two $7/8$" black buttons for eyes

$3/8$ yard each of blue, red, and yellow heavy polyester satin fabric for balloons

Three pieces of cardboard, $8^1/2$" x 11"

Polyester fiberfill

One yard each of three different colored ribbons

Four small plastic rings sold for crochet to be used to hang the wall hanging

INSTRUCTIONS

All seam allowances are $1/4$" unless otherwise indicated.

1. As instructed in chapter 1, transfer the patterns to paper, pin to the wrong side of the fabric, and cut out.

2. Place the two head pieces, right sides together, on a piece of batting. Stitch, using a $1/4$" seam allowance, leaving a 2" gap in the stitching for turning. Repeat for the body and the arms.

3. Place the leg pieces, right sides together, on a piece of batting. Stitch, leaving the straight edge open. Repeat for the ears, using a double thickness of batting.

4. Turn all pieces right side out. Press. Whip-stitch the openings closed.

5. Position all body parts on the body. The head and the arm resting at the bear's side will overlap the body. The legs and the arm holding the balloons will be overlapped by the body. Pin in place. When you are happy with their positions, whipstitch them to the body.

6. Position and whipstitch the ears to the back of the head.

7. Position the eyes and nose on the bear's face. Glue the nose and sew on the eyes. Thread a tapestry needle with embroidery floss. Knot one end. Bring the needle up from the back of the head just under the center of the bottom of the nose. Put it back in the head $1/2$" below the nose and $1^1/4$" to the left.

Bring the needle back up ¹/₂" below the nose, between the corner of the mouth and the thread. Put the needle back in the felt ¹/₂" below the nose and 1¹/₄" to the left. Knot the thread on the back.

8. Sew one ring to the center back of the head.

9. Sew the three remaining rings to the top, narrower end, of the pieces of cardboard, punching two holes in the cardboard first, if neccessary.

10. Sew a row of gathering stitches around the edges of the balloons, ¹/₄" from the edge.

11. Place a cut piece of cardboard on the wrong side of each balloon. Pull up on the ends of the gathering threads. When you have pulled up on the threads until you have formed a pocket in the front of the balloon but can still fit your hand in, stuff the balloon with the fiberfill. Finish pulling up on the threads until the fabric is gathered snugly around the cardboard. Tie knots in the threads. Smooth the gathers.

12. Glue one end of each of the three pieces of ribbon to the bottom back of the three ballons.

13. Hang the balloons on the wall. Hang the bear. Place the free ends of the balloon ribbons in the bear's paw and with a small stitch or a dab of glue attach the ribbons to the bear's paw.

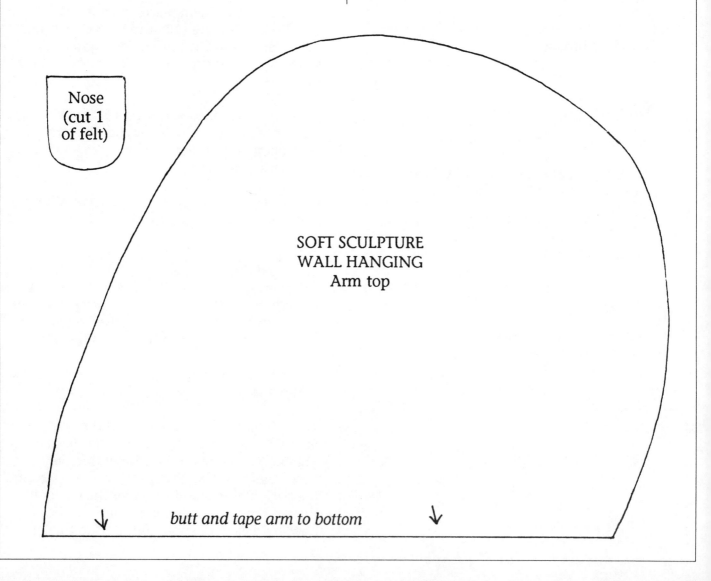

Nose
(cut 1
of felt)

SOFT SCULPTURE
WALL HANGING
Arm top

butt and tape arm to bottom

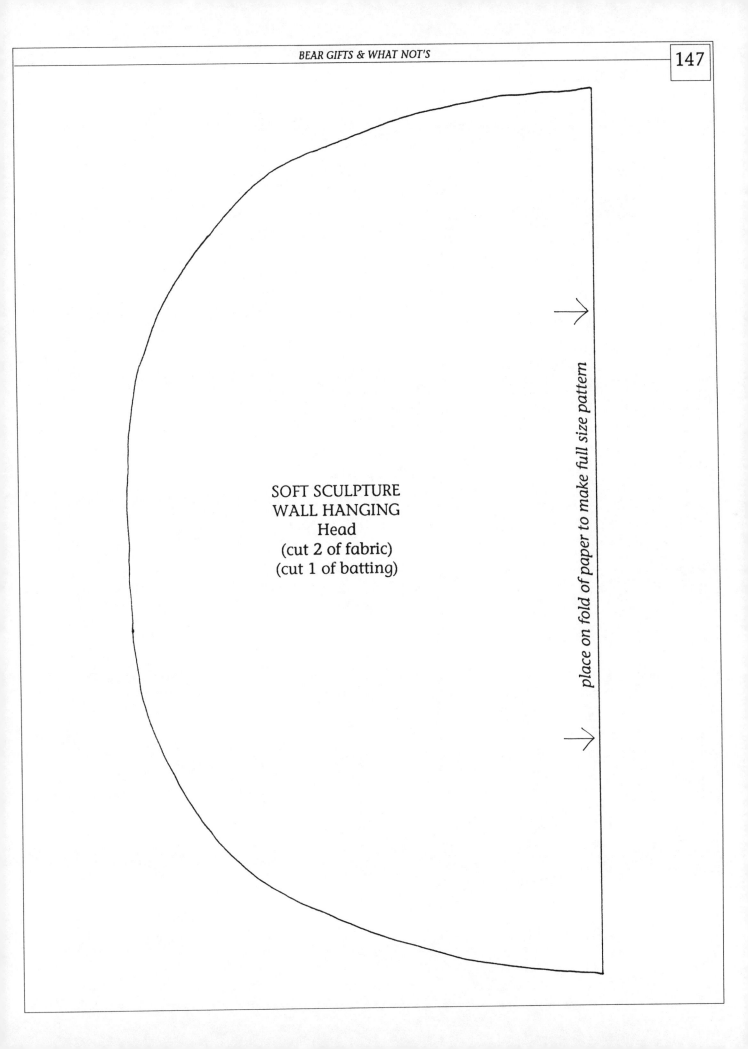

SOFT SCULPTURE
WALL HANGING
Head
(cut 2 of fabric)
(cut 1 of batting)

place on fold of paper to make full size pattern

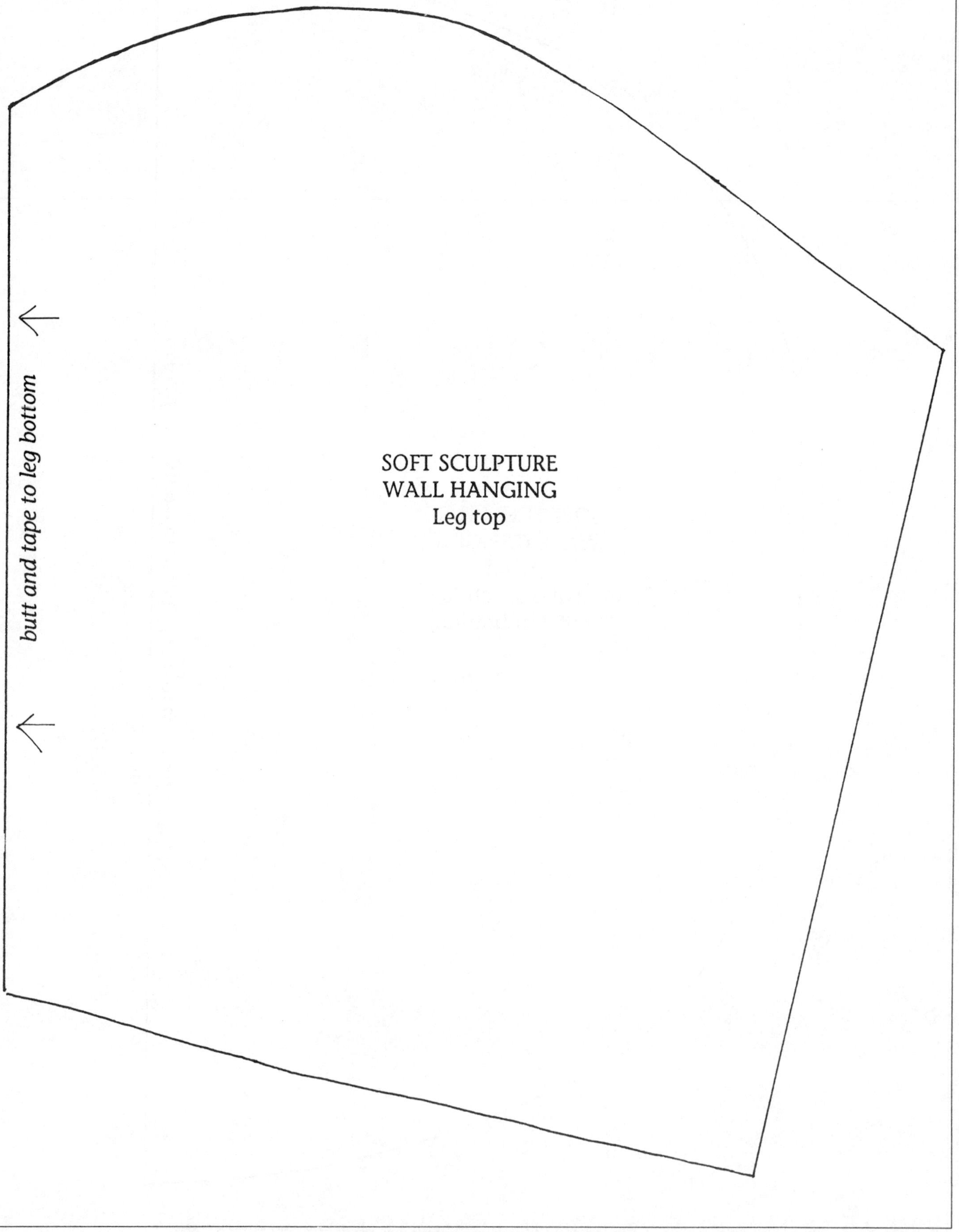

butt and tape to leg bottom

SOFT SCULPTURE
WALL HANGING
Leg top

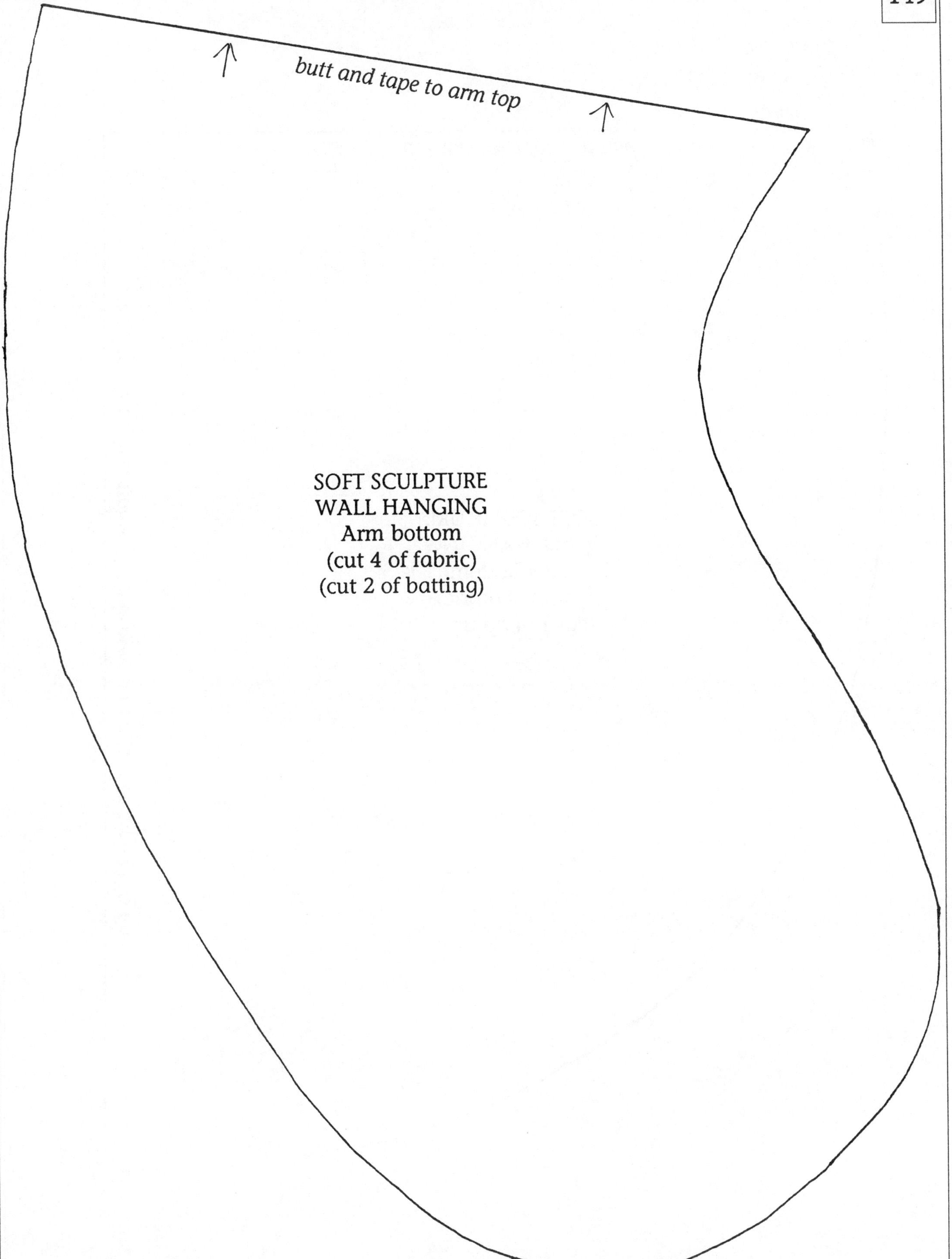

butt and tape to arm top

SOFT SCULPTURE
WALL HANGING
Arm bottom
(cut 4 of fabric)
(cut 2 of batting)

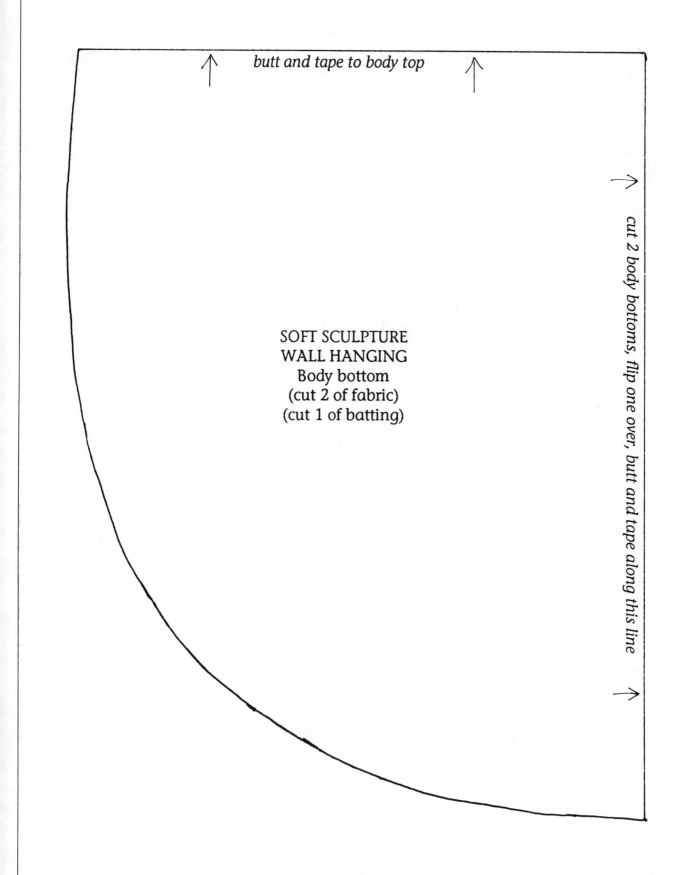

butt and tape to body top

SOFT SCULPTURE
WALL HANGING
Body bottom
(cut 2 of fabric)
(cut 1 of batting)

cut 2 body bottoms, flip one over, butt and tape along this line

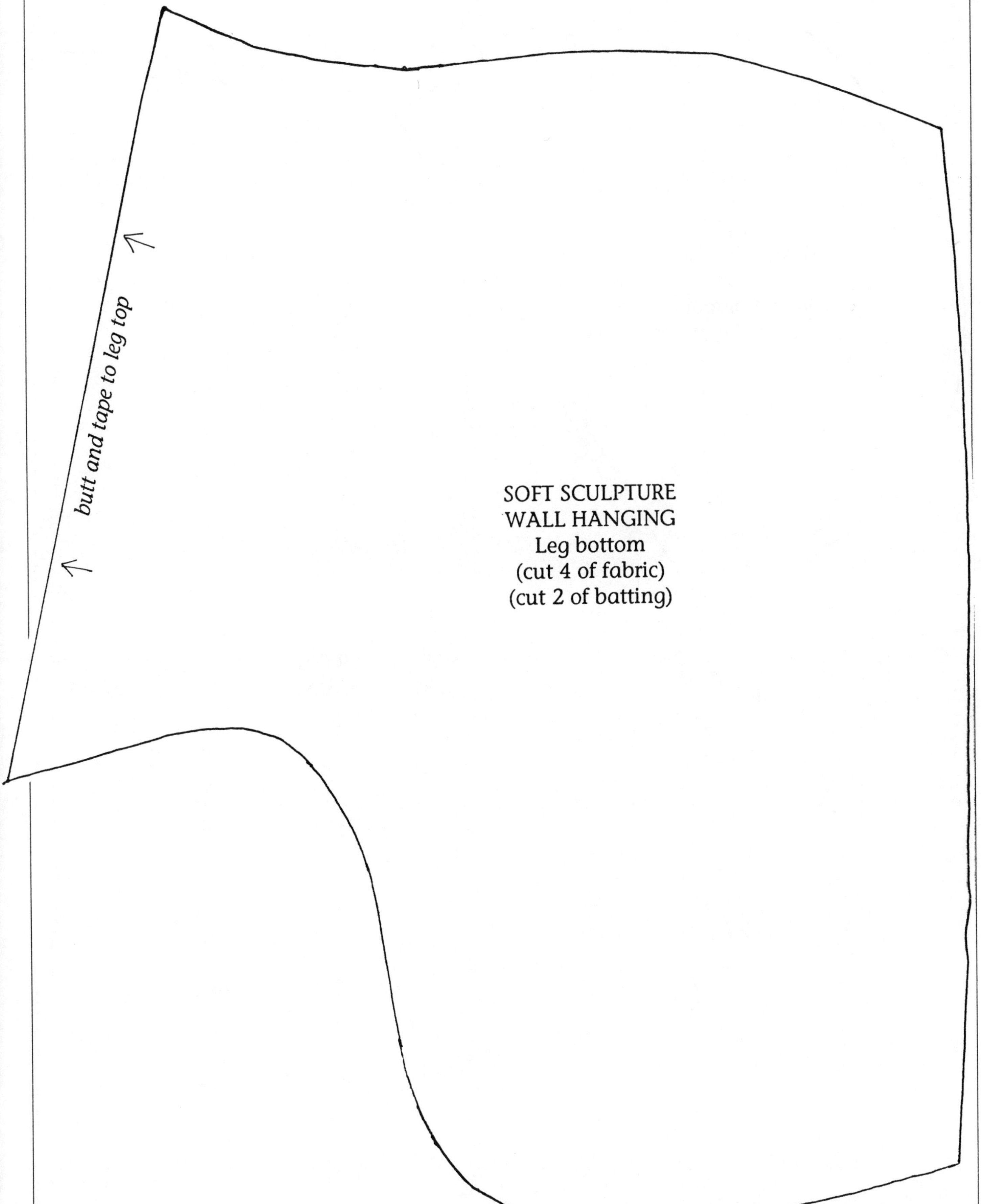

butt and tape to leg top

SOFT SCULPTURE
WALL HANGING
Leg bottom
(cut 4 of fabric)
(cut 2 of batting)

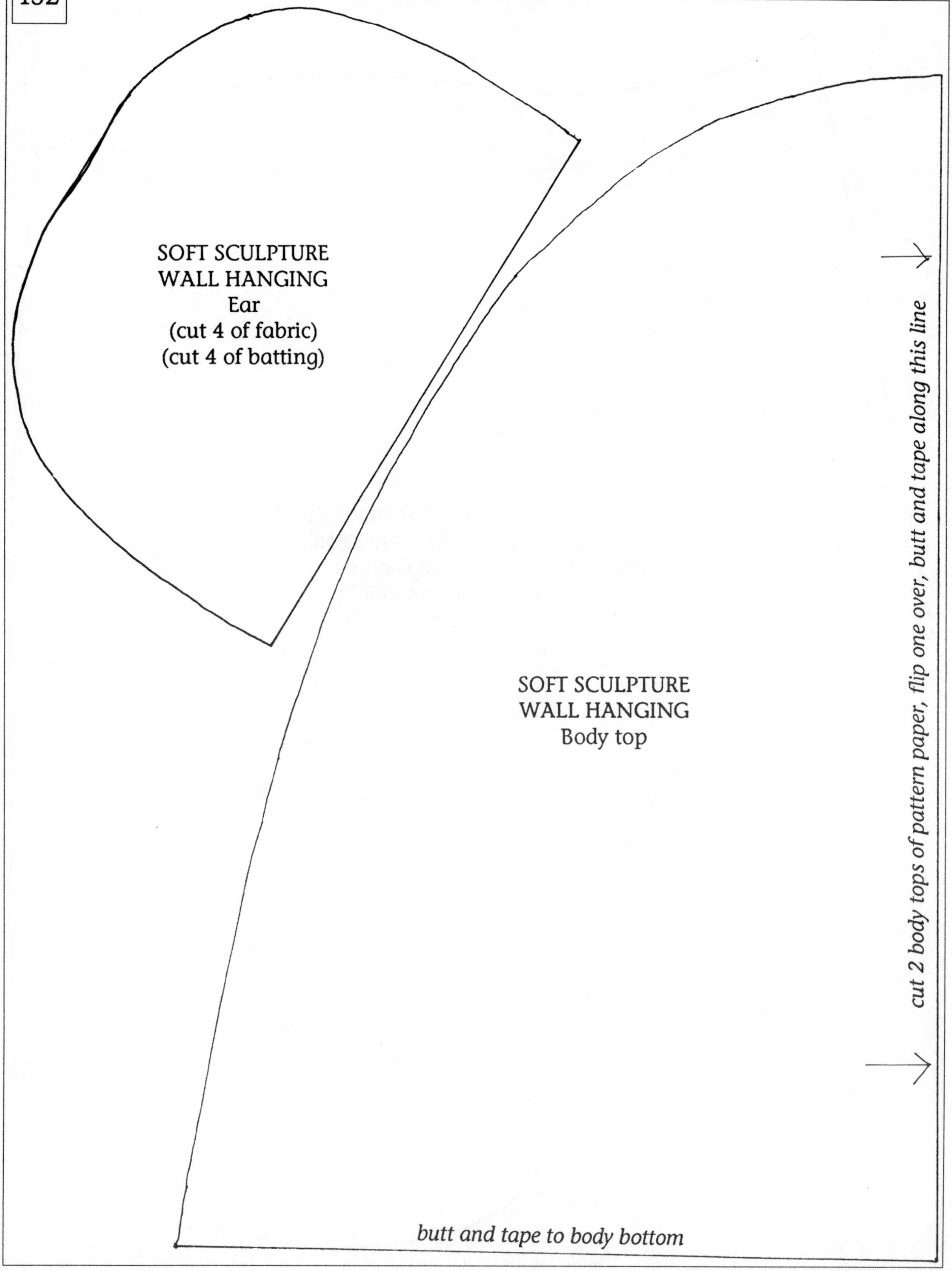

SOFT SCULPTURE
WALL HANGING
Ear
(cut 4 of fabric)
(cut 4 of batting)

SOFT SCULPTURE
WALL HANGING
Body top

cut 2 body tops of pattern paper, flip one over, butt and tape along this line

butt and tape to body bottom

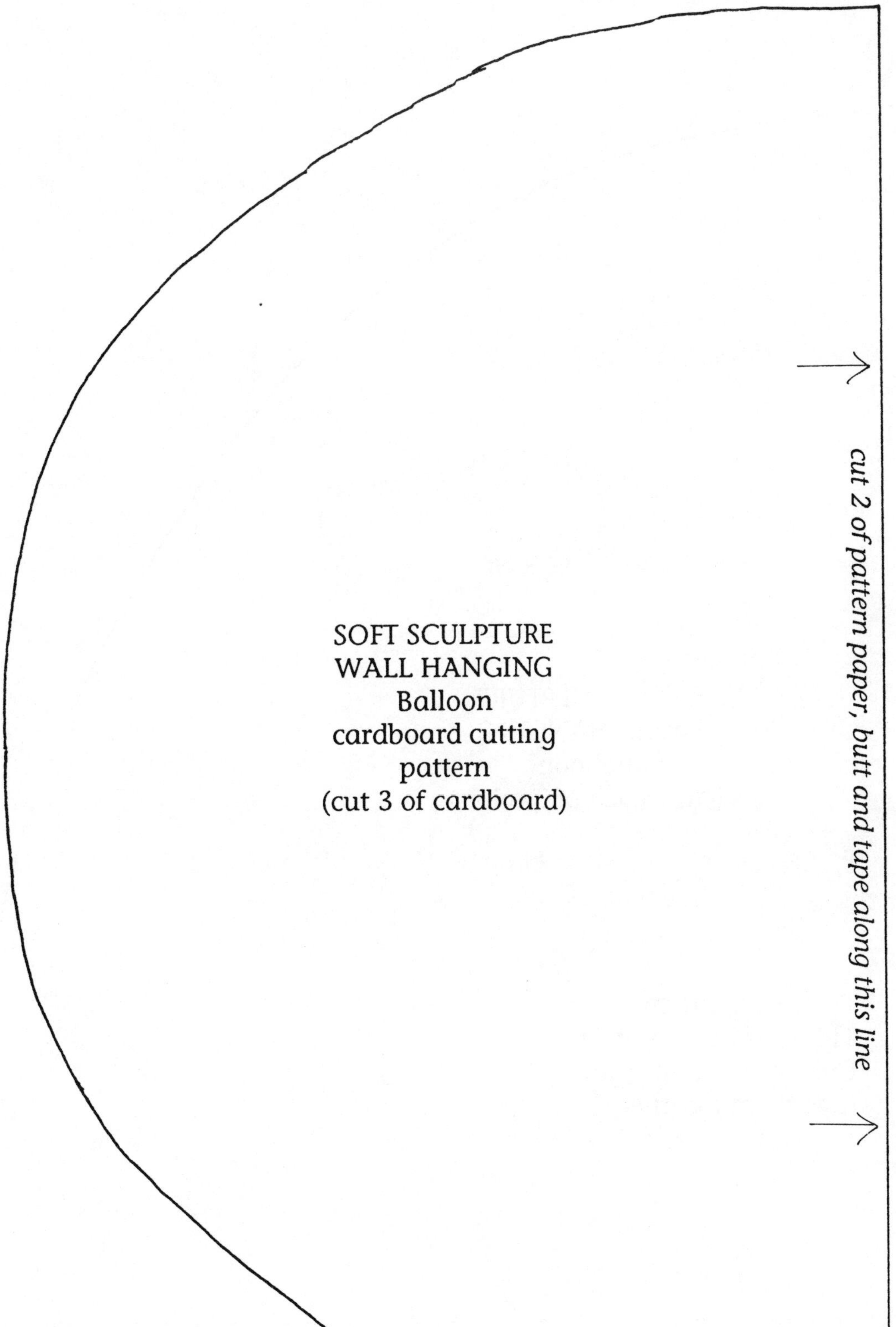

SOFT SCULPTURE
WALL HANGING
Balloon
cardboard cutting
pattern
(cut 3 of cardboard)

cut 2 of pattern paper, butt and tape along this line

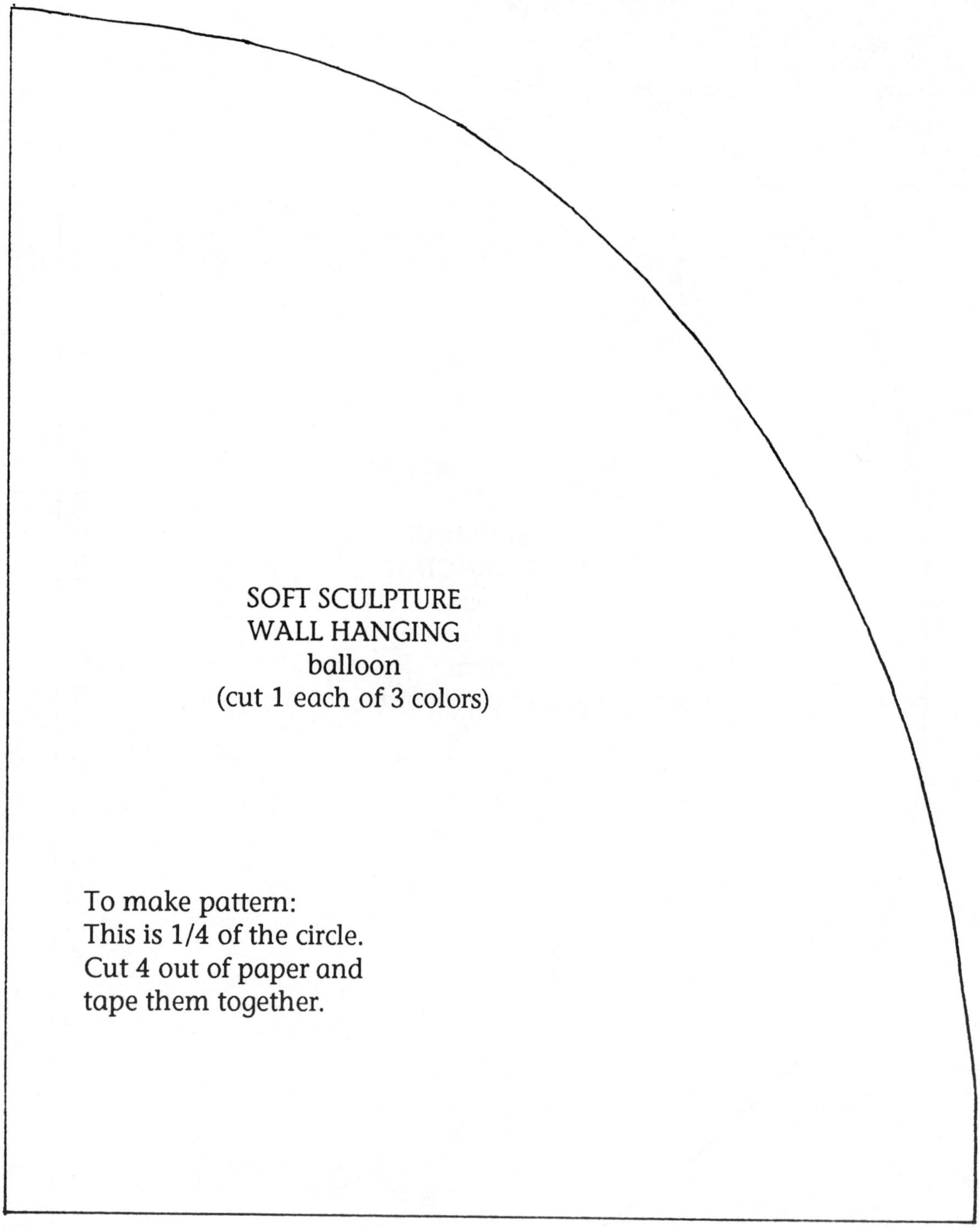

SOFT SCULPTURE
WALL HANGING
balloon
(cut 1 each of 3 colors)

To make pattern:
This is 1/4 of the circle.
Cut 4 out of paper and
tape them together.

FOR TEDDY'S CRADLE

Mattress and Pillow

MATERIALS

$5/8$-yard pillow ticking

Matching thread

Polyester stuffing

INSTRUCTIONS

1. Cut two pieces of the pillow ticking $9^1/2$" x 18" for the mattress and one piece $8^1/2$" x $12^1/2$" for the pillow, with the stripes running in the direction of the long measurement for the mattress and the short measurement for the pillow.

MATTRESS:

2. Using a $1/4$" seam, stitch around the mattress pieces, leaving a 3-inch opening along one side for turning. Trim the corners. Turn.

3. Stuff with polyester fiberfill. Close the opening by hand.

4. Push the tip of one corner into the mattress, bringing the two side seams together and making the corner square. Tack in place. Repeat for the remaining three corners.

PILLOW:

5. Fold pillow piece in half along a stripe, right sides together. Stitch, leaving an opening in the short end for stuffing. Trim corners. Turn.

6. Stuff.

7. Stitch the opening closed.

Sheets & Pillowcases

MATERIALS

$3/4$ yard sheet material

Matching thread

$1/4$"-wide elastic

INSTRUCTIONS

1. Cut the top sheet 14" x 22", the fitted sheet 11" x 20", and pillowcase $6^1/2$" x 12".

TOP SHEET:

2. Press under $1/4$" on the long sides. Press under another $1/4$". Topstitch.

3. Repeat for one short side.

4. Turn under $1/4$" on the remaining short side. Turn under $1^3/4$". Topstitch close to the $1/4$" turned-under edge.

FITTED SHEET:

5. Fold under $1/4$" all around the edge. Fold under another $1/4$". Topstitch.

6. Cut two pieces of elastic 10" long.

7. Pin the center of a piece of elastic to the wrong side of the center edge of one short end of the sheet. Pin the other ends to the edge of the sheet 5" from the corner on the long side of the sheet. Starting at one end of the elastic, zigzag stitch the elastic to the wrong side of the sheet edge stretching the elastic as you go. Repeat for the other end of the sheet.

PILLOWCASE:

8. Fold the pillowcase in half along the middle of its measurement. With a $1/4$" seam allowance stitch the side seams.

9. Turn under $1/4$" on the opening of the pillowcase. Turn under $1^1/2$". Topstitch close to $1/4$" turned-under edge.

TEDDY'S PATCHWORK QUILT

Envision your bear cuddled up in his cradle, warmed by his patchwork quilt. Or entertaining friends with a yummy picnic spread—featuring a lovely quilt made by you.

Following the step-by-step instructions below you can bring these scenes to life. Use of a patchwork technique known as "strip piecing" makes for speedy and accurate construction of the quilt. A quilting pattern is included as an optional finishing step.

Have fun and let your creativity loose when selecting fabrics. Your quilt could match Teddy's favorite room or outfit. Both all-cotton and cotton/polyester blends are appropriate. Muslin and calico make a nice quilt. For an Amish look, you may choose black cotton instead of muslin and a bright color such as red or royal blue in place of the calico.

MATERIALS

Finished size is 19 1/2" x 19 1/2".

1/4 yard muslin

3/4 yard calico

Matching thread

20" x 20" piece of batting

INSTRUCTIONS

1. As purchased from the fabric store, the raw (cut) edge of the fabric will be uneven. Using a yardstick or straight edge find the straight grain of the fabric, perpendicular to the selvage (finished edge) of the fabric. Draw a line across the fabric. Cut along this line. Use this as the starting point for cutting the quilt pieces.

2. Cut the fabric according to the illustrations. You will have:

CALICO:

Strips:	Two 2" x 20"	
	One 2" x 10"	
Border:	Two 3 1/2" x 20"	
	Two 3 1/2" x 14"	
Backing:	One 20" x 20"	

MUSLIN:

Strips:	One 2" x 20"	
	Two 2" x 10"	

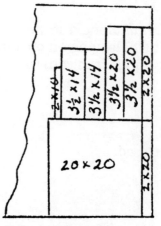

Muslin cutting guide.

Note: The key to sucessful patchwork is **ACCURACY**. Cut carefully and when piecing, pin first to make sure pieces match squarely and smoothly.

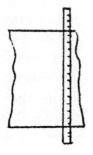

Calico cutting guide.

Piece the blocks as instructed in steps 3–11:

Note: All seam allowances are ¹/₄" which is the distance between the needle and the edge of the presser foot of your sewing machine. So, instead of lining up the raw edges with the ⁵/₈" line on your machine throat plate, just line them up with the right edge of the presser foot.

3. Match the one 2" x 20" strip of muslin with one of the 2" x 20" calico strips, right sides together. Stitch one long side. Match the other 2" x 20" calico strip to the muslin strip, right sides together. Stitch. Now you will have a muslin strip with a calico strip sewn to each side.

4. Do the same for the 2" x 20" strips. This time the one calico strip will be in between the two muslins.

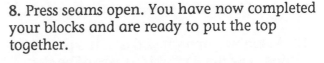

5. Press all seams open.

6. Carefully mark lines 2" apart along the length of both strips. You will have 4 lines on the 10"-long piece, and 9 lines on the 20"-long piece. Cut, making ten pieces from the 20"-long piece and five pieces from the 10"-long piece.

7. Sew five calico-muslin-calico pieces to five muslin-calico-muslin pieces along the long edge, right sides together. Sew the remaining five calico-muslin-calico pieces to the muslin-calico-muslin piece above to form the block as illustrated.

8. Press seams open. You have now completed your blocks and are ready to put the top together.

9. Piece the blocks together. Sew three pieced-blocks to three plain muslin blocks, right sides together. Sew the remaining plain muslin block to the other side of the pieced blocks, right sides together.

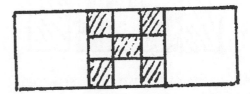

10. For both of the remaining two, sew a pieced block to the muslin block so that the muslin will be the center block.

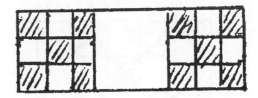

11. Press seams open. Sew these three strips together along the long edges to form the alternate blocks of the quilt as shown. Press.

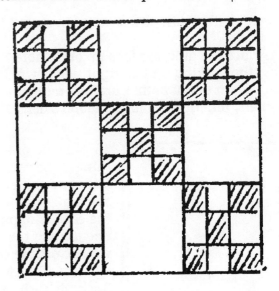

Make the border as instructed in steps 12–13:

12. Along two opposite sides of the pieced section, sew the 3½" x 14" strips of border calico, one on each side. Press.

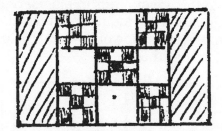

13. Along the other two sides, sew the 3½" x 20" border strips of calico, one on each side, overlapping the two strips just sewn to form a square. Press. Your quilt top is now complete.

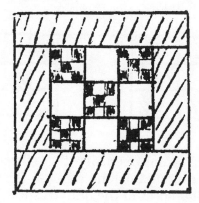

Assemble the quilt as instructed in steps 14–16:

14. Place the quilt top face up on a table. Lay the backing on top, right side down. Lay batting on top of both. Carefully matching corners, pin all three layers along sides.

15. Starting one third of the way from one corner, stitch all around the edges stopping one third of the way across the edge where you started. Backstitch where you begin and end.

16. Turn the quilt right side out. Batting will be inside. Turn under ¼" on the remaining open edge. Pin and slip stitch the opening closed. Your quilt is complete. You may elect to quilt as instructed below or present your new creation to Teddy now.

17. Quilting (optional): Trace and cut out the heart quilting template. Centering the template in each of the four plain squares in turn, trace around it lightly with a pencil or disappearing fabric marker. With a running stitch, quilt on the lines. Start by knotting the end of the thread and pushing the needle through just the top layer of fabric and bring it up on the line where you wish to start quilting, lodging the knot in the batting. End by knotting the thread and, after putting the needle into the cloth for the final stitch, run the needle through the quilt top and batting and up through the cloth, lodging the knot in the batting. You have to give a little tug to get the knot to pop through the fabric. Clip the thread where it emerges.

Quilting Templet

LACE TEDDY BEAR SACHETS

Romantic remembrances of Victorian times, these easy-to-make sachets will scent your Valentine's dresser drawers, grace your dressing table, or even adorn your Christmas tree. A perfect gift!

MATERIALS

7" x 14" piece of lace fabric

Matching thread

Four or more colors of $1/8$"-wide ribbon

Potpourri

Velvet leaves

Ribbon rose

INSTRUCTIONS

Use pattern on page 132.

1. Transfer the pattern to heavy paper or cereal box cardboard as instructed in chapter 1.

2. Cut two fabric pattern pieces for each ornament.

3. With right sides together, zigzag stitch the two pieces, starting and ending at the dots indicated on the pattern, thus leaving an opening for stuffing.

4. Fill with potpourri over a newspaper, gently shaking the ornament to get the mixture to fill the legs and arms in turn.

5. Sew the opening closed.

6. Trim the seam allowances close to the stitching.

7. Tie the ribbons together as one in a bow around the bear's neck.

8. Glue a ribbon rose on one ear.

9. Double thread a needle with embroidery floss, run it through the back of the head at the top, tie a knot to make the hanger about two inches long, and clip the thread.

SHADOW APPLIQUE QUILT

MATERIALS

¹/₂ yard red cotton fabric, cut into one 16" x 16" square and two 11" x 16" pieces

Matching thread

Solid pink cotton fabric

Solid colored and calico scraps

Embroidery floss

16" x 16" piece of white voile or organza

16" x 16" piece of muslin or other scrap fabric, for lining for quilting pillow front

16" x 16" piece of batting

One package red extra-wide double-fold bias tape

Glue stick

Water-soluble fabric marker

INSTRUCTIONS

Use pattern on pages 143 and 144.

1. Transfer the designs from the book to paper as instructed in chapter 1. Mark and cut out the heart from the pink fabric. Do the same for the bear, ribbon, flowers, and remaining pattern pieces. Cut the edges very cleanly, leaving no frayed threads. Handle these pieces as little as possible.

2. Position the pink heart in the center of one red square of foundation fabric. Dab small amounts of glue stick on the back of the heart. Press it in place. Pin the pieces in place over the pink heart overlapping the flowers over the leaves as in the pattern, adjusting their positions until you are happy with their placement. Dab a small dot of glue stick to the back of each pattern piece and press in place.

3. Lay the voile over the glued design. Pin in place. With long stitches, baste through the two layers about one inch from the design.

4. Using a single strand of embroidery floss, stich around each cut out piece of the design, just catching the very edge threads of the pieces with each stitch, with as short a stitch as possible on the underside and a long (about ¹/₄") stitch on the front. Use a double strand of embroidery floss for the edges of the pink heart to give it greater definition. You may choose embroidery floss colors to match or contrast with the fabric pieces.

5. Embroider the face of the bear, and the fold lines on the ribbon.

6. Place your work in a sink or basin of cool water and let it soak for a few minutes to soften the glue. Rinse under cool water. Roll in a towel. Air dry or press with your iron.

7. With a ruler and a water-soluble marker, draw quilting lines on the pink heart. Lay the second piece of red fabric on your work surface, place the batting over it, and lay the quilt front on top, right side up. Pin the three layers together all around the edges and around the heart. Using two strands of embroidery floss, quilt along these lines. Quilt around the heart, about ¹/₈ inch away from it, including in the outline quilting design pieces which extend out of the heart and onto the red foundation fabric.

8. Handstitch the bias tape all around the edges of the quilt.

C H A P T E R • 7

FURNISHINGS: THE BEAR MINIMUM

$\heartsuit$ $\heartsuit$ $\heartsuit$

Now that your bear has emerged miraculously from a bit of fabric and thread, you have stitched him up a complete wardrobe, and he has added his special brand of joy to your holiday celebrations, you can make him his own bear-sized furniture. Most of this furniture is already assembled and finishing takes just a few simple steps. Your local craft shop often has unfinished wood items similar to those available from mail order sources.

GENERAL INSTRUCTIONS

MATERIALS

Fine sandpaper

Very fine sandpaper

Wood filler

Tack cloth

Stain or paint for base coat

Water-base varnish

Two sponge brushes

INSTRUCTIONS

1. Fill any nail or staple holes in the wood with wood filler. Allow to dry.

2. Give your unfinished wooden item a light sanding with fine sandpaper before staining or painting a base coat. Clean with a tack cloth.

3. Stain: You may purchase a stain or dilute acrylic paint with water to the consistency of stain. You may wish to apply two or more applications of stain, depending on the covering capacity of the stain and the desired effect. Sand lightly after each application with very fine sandpaper. Clean with the tack cloth.

Paint: The two painted pieces in this book, the cradle and the shelf, were painted with a water-base solid color acrylic latex paint, as this was available in the desired color. You may choose any paint you wish, following the manufacturer's instructions for application. Sand lightly with very fine sandpaper. Clean with a tack cloth.

4. To seal the paint or stain: Apply two or more coats of varnish, sanding with very fine sandpaper between coats. Clean with a tack cloth.

Note: As you stencil, remember that by varnishing you have sealed the wood and can therefore remove any mistakes with a paper towel and rubbing alcohol.

STENCILING

A highly adaptable craft, stenciling can be applied to paper, wood, fabric, and many other surfaces. Stenciling is an easy method to achieve handcrafted results even for those reluctant to try free-hand painting or drawing. Using quick drying, water-clean-up acrylic paints, these projects will be a breeze. The most important factor in any stenciling project is to remember to work with a dry brush. With too much paint on the brush, the paint will run under the edges of the stencil and will ruin a clean crisp edge. The same is true of a wet brush or paint which is mixed with too much water.

The procedure is simple. A design is chosen, say a heart with a circle of dots around it. We'll make our heart red and our dots blue. A piece of stencil paper—see-through mylar frosted on one side is a good choice—is laid on top of the design and the pattern for the heart is traced on to it. Another piece of mylar is placed over the design and the dots are traced. The hearts and the dots are cut out with a sharp craft knife. The heart stencil is placed in position on the surface to be stenciled. A dry stencil brush is then loaded with paint and the paint is applied with an up-and-down motion until the cut out area is fully painted. Once the paint has dried, which is just a matter of minutes for acrylic paint, the stencil is removed, and the dot stencil is placed in position and paint is applied.

Practice on paper until you are confident that you have a feel for the correct paint consistency.

After your stenciling has dried you may wish to apply a coat of varnish to your new creation to protect it from the antics of your rambunctious bears and their friends.

INSTRUCTIONS

1. Transfer the stencil designs from the book onto tracing paper as instructed in chapter 1 for transferring patterns.

2. Cut a piece of mylar about an inch wider all around than the design. Cut one piece for each color in the design.

3. Place a piece of the cut mylar over the design, frosted side up. With a pencil, trace all elements labeled one color. Also mark other elements of the design as references for placement. Put aside. Repeat for all colors in the design.

4. Lay each marked piece of mylar in turn on a piece of thick cardboard and cut out the design with a craft knife.

5. Squeeze out a small amount of paint onto your palette or waxed paper. Acrylics dry out quickly. With a dry brush, push your brush straight down into the paint, turning it in a circular motion to pick up the paint. Dab it on a folded paper towel so that the ends of the bristles of the brush are completely full of paint, but the brush is dry.

6. Place the stencil in position on a piece of paper. Starting at the outside edges of the cut-out stencil design, dab the paint with an up-and-down motion, filling the entire cut out area with paint. The brush must be dry. Continue to load the brush with paint, and stencil until the design is complete.

MATERIALS

Mylar, .004mm frosted on one side, or other stencil paper, available at craft stores

Craft knife

Stencil brushes or sponge stencil applicators, one for each color

Small round brushes, such as a number three

Acrylic paints: These can be artist quality tube paints, squeeze bottle paints such as Ceramacoat™, jar acrylics, or special stencil paints

Palette knife

Waxed palette, paper plate or an old plate

Soft paper towels

Rubbing alcohol for cleaning brushes and stencils

7. Clean up: As soon as you are finished with a brush, rinse it in water, brushing the bristles on your palm to get the paint out of the center of the brush. If some stubborn paint remains, you may wish to slosh the brush around in some rubbing alcohol. Rinse. Soak your stencils in water and gently scrub the paint off. A paper towel soaked in alcohol will help to remove dried patches.

ROCKING HORSE

MATERIALS

Unfinished rocking horse—available from craft shops or Cabin Craft (see Sources)

Stain: Colonial maple was used for the rocking horse in this book, but choose what you like.

Acrylic paints: These can be artist-quality tube paints, squeeze bottle paints such as Ceramacoat™, or jar acrylics. You will need to mix or buy the following colors: Dark or barn red, forest green, gold, colonial blue, brown, and black.

Palette knife

Chalk

Number 3 round brush

Number 3, 4, 5, or 6 flat brush

Stencil mylar

Craft knife

Stencil brushes

Waxed paper palette, paper plate, or old plate

Soft paper towels

Rubbing alcohol for cleaning brushes and stencils

INSTRUCTIONS

1. Stain and varnish the rocking horse as instructed in the general instructions in the beginning of this chapter.

2. As also instructed in the beginning of this chapter, trace the designs for the saddle and rocker from the book onto stencil mylar and cut them out.

3. Trace the design for painting the horse's head from the book. Go over the lines with the chalk. Place on the appropriate side of the horse's head. Rub the back of the paper with a stylus or similar instrument to transfer the design. Tape the paper to a window or light box. Trace the design onto the back of the paper. Go over the design with the chalk and transfer the design to the other side of the horse's head as before.

4. Put some brown paint on your palette. Add a little water with your palette knife and mix the paint. Using the flat brush go over your chalked lines for the edges of the mane and forelock and around the ear. The paint should give a stain effect, letting the wood show through. Cover the entire mane and forelock with the watered-down paint. Use the paint straight out of the tube and at various watered-down consistencies to streak the mane, giving the effect of wisps of hair. Run a few faint streaks of black through the hair.

5. With the #3 round brush, go over the edge of the ear where it contacts the mane and forelock, using just a hint of water-thinned black paint. Experiment on paper first until you are happy with the consistency.

6. Paint the inside of the ear a light pink.

7. With the flat brush, paint the bridle dark or barn red.

8. With the #3 round brush, carefully paint the eyelashes and the nostril.

9. Paint the eye medium-blue. Allow to dry. Dot a small pupil of white on the eye.

10. Stencil the bridle with gold paint, over the now dry dark red. With the #3 round brush, dot between the stenciled hearts with blue paint. Allow the head to dry. Turn it over and paint the other side.

11. Paint the saddle area dark red. Allow to dry. Stencil the hearts gold. Allow to dry. Stencil the tear-dropped shaped stencil green. Allow to dry. Stencil the gold hearts

on the edge of the saddle, moving the stencil as you go. Allow to dry. With the #3 round brush, paint the blue dots as indicated on the patterns.

12. Measure up 1/2 inch from the base of the hooves and draw a line. Repeat all around the hooves. With the flat brush, paint the hooves black.

13. Stencil the hearts on the runner red. Stencil the tear-dropped shaped stencil green. With the #3 round brush, paint the blue dots as indicated on the pattern. Repeat for the other runner.

ROCKING HORSE HEAD

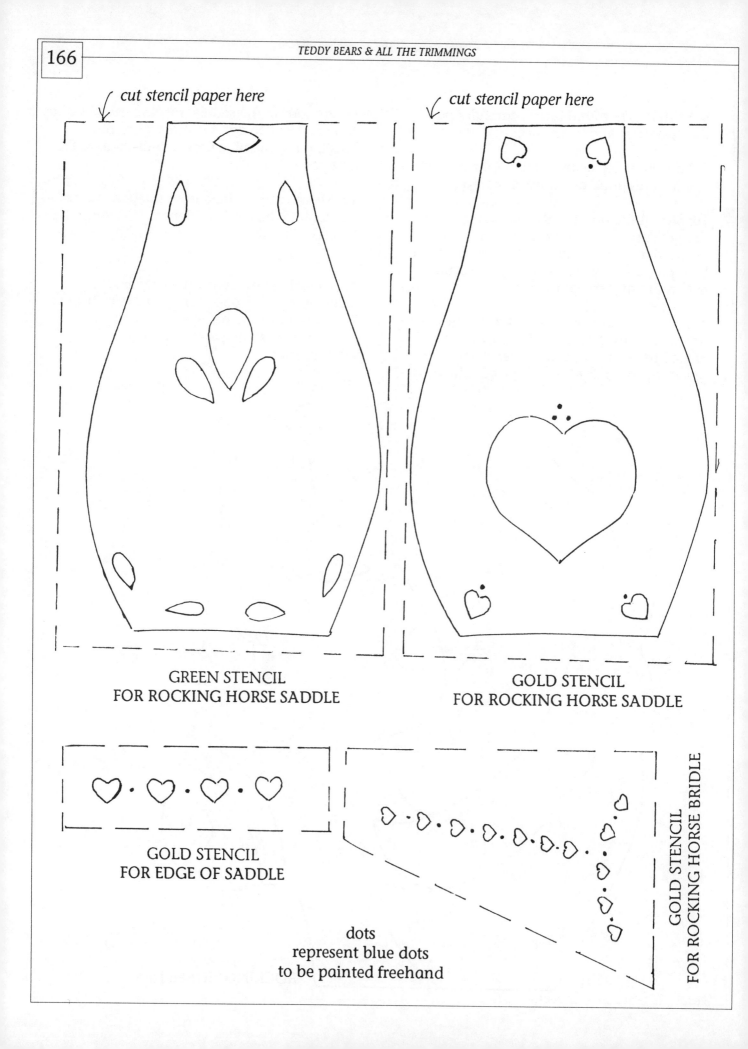

cut stencil paper here

cut stencil paper here

**GREEN STENCIL
FOR ROCKING HORSE SADDLE**

**GOLD STENCIL
FOR ROCKING HORSE SADDLE**

**GOLD STENCIL
FOR EDGE OF SADDLE**

**GOLD STENCIL
FOR ROCKING HORSE BRIDLE**

dots
represent blue dots
to be painted freehand

ROCKING HORSE RUNNER

Cranberry Red Stencil

butt and tape to above

butt and tape to above

butt and tape to below

Forest Green Stencil

butt and tape to above

butt and tape to above

butt and tape to below

dots represent blue dots

WAGON

Teddy will love giving his friends rides in this wagon. This project involves a simple two-color stencil and can be completed in a day. The most difficult and time-consuming element is waiting for the stain and varnish to dry between coats.

MATERIALS

Unfinished wagon: available from craft shops or Cabin Craft (see Sources)

Stain: Colonial maple was used for the wagon in this book, but select what you wish.

Acrylic paints: These can be artist-quality tube paints, squeeze bottle paints such as Ceramacoat™, or jar acrylics. You will need to buy the following colors: dark or barn red, forest green, black, and colonial blue.

Palette knife

Number 3 round brush

Stencil mylar

Craft knife

Stencil brushes

Waxed paper palette, paper plate, or old plate

Soft paper towels

Rubbing alcohol for cleaning brushes and stencils

INSTRUCTIONS

1. Stain and varnish the wagon as instructed in the general instructions in the beginning of this chapter.

2. As also instructed in the beginning of this chapter under the general stenciling instructions, trace the stencil designs from the book onto stencil mylar and cut them out.

3. On the back and the front of the wagon, stencil the hearts gold. Let dry. Stencil the tear-dropped shaped stencil green. Allow to dry. With the #3 round brush, paint the blue dots as indicated on the pattern.

4. To make the spokes, using a soft lead pencil and a ruler, draw a vertical line on the face of a wheel through the center of the wheel. Draw a horizontal line across the wheel at a right angle to the first line. Make a dot on the edge of the wheel equidistant between these two lines in each of the four pie pieces. Connect the dots. With the #3 round brush and some rather thin but not watery paint, paint these spokes with an even black line. Paint the tire tread black. Repeat for the remaining three wheels.

5. Screw the wheels to the wagon. Paint the heads of the screws black.

6. Glue the shaft to the center front of the wagon, under the box.

CRADLE AND SHELF STENCIL
(Hearts are two different sizes; therefore just bottom is shown for placement.)

DARK GREEN

Dots represent blue dots to be painted freehand

WAGON STENCILS

DARK RED

Dot represent blue dot to be painted freehand

DARK GREEN

TRICYCLE

Your bear will spend many a happy hour riding this tricycle. This project will take you an extremely short amount of time and effort to complete. The quality of the results is certain to surprise you. The tricycle makes a perfect gift for boys who have favorite bears and dolls they like to play with.

MATERIALS

Unfinished tricycle: available from craft shops or Unfinished Business (see Sources)

Dark or barn red acrylic paint or specially formulated base coat: available from craft shops, Unfinished Business, Cabin Craft, and Florida Supply (see Sources)

Water-base varnish

Fine sandpaper

Very fine sandpaper

Sponge brushes

INSTRUCTIONS

1. Prepare the tricycle as instructed under the general instructions at the beginning of this chapter, using watered-down paint as your stain.

2. On your final sanding before varnishing, pay extra attention to areas such as the handle bars, the front of the seat, and the back runners where little feet would have worn the paint, sanding down to let some natural wood peek through to simulate wear. Sand all edges to show some of the wood through the stain.

3. Apply varnish as instructed in the general instructions at the beginning of this chapter.

CRADLE

Your bear will look forward to bedtime in his very own cradle complete with sheets and a handmade quilt (see chapter 6). Paint the cradle to match the shelf holding your bear's clothes and he will have his own bedroom set.

MATERIALS

Unfinished cradle: available from craft shops or Cabin Craft (see Sources)

Base coat paint

Acrylic paints: These can be artist-quality tube paints, squeeze bottle paints such as Ceramacoat™, or jar acrylics. You will need to mix or buy the following colors: dark or barn red, forest green, colonial blue, brown, black, and pink.

Palette knife

Number 3 round brush

Stencil mylar

Craft knife

Stencil brushes

Sponge brush

Waxed paper palette, paper plate, or old plate

Soft paper towels

Rubbing alcohol for cleaning brushes and stencils

INSTRUCTIONS

Use stencil patterns on pages 169 and 193.

1. Prepare and paint the cradle as instructed at the beginning of this chapter in the general instructions.

2. Trace and cut the stencil, including the two stencils for the bear as also instructed in the beginning of this chapter under the general stenciling instructions.

3. Stencil the tear-shaped stencil green under the cut-out heart on both the front and the back of the back piece of the cradle. With the #3 round brush, paint three red dots over the heart as indicated on the pattern.

4. Center the brown bear stencil on the front of the cradle and stencil. Allow to dry. Place the pink stencil over the bear and stencil. With the #3 round brush, paint the face and claws on the bear.

HANGING SHELF

Painted to match your teddy's cradle, this shelf is the perfect place to hang his clothes. Choose any background color you and Teddy desire, or stain the shelf rather than paint it.

The hangers can be left natural, stained or painted with a watered-down acrylic paint. You may wish to use a paper towel or rag to do this.

MATERIALS

Unfinished shelf: available from craft shops or Unfinished Business (see Sources)

Base coat paint

Acrylic paints: These can be artist-quality tube paints, squeeze bottle paints such as Ceramacoat™, or jar acrylics. You will need to mix or buy the following colors: dark or barn red, and forest green.

Palette knife

Number 3 round brush

Stencil paper or mylar

Craft knife

Sponge brushes

Stencil brushes

Waxed paper palette, paper plate, or old plate

Soft paper towels

Rubbing alcohol

Two chair buttons or hole plugs—available from craft shops or Unfinished Business (see Sources)

Glue

INSTRUCTIONS

Use stencil pattern on page 169.

1. Prepare and paint the shelf as instructed at the beginning of this chapter in the general instructions.

2. Trace and cut the stencil as instructed in the beginning of this chapter under the general stenciling instructions.

3. Stencil the tear-shaped stencil under the cut-out hearts green.

4. With the #3 round brush, paint the dots as indicated on the pattern.

Hangers

MATERIALS

6 mm round reed—available from craft shops or Florida Supply (see Sources)

Pruning shears for cutting cane

Piece of wood, approximately 8" x 12"

Nails

Paint or stain, optional

INSTRUCTIONS

1. Transfer pattern guide onto the board. Nail nails into designated holes.

2. Cut reed into 15-inch lengths, cutting the ends at the angle.

3. Soak the reed for half an hour.

4. Bend a piece of reed around the nails onto the form, pushing it down to the bottom of the form.

5. Repeat with the remainder of the reed pieces, making as many hangers as desired.

6. Allow to dry. Remove from the form.

7. If you wish to paint the hangers, dilute some acrylic paint with water to the consistency of stain. Apply to the hangers and allow them to dry.

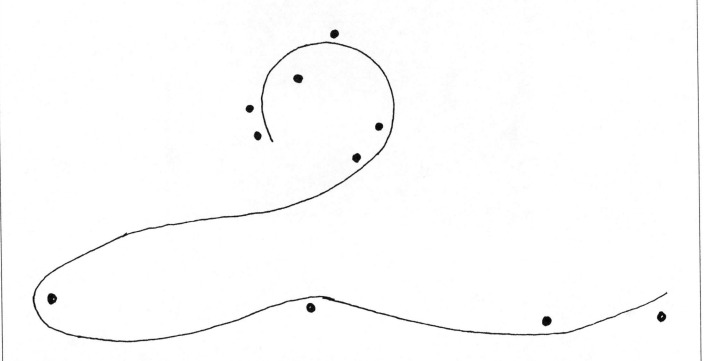

pattern for reed hangers for shelf

CHAPTER • 8

A TEDDY BEAR BIRTHDAY PARTY

♡ ♡ ♡

Birthday parties are just plain special—special for the birthday person and special for all the lucky invited guests. Nowadays, it has become fashionable for kids' parties to be a game of one-upmanship, with kids being feasted and entertained to the point of being overwhelmed.

For all of us who remember these special times, when a cake, a party favor and hat, along with some fun and games were what birthday parties were all about, here's a teddy bear party from start to finish. All you need are some smiling-faced guests—each arriving with a favorite (or two) bear—and you're guaranteed a party kids will enjoy and long hold dear in their memories.

For party games, many children will be delighted to make up stories and situations for their bears. You can play bear dress-up, letting each child dress his or her bear in jewels, or lace, or sunglasses, or hard hat and then tell the group a story about how Teddy happens to be dressed that way. And, of course, there are always bear stories to read and "Pin the Honey Pot on the Bear" to play.

For little girls who are "into" dressing up, you can turn your bear party into a bear tea party. Let each child dress herself in "Victorian" garb, choosing from an array of long skirts, straw bonnets, costume jewelry, barrettes, feathers, and scarves, and some makeup too. Once they are each properly attired they may sit along with their bears at a formally set table for tea and cakes. Now that's a party 5-and 6-year-olds can get into.

TEDDY BEAR BIRTHDAY CAKE

Handed down in our family, this superb chocolate cake is easily cut and assembled into a bear and then frosted. It makes the perfect center of attraction for your festive birthday table spread.

INGREDIENTS

²/₃ cup butter, margarine, or shortening, softened

2 cups sugar

2 eggs

2 teaspoons vanilla

4 squares chocolate

2²/₃ cups cake flour

2 teaspoons baking powder

1 teaspoon salt

2 teaspoons baking soda

2 cups boiling water

INSTRUCTIONS

1. Cream the butter and the sugar.

2. Add the eggs and the vanilla. Beat until light.

3. Melt the chocolate and stir it into the egg mixture.

4. Sift the dry ingredients together.

5. Add the dry ingredients alternately with the boiling water, starting and ending with the dry ingredients.

6. Divide the batter into a greased and floured 11" x 13" pan and an 8"-round cake pan.

7. Bake at 350 degrees for 30-40 minutes.

8. Turn the cake onto a wire rack to cool.

9. Transfer the patterns for the bear cake from the book onto paper as instructed in chapter 1. Place the large cake on a cutting board. Lay the head and ear pattern pieces on top of the cake as in the diagram. Cut them out with a sharp knife. Cut along the two lines as shown in the diagram. Round off two adjacent corners on each of the four cake pieces. These will be the arms and legs. Assemble the pieces into a bear on a large platter.

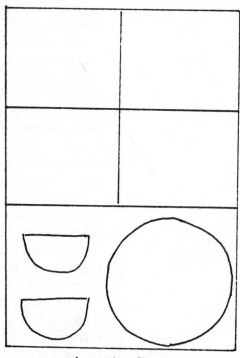

cake cutting diagram

Frosting

INGREDIENTS
1 cup butter, softened
2 packages (2 lbs.) confectioner's sugar
2 teaspoons vanilla
4 tablespoons cocoa
8–10 tablespoons milk
Black and red food coloring

INSTRUCTIONS

1. Cream the butter. Add one-third of the confectioner's sugar, blending well. Add the vanilla. Add more confectioner's sugar and then a few tablespoons of the milk if the frosting becomes dry. Keep adding the sugar and a little milk when needed.

2. Remove three tablespoons of frosting to a separate, small bowl. Add red food coloring and mix. This is for the bear's paw pads and heart.

3. Remove three tablespoons of frosting to another separate, small bowl. Add black food coloring and mix. This is for the bear's eyes, nose, and claws.

4. Add the chocolate to the frosting in the large bowl. Mix.

5. Assemble the bear cake pieces on a large platter. Frost the entire bear with the chocolate frosting.

Decorating the cake:

1. Frost the bear with the chocolate frosting.

2. Take a small glob of black frosting on the tip of a knife. Put it on the face for an eye. Repeat for the other eye and the nose. Moisten your finger and smooth the eyes into circles and the nose into a triangle.

3. Put a glob of red frosting in position for the paw pads and heart. With a moistened finger make circles for the paw pads and a heart on the bear's chest.

4. Take a bit of black frosting on a sharp knife and run it on the frosted paw for claws. Make two more claws for the first paw. Wash off the knife and repeat for all the paws.

5. Tie a bow out of ribbon and place it under the bear's chin.

6. Using a tube of cake-writing frosting, write "Happy Birthday" to someone special if you wish. You might also want to write "Love" on the bear heart.

TEDDY BEAR CAKE
Head

TEDDY BEAR CAKE
Ear

STENCILED BLOCK CANDLE HOLDERS

You may want to surround your cake with birthday candles in these attractive blocks, or put one candle at each place setting.

MATERIALS

In addition to the materials listed under general stenciling instructions at the beginning of chapter 7, you will also need:

Thirteen 1½" unfinished wooden blocks —available from your local craft store or from Unfinished Business (see Sources)

Water-base varnish

Fine sandpaper

Colonial maple stain, or color of your choice

Acrylic paint colors including: cranberry, brown, pink, blue, yellow, and black

Letter stencils, 1" to 1¼" in height to spell "Happy Birthday"—available from your local craft store or Florida Supply (see Sources)

Drill with a ¹⁵/₆₄" bit

Birthday candles

INSTRUCTIONS

1. Follow the general instructions in the beginning of chapter 7 to cut your stencils.

2. Drill holes in the center top of each block.

3. Lightly sand the blocks. Clean them with a tack cloth or damp paper towel. Apply a coat of stain. Allow to dry. If the grain has raised, sand lightly and clean with a damp paper towel. Repeat, if desired. Apply two or three coats of water-based varnish, sanding and cleaning after each coat.

4. Center each letter stencil over the front of the block and stencil with cranberry paint.

5. Stencil the bears to the back of the block, opposite the letter. When dry, hand paint black eyes and noses to the bears' faces.

6. Stencil each individual ballon to the two remaining sides of the blocks, using stencil for each color. (I chose yellow, pink, and blue for my balloons.)

7. Paint faint strings for the balloons. Paint cranberry bows under the bears' chins.

Balloon Stencil Key   Balloon Stencil I   Balloon Stencil II   Balloon Stencil III

STENCILS FOR BLOCKS

PIN THE HONEY POT ON THE BEAR

This variation on an old favorite is simple to make. Choose various colored felt for the honey pots, a different color for each player. With their velcro stickers these little child-safe honey pots will stick to the bear's tummy target.

MATERIALS

$3/4$ yard brown or beige felt, 72" wide

Pink felt

Black felt

Off-white felt

Various colored felt, one color for each honey pot

$1^1/2$ yard craft fuse or heavy weight fusible interfacing, 44" wide

$1/3$ yard brown or beige robe velour or terry cloth

Matching thread

Two black buttons for eyes

Black embroidery floss

Craft glue

Two round plastic circles for hanging

One inch of fusible velcro per honey pot

4" x 24" piece of thin cardboard

Permanent marker

INSTRUCTIONS

1. Prepare the patterns as instructed in chapter 1. Trace the bear body parts and honey pots onto the felt and cut out. Trace bear parts and honey pots onto interfacing. Cut out about $1/8$" inside of the lines. Cut the honey pot labels out of the off-white felt. Cut two tummys out of the velour.

2. Fuse interfacing to backs of all bear parts and honey pots. Fuse the wrong side of the "grabber" (try it on the velour to be sure you use the side of the velcro that will stick on the tummy) side of the velcro to the backs of the honey pots.

3. Write "honey" on the honey pot labels with the permanent marker. Glue them on the honey pots.

4. Pin the head and arms on the bear's body. Pin the legs under the bear's body. Adjust their positions until you are pleased with the look of the bear. Glue them in place. Pin the ears in place. Glue the ears to the back of the head.

5. Glue the pink foot pads to the bear's feet.

6. Pin the two tummies together, right sides facing. Stitch, leaving a three-inch gap in the stitching. Turn. Press. Stitch the opening closed. Pin the tummy in place on the bear's body. Whipstitch in place.

7. Sew the bear's eyes to his face. Glue on his nose. Thread a tapestry needle with embroidery floss. Knot one end. Bring the needle up from the back of the head just under the center of the bottom of the nose. Put it back in the felt $1/2$" below the nose and $1 1/4$" to the left. Bring the needle back up $1/2$" below the nose, between the corner of the mouth and the thread. Put the needle back in the felt $1/2$" below the nose and $1 1/4$" to the right. Knot the thread on the back.

8. Sew the rings to the backs of the ears.

9. Glue the cardboard to the back of the bear from the top of one arm across the bear's chest to the top of the other arm so that none is showing on the front of the bear. The cardboard will stiffen the bear so that he will hang flat against the wall rather than curl toward the center

10. To play: Blindfold each player when his turn comes up, turn once, and head in the direction of bear with honey pot in hand. Winner places honey pot closest to bear's tummy!

PIN THE HONEY POT ON THE BEAR
Foot Pad
(cut 2 of pink felt)

PIN THE HONEY POT ON THE BEAR
Honey Pot

PIN THE HONEY POT
ON THE BEAR
Honey Pot Label

PIN THE HONEY POT ON THE BEAR
Ear
(cut 2 of felt)
(cut 2 of interfacing)

Nose
(cut 1 of
black
felt)

PIN THE HONEY POT ON THE BEAR
Head and Tummy
(cut 1 of felt for head)
(cut 2 of velour for tummy)
(cut 1 of interfacing)

 place on fold of pattern paper and cut out

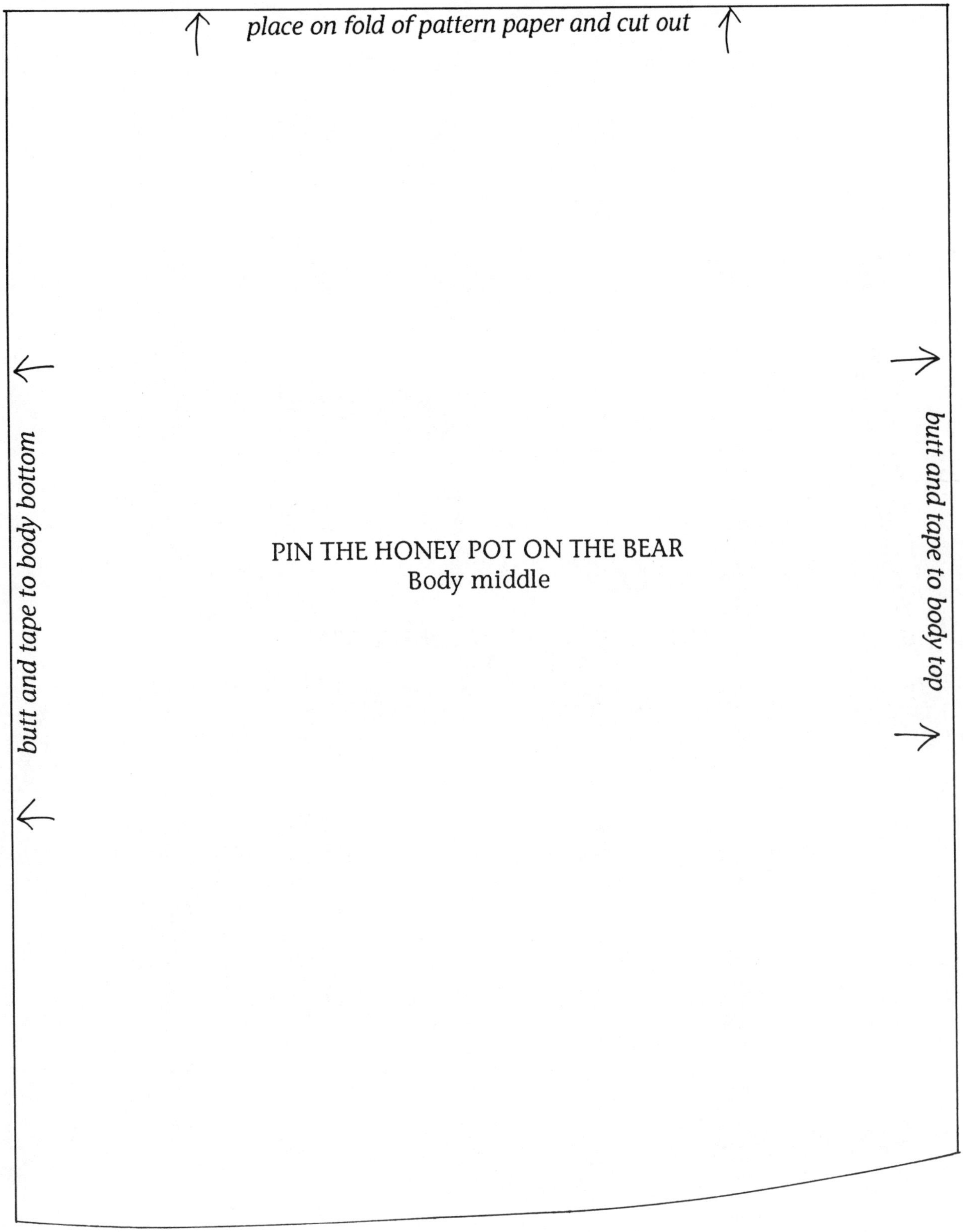

place on fold of pattern paper and cut out

butt and tape to body bottom

butt and tape to body top

PIN THE HONEY POT ON THE BEAR
Body middle

place on fold of pattern paper and cut out

PIN THE HONEY POT ON THE BEAR
Body top

butt and tape to body middle

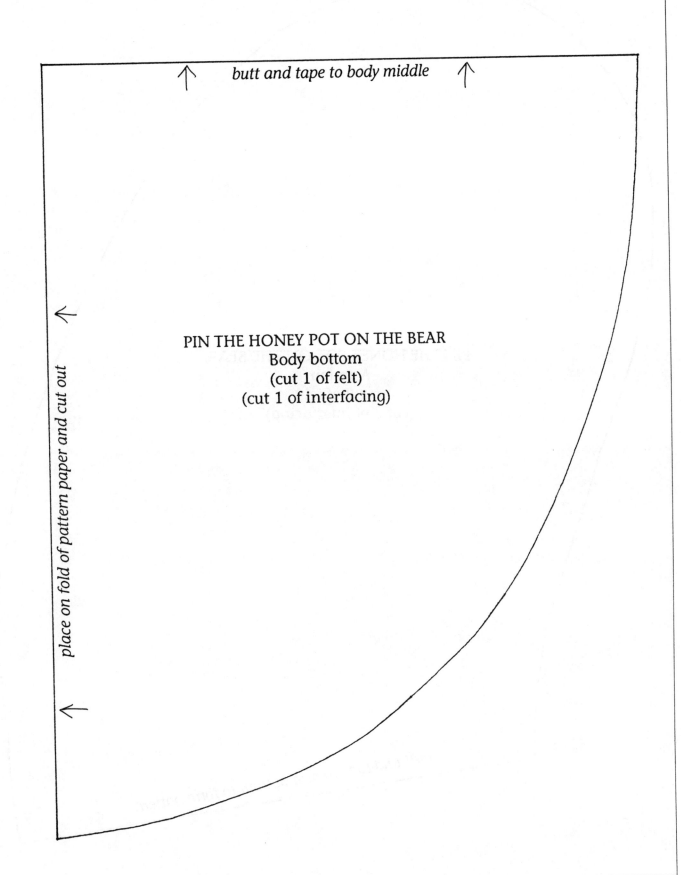

butt and tape to body middle

PIN THE HONEY POT ON THE BEAR
Body bottom
(cut 1 of felt)
(cut 1 of interfacing)

place on fold of pattern paper and cut out

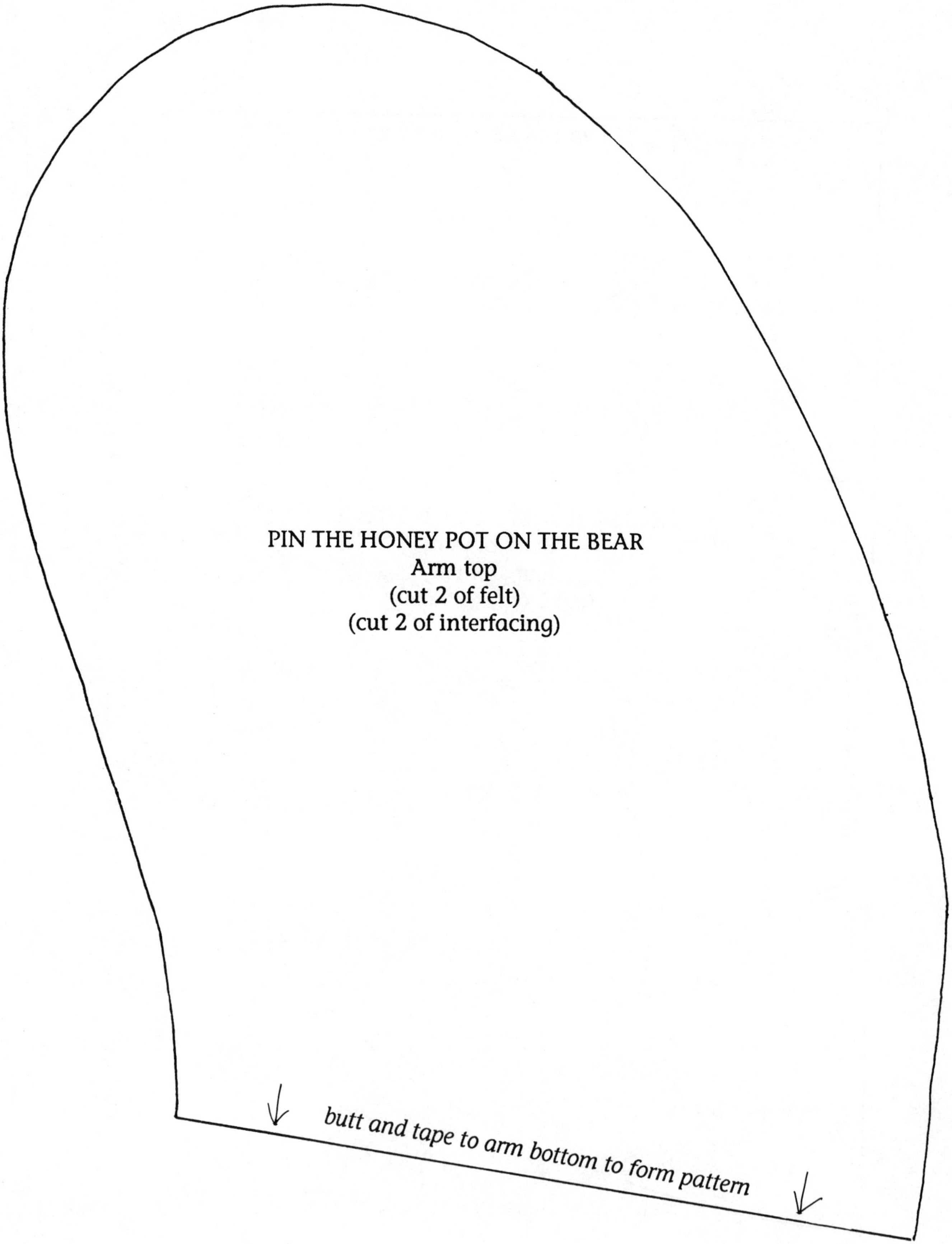

PIN THE HONEY POT ON THE BEAR
Arm top
(cut 2 of felt)
(cut 2 of interfacing)

↓   *butt and tape to arm bottom to form pattern*   ↓

butt and tape to arm top to form pattern

butt and tape to complete pattern

PIN THE HONEY POT ON THE BEAR
Arm bottom

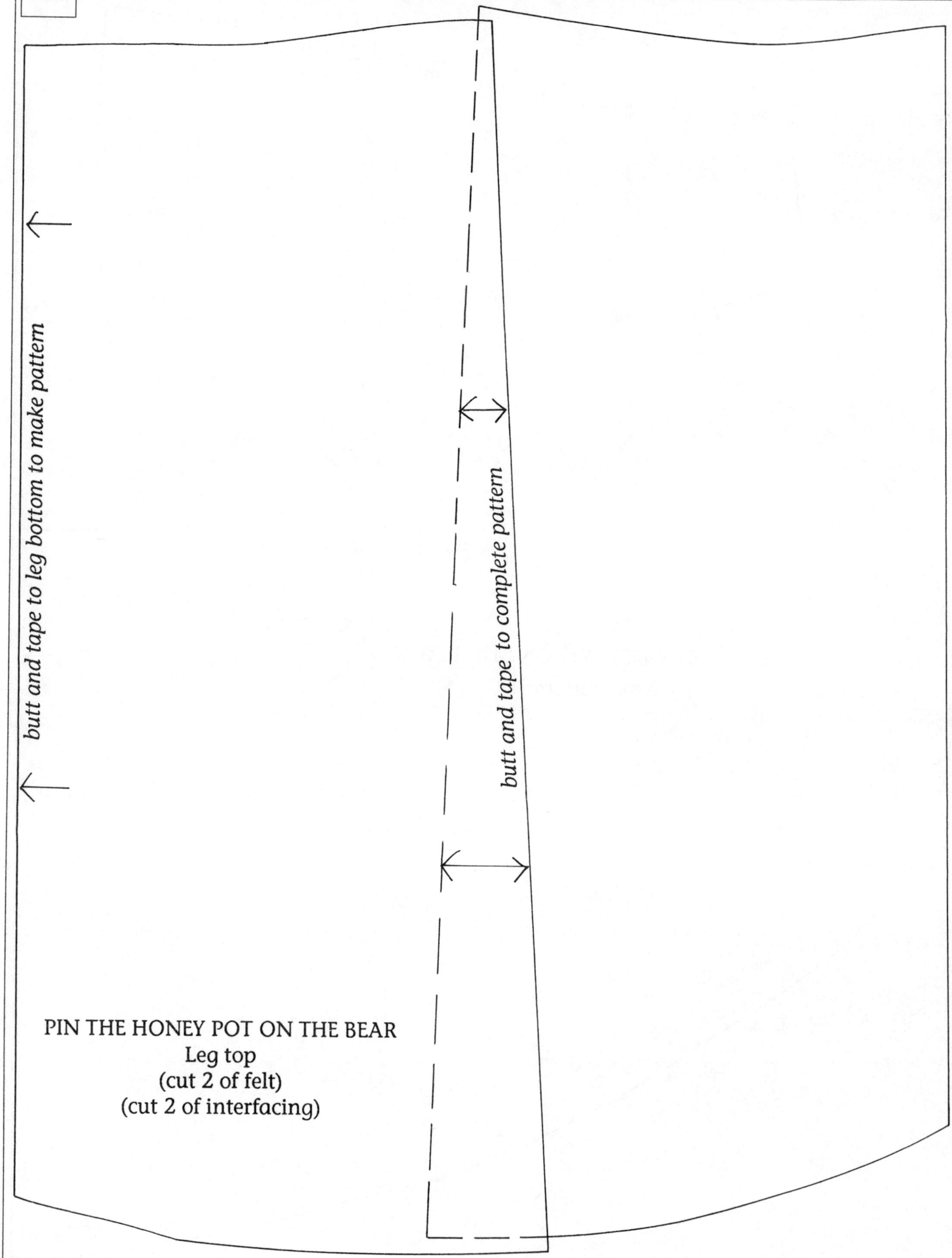

butt and tape to leg bottom to make pattern

butt and tape to complete pattern

PIN THE HONEY POT ON THE BEAR
Leg top
(cut 2 of felt)
(cut 2 of interfacing)

PIN THE HONEY POT ON THE BEAR
Leg Bottom
(cut 2 of felt)
(cut 2 of interfacing)

butt and tape to leg top to form pattern

butt and tape to complete pattern

TEDDY BEAR PARTY FAVORS/PLACE CARDS

Personalized with the names of the party guests, these inexpensive crates are easily adorned with painted cut-outs, and the kids will take them home with their happy memories of the teddy bear birthday party.

MATERIALS

Small wooden basket or mini-crate, with or without handle, available at craft shops

Wooden teddy bear cut out in scale with basket

Fine sandpaper

Acrylic paints

Number 3 round brush

Number 3, 4, 5 or 6 flat brush

White craft glue or a glue gun

Ribbon

INSTRUCTIONS

1. Sand the rough edges of the wooden items. Wipe them off.

2. Using the flat brush paint the crate or basket with the white base coat. Two thin coats will give the paint a slightly translucent appearance, letting the wood texture show through. Acrylic paints dry so quickly that if you paint them in assembly line fashion the first item will be dry by the time you've given all of them a first coat.

3. Using the flat brush, paint the bears with a beige or brown base coat.

4. Paint the hearts the bears hold pink.

5. Using the round brush, paint blue bows on the bears' necks.

6. Using the round brush, paint a red or pink heart on the bears' chests.

7. Using the round brush, paint dots for eyes on the bears.

8. Depending on whether your cut-out is a front or a side view you may wish to paint a nose and face and claws on them.

9. Using just the tip of the round brush and holding it straight up and down, use a gentle dabbing motion to dot a series of dots along the outside edge of the heart. Load more paint on the brush frequently to keep the dots of uniform size.

10. Using the round brush or a fine tip permanent marker, paint or write a name on the heart.

11. Tie a bow around the handle of the basket. Fill with candies or raisins and peanuts.

STENCILED BIRTHDAY CARDS OR INVITATIONS

You may want to surround your cake with birthday candles in these attractive blocks, or put one candle at each place setting.

MATERIALS

In addition to the materials listed in the general stenciling instructions at the beginning of chapter 7, you will also need:

Plain greeting cards or writing paper, folded in half

Envelopes to match

Acrylic paint colors including brown, red, black, and white

INSTRUCTIONS

1. Prepare the stencils as instructed in the general stenciling instructions at the beginning of chapter 7.

2. Place the bear stencil towards the bottom left hand corner of the paper, leaving room at the top right hand corner to stencil the balloons. Stencil the bear. Allow to dry.

3. Lay the stencil for the paws, heart, and muzzle of the bear in position over the bear. With the pink paint, stencil these parts. Allow to dry.

4. Stencil each individual balloon, one at a time.

5. With black paint and the number three brush, paint the eyes, nose, and mouth of the bear in the desired locations. Add the balloon strings with a very small amount of paint and a light touch.

STENCILED PARTY PLACEMATS

You may want to have the guests make their own placemats and party hats.

Follow the instructions for the stenciled cards above, centering the bear design in the center of a sheet of plain or colored paper. With a ruler and a felt tip marker, add a single or double line border close to the edge of the paper.

STENCILED PARTY HATS*

for bears and kids

Cut the hats out of thin white posterboard, using the hat patterns. Center the design so that the seam will be in the back and the stencil will be in the center front of the hat. Stencil. Glue the long, straight sides of the hat together, overlapping along the fold line. Punch holes at the dots at the bottom sides of the hat indicated on the pattern. Knot a piece of elastic thread. Run the unknotted end through one hole. Run the elastic through the other hole. Try on. Adjust. Knot.

STENCILED WRAPPING PAPER & GIFT CARDS

These stencils can be used for a variety of fun projects. You may use the small bears and balloons from the birthday candle holder block design for an all-over stencil for wrapping paper or for the front of small gift cards to punch holes in and attach with ribbons to presents. The large bear stencil would be delightful centered on the front of a gift.

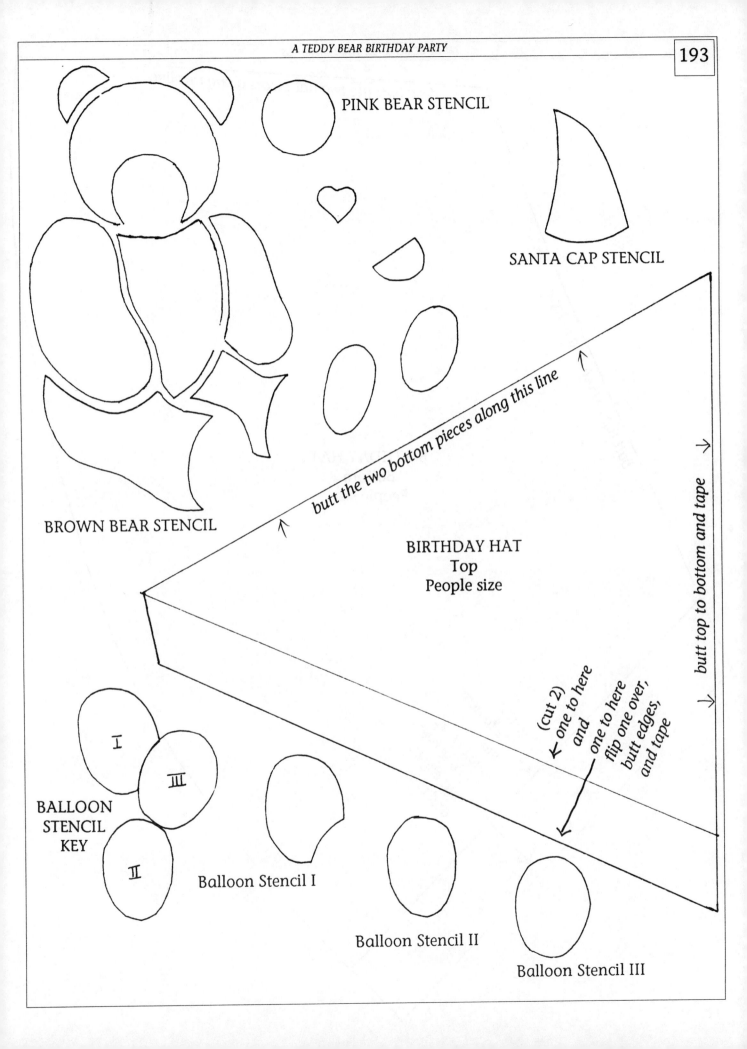

PINK BEAR STENCIL

SANTA CAP STENCIL

BROWN BEAR STENCIL

butt the two bottom pieces along this line

BIRTHDAY HAT
Top
People size

butt top to bottom and tape

(cut 2)
one to here
and
one to here
flip one over,
butt edges,
and tape

BALLOON
STENCIL
KEY

I

III

II

Balloon Stencil I

Balloon Stencil II

Balloon Stencil III

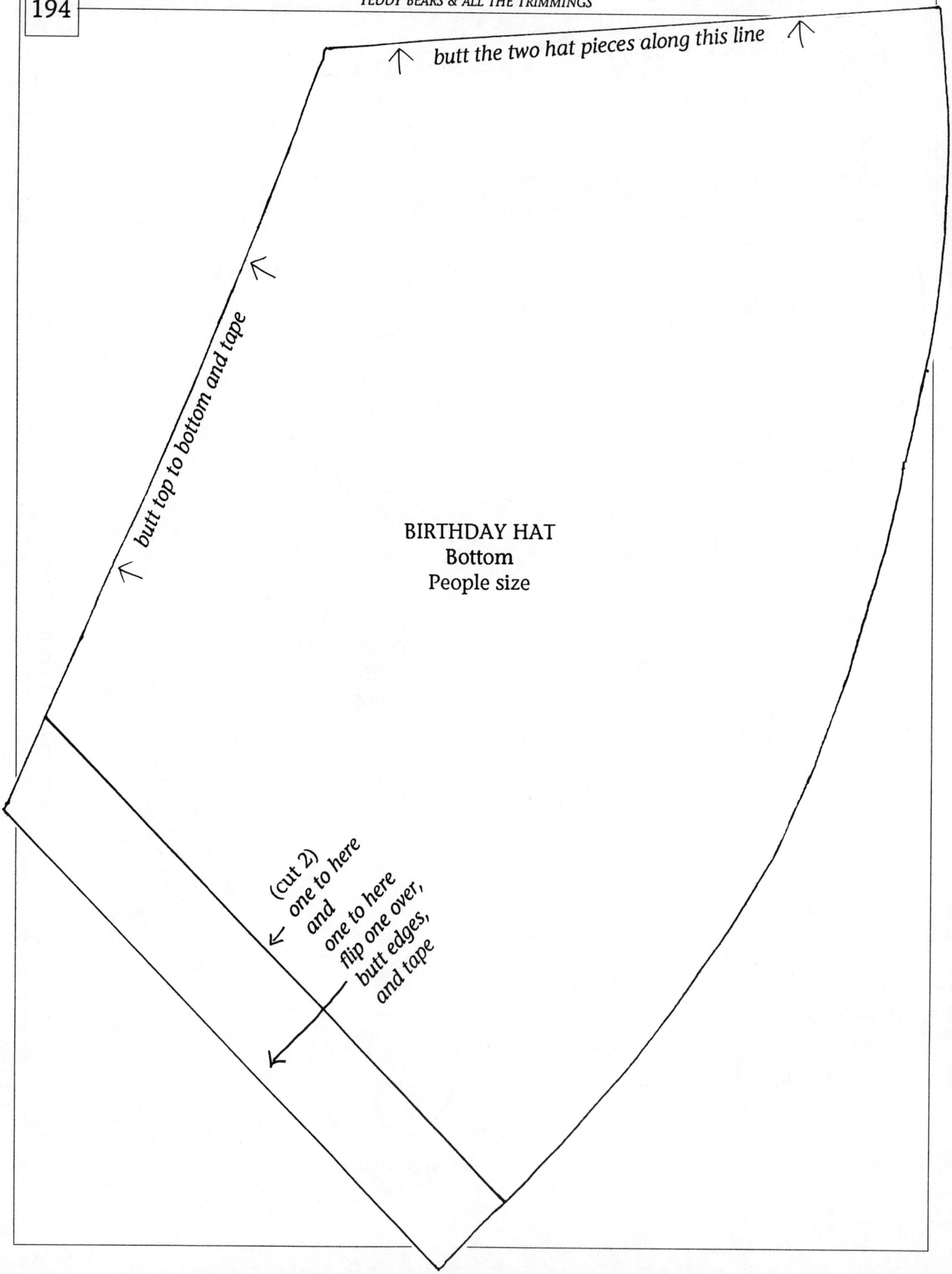

butt the two hat pieces along this line

butt top to bottom and tape

BIRTHDAY HAT
Bottom
People size

(cut 2)
one to here
and
one to here
flip one over,
butt edges,
and tape

CHAPTER • 9

BEAR CRAFTS
FOR
KIDS

There are many ways to enjoy teddy bears. Playing quietly with them is a fond memory many of us hold dear, reading with a favorite bear patiently seated beside us can make a lonely night more friendly, making bears and their trimmings is something many of us enjoy because giving bears is the greatest thrill of all, save one.

That one bear activity that is more special than giving, is sharing time with youngsters, helping children make bear crafts. Kids love anything to do with bears, and making bear-related crafts and gifts is high on the list of fun, educational activities. What could be more appropriate than a handmade bear gift from a child to a grandparent, teacher or neighbor!

CRAYON PAINTING

Crayon painting is fun. The results are superb, especially when one considers the simplicity and ease of the procedure, and the few supp-lies, all readily available, needed. This is an excellent craft for children. Young children can do the crayon painting themselves, but will need help completing the projects. These crafts are especially nice if you wish to encourage older children to make their own gifts for giving.

Crayon-Painted Stocking

MATERIALS

³/₄ yard muslin for each stocking

Matching thread

Fine point permanent marker such as Sharpie™

Crayons

Gold metallic embroidery floss

¹/₂ yard of 5¹/₂"-wide, gathered eyelet

Polyester batting

Extra wide double-fold bias tape

INSTRUCTIONS

Use stocking pattern on pages 135, 136, 137, and 138.

1. Transfer the stocking pattern onto heavy paper, joining the three pieces with tape as indicated on the stocking patterns. Trace and cut four stocking pieces out of muslin and cut two pieces of batting for each stocking you wish to make.

2. Trace the design patterns as instructed in the first chapter of this book. Tape the pattern to a window or on a light box. Tape the stocking over the design, centering the design over the lower leg or ankle portion of the stocking so that the eyelet will not cover the design when the stocking is completed. Trace the design with soft pencil or disappearing marker onto the muslin.

3. Place the stocking front on a piece of cardboard. With a light touch, go over your traced design with the permanent marker.

4. Color in the design areas with crayons.

5. Using a dry iron set on the cotton heating setting, press the design, protecting it with a single layer of brown paper bag (with no writing), until the crayon "melts" into the fabric.

6. Mark quilting lines on the decorated front and plain back with a soft led pencil or disappearing marker in a grid with the lines one inch apart, skipping the design area on the stocking front. If you have a cardboard cutting board marked with a grid, just place the fabric over the cutting board, diagonally across the grid lines, and trace.

7. Lay a plain stocking piece down. Place batting and then the decorated stocking piece on top, right side up. Match edges. Pin. Repeat for the stocking back using the two remaining plain muslin stocking pieces and having the toe of the stocking point in the opposite direction of the stocking front so that you have a front and a back.

8. Using the gold thread, quilt along the marked lines on the front and back of the stocking. Make long running stitches, showing about an inch of thread on the top, taking short stitches in between to show as little a stitch as possible underneath and maximizing the gold thread showing on top.

9. Stitch the stocking front and back, right sides together, using a $1/4$" seam allowance. Leave the top open. Turn.

10. Trim the eyelet to 17 inches in length. Stitch the raw edges together using a $1/4$" seam. Trim the seam. Pin the wrong side to the right side of the stocking top, having top edges even. Baste in place.

11. Sew bias tape on top edge of stocking, enclosing the raw edge of the stocking and the top of the eyelet.

12. Cut a piece of bias tape 5 inches long. Fold it in half lengthwise, with one half a $1/2$" longer than the other half. Turn this extension under. Pin this hanger to the top of the stocking and tack in place.

Crayon Painted Tree Skirt

MATERIALS

Two pieces of 45"-wide muslin, $1^1/4$ yards each

Fine point permanent marker such as Sharpie™

Crayons

Gold metallic embroidery floss

Two packages cranberry extra wide double-fold bias tape

45"-square piece of polyester batting

INSTRUCTIONS

1. Fold one piece of muslin in half and in half again. Press folds to use them as markings for pattern design placement. Tie a string to a pencil at one end and a pin at the other making the string 22" between the two. Place the pin at the center of the folded point (which will become the center of the tree skirt). Holding the pin, place the point of the pencil at the folded edge of the fabric 22" from the pin. Draw an arc. Cut. Repeat with a string $2^1/2$" long for a center hole. Cut out the hole. Cut along one fold to make an opening.

2. Trace patterns as instructed in the first chapter of this book. Tape the pattern to a window or a light box. Trace the half-bow pattern on tracing paper. Repeat on another piece of tracing paper. Turn one of them over and trace the design onto the back of the paper. Trim the patterns along the slashed lines. Butt and tape the two pieces together to form the complete bow pattern. Trace one of each of the three teddy bear designs on each of the three remaining uncut folds, about four inches from the outside edge of the tree skirt. Trace the bow design in between the bear designs four times according to the picture of the finished tree skirt.

3. With a light touch go over your traced design with the permanent marker, placing cardboard under the design area you're working on—or you'll regret it!

4. Color in the design areas with crayons.

5. With a dry iron set on the cotton heat setting, press the design, protecting it with a single layer of brown paper bag (with no writing), until the crayon "melts" into the fabric.

6. Mark quilting lines on the decorated tree skirt with a soft lead pencil or disappearing marker in a grid with the lines one inch apart, skipping the design areas. If you have a cardboard cutting board marked with a grid, just place the fabric over the cutting board diagonally across the grid lines and trace.

7. Place the square of muslin for the skirt backing on your work surface, lay the batting over it, and the decorated tree skirt on top, right side up. Pin through all layers.

8. Using the gold thread, quilt through all three layers following the markings. Make long running stitches, showing about an inch on the top of the tree skirt, taking short stitches in between to show as small a stitch as possible underneath and maximizing the gold thread showing on top.

9. Trim the bottom two layers even with the tree skirt top.

10. Stitch the bias tape all around the outside edge of the tree skirt.

BOW FOR CHRISTMAS TREE SKIRT

Make a reverse copy and butt and tape the two together. See instructions for Tree Skirt.

FLOUR/SALT DOUGH ORNAMENTS

The trick to making these ornaments is to knead the dough the full ten minutes and to use it freshly mixed. They are so easy to make that you can mix up a full batch to make extra ornaments to give away, or cut the recipe in half for fewer ornaments. These make nice birthday party favors, too.

INGREDIENTS

4 cups white flour

1 cup salt

$1\frac{1}{2}$ cups water

MATERIALS

Acrylic paints

Brushes

Satin-finish polyurethane or water-base varnish

Cookie sheets

Drinking straw or nail

Garlic press

INSTRUCTIONS

1. Mix the flour and salt thoroughly.

2. Add one cup of the water and mix. Add the remaining $\frac{1}{2}$ cup of water a little at a time, working it in well after each addition.

3. Turn onto a floured surface and knead for 10 minutes.

4. Place in a plastic bag. This dough will keep for about 5 days stored in the refrigerator, but is best used right away.

BAKING & FINISHING

1. Bake at 250 degrees until hard. This may take a couple of hours so bake for half an hour and then set your timer for another half hour and check again. To test for doneness, allow it to cool slightly and press. If it gives, it isn't cooked enough. Allow to cool.

2. Paint the ornament.

3. Spray or brush a thin application of varnish on the ornament. Allow it to dry. Repeat twice so that you have three coats.

4. Run a piece of embroidery floss through the hole and hang the ornament.

Teddy Bear Snowman

1. Lightly flour a cookie sheet.

2. Break off a ball measuring about $1\frac{1}{4}$" in width. Roll into a smooth ball. Press it down evenly to flatten it to $1\frac{3}{4}$" in width. Place on cookie sheet. This will be the body.

3. Break off a 1" ball of dough. Roll it into a smooth ball. Press it down to flatten it to $1\frac{1}{2}$" wide. Brush the top of the body with water where you want to attach the head. Lay the head on the cookie sheet overlapping the top of the body. Gently press the head into place.

4. Break off a 2" ball of dough. Roll it into a ball. Cut the ball into two even pieces. Roll one piece into a log of even width, about $1\frac{1}{2}$" long. Bend the dough in the middle of the log to form a bend at the bear's elbow. Brush the body with water where you wish to attach the arm. Gently press the arm into place. Repeat for the other arm.

5. Press out a small piece of dough on a counter top or cutting board as if making a pie crust. Cut out a 1" square and a piece $1\frac{1}{2}$" x $\frac{1}{2}$". Attach these pieces to the top of the head to form the snowman's top hat.

6. Cut a long, thin piece of dough, about $\frac{1}{4}$" wide and 4" long. Attach it to the snowman's neck for a scarf, moistening the body first.

7. Push a small amount of dough through a garlic press. Cut it off with a knife when it protrudes $\frac{1}{4}$". Attach to the ends of the scarf.

8. Form tiny round balls for the eyes. Moisten the head where the eyes are to go, and press them in place.

9. Push a straw or nail through the top of the hat to make a hole for hanging.

10. Roll two small pieces of dough into flat circles for ears. Press your thumb into the center to make them concave. Experiment until you have the desired size and shape. Attach to the head.

11. After baking the ornament, paint the bear white, the hat black, and the scarf red.

12. Varnish and complete.

Furry Teddy Bear

1. Break off a ball of dough about $1\frac{1}{2}$" in width. Roll into a slightly flattened oval to form the body. Place on cookie sheet.

2. Roll a $1\frac{1}{4}$" piece of dough into a ball, flatten it slightly, and attach to the top of the body, moistening the top of the body first.

3. Break off a piece of dough about $2\frac{1}{4}$" wide. Roll it into a ball. Cut in half evenly. Roll each into a log about $1\frac{1}{2}$" wide. Make a bend in the elbow. Moisten the body where you wish to attach the arms. Press into place.

4. Roll a 3" ball of dough and cut it in half. Make two logs for legs, wider at the top and bending out slightly at the ankles. Attach to moistened body.

5. Make ears as above.

6. Push dough through a garlic press, cutting it off when it extends about $\frac{1}{4}$". Gently press onto moistened bear. Repeat until the bear is entirely covered.

7. Make a small ball for the muzzle. Press it flat. Attach to the face of the bear. Make a tiny flattened ball for the nose. Attach it to just above the center of the muzzle. Make tiny balls for the eyes. Attach them to the face above the muzzle.

8. Make a hole with the straw or nail to hang the bear. Or, if you're afraid it will ruin your bear's head, glue the hanger to the bear's head after painting and varnishing.

9. After baking, paint the bear brown or beige and his features black.

10. Varnish and complete.

SOURCES

by Diane
1126 Ivon Avenue
Endicott, NY 13760
Catalog: SASE #10 and two stamps

Diane offers easy-to-follow patterns and kits for 47 traditional and personality-plus bears as well as 60 soft animal designs. She will send you a free listing of high quality fabric furs, growlers and squeakers, noses, eyes, and joint sets.

Cabin Craft Midwest, Inc.
1225 W. First St.
P.O. Box 270
Nevada, Iowa 50201
Catalog: $3.00

A large selection of ready-to-to finish wooden items, many pictured painted, with instruction booklets also available, fills this inspiring, full color catalog. Also paints, brushes, books, and painting accessories. This is the source for the rocking horse, cradle and wagon featured in this book.

Edinburgh Imports, Inc.
P.O. Box 722
Woodland Hills, CA 91365–0722
Price and Information List for a long SASE

Elke Block offers premium quality teddy bear supplies including mohair, alpaca, and merino furs, woven-backed synthetics, glass eyes, felt, growlers, bear patterns and kits from important bearmakers.

Florida Supply House, Inc.
P.O. Box 847
Bradenton, FL 33506
Catalog: $2.00

Thousands of craft items at very reasonable prices fill this catalog. This is the source for the Christmas sleigh.

Gaillorraine Originals
P.O. Box 137
Tehachapi, CA 93561
Catalog: $2.00

Jointed bear patterns & bear-making supplies.

Home Sew
Dept. JD
Bethlehem, PA 18018
Catalog: Free

This little catalog is overflowing with basic, and not-so-basic, sewing needs such as thread, elastic, lace, trims and much, much more. But the real joy of the Home Sew catalog is the low prices.

The Teddy Works
5-15 49th Avenue
Long Island City, NY. 11101
Catalog: Free

The color catalog features everything imaginable for the bear-maker including furs, plastic joints, eyes, growlers, and the parasol, and straw hat seen in this book.

Unfinished Business, Inc.
P.O. Box 246
Wingate, N.C., 28174
Catalog: $3.00

Over 500 unfinished wooden items and parts ready to paint, stencil, or stain. Also paints and brushes. Tricycle, blocks and shelf are featured in this book.

BIBLIOGRAPHY

Bialosky, Peggy, Alan Bialosky, and Robert Tynes. *Make Your Own Teddy Bear*, New York: Workman Publishing Company, Inc., 1982

Bishop, Adele, and Cile Lord. *The Art of Decorative Stenciling*, New York: Penguin Books, 1976

Hutchings, Margaret. *Teddy Bears and How to Make Them*, 1964; rpt. New York: Dover Publications, Inc. 1977

Linsley, Lesley. *First Steps in Stenciling*, New York: Doubleday and Co., Inc., 1986

Moore, Marsha Evans. *The Teddy Bear Book*, New York: Alan D. Bragdon Publishers, Inc., 1984

Puckett, Marjorie. *Shadow Quilting*, New York: Charles Scribners & Sons, 1986

The Reader's Digest Association, Inc. *The Reader's Digest Complete Guide To Sewing*, 1976 rpt. New York: Reader's Digest Association, 1978

Singer Sewing Reference Library. *Singer Sewing Essentials*, Minnesota: Cy DeCosse, Inc., 1984

To order more good books from
WILLIAMSON PUBLISHING

To order additional copies of **Teddy Bears and All The Trimmings**, please enclose $12.95 per copy plus $1.50 shipping and handling to Williamson Publishing Co. at the address listed on the last page.

DOING CHILDREN'S MUSEUMS
A Guide to 225 Hands–On Museums
by Joanne Cleaver

Turn an ordinary day into a spontaneous "vacation" by taking a child to some of the 225 participatory children's museums, discovery rooms, and nature centers covered in this one-of-a-kind book. Filled with museum specifics describing age-appropriate exhibits, facilities, specialties, toddler playspaces, other nearby attractions and eateries. Cleaver has created a most valuable resource for anyone who loves kids!

224 pages, 6x9, illustrations
Quality paperback, $12.95

Easy-to-Make
GIFTS FOR THE BABY
by Cindy Higgins

There's still nothing nicer than a home-crafted, straight from the heart, gift for babies and toddlers. Somehow store-bought just doesn't measure up. Here are 65 gifts—everything from practical carry-all totes to huggable bunnies and two-sided dolls to clever wooden toys, rocking chairs, clown book shelf, and toy soldier clothes racks. Plus quick and easy quilts, blankets, kids backpacks. Best of all—simple directions and many projects to make in an hour or less!

144 pages, 8x10, illustrations
Quality paperback, $8.95

PARENTS ARE TEACHERS, TOO
Enriching Your Child's First Six Years
by Claudia Jones

Be the best teacher your child ever has. Jones shares hundreds of ways to help any child learn in playful home situations. Lots on developing reading, writing, math skills. Plenty on creative and critical thinking, too. A book you'll love using!

192 pages, 6x9, illustrations
Quality paperback, $9.95

GOLDE'S HOMEMADE COOKIES
by Golde Hoffman Soloway

"Cookies are her chosen realm and how sweet a world it is to visit."
Publishers Weekly

Over 100 treasured recipes that defy description. Suffice it to say that no one could walk away from Golde's cookies without asking for another...plus the recipe.

144 pages, 8¼x7¼, illustrations
Quality paperback, $7.95

THE BROWN BAG COOKBOOK:
Nutritious Portable Lunches for Kids and Grown-Ups
by Sara Sloan

Here are more than 1,000 brown bag lunch ideas with 150 recipes for simple, quick, nutritious lunches that kids will love. Breakfast ideas, too!

192 pages, 8¼x7¼, illustrations
Quality paperback, $8.95

PUBLIC SCHOOLS USA
A Comparative Guide to School Districts
by Charles Harrison

"How are the schools?" is the question most asked by families on the move whether its cross-town, cross-state or cross-country. Finally, here's the answer as over 500 school districts in major metropolitan areas nationwide are rated on everything from special programs for high-or-low achievers to SAT scores, to music and art programs, to drop-out rates. If your children's education matters to you, here's a book you'll want to own.

368 pages, 8½x11
Quality paperback, $17.95

PARENTING THROUGH THE COLLEGE YEARS
From Application Through Graduation
by Norman Giddan, Ph.D., and Sally Vallongo

Don't drop out when your kids go off to college! They may need you in a different capacity, but they need you just the same. Here's all about this amazing 4 years in the life of parents and their almost-adult children. A lifesaver in many, many ways!

192 pages, 6x9
Quality paperback, $9.95

SIMPLY ELEGANT COUNTRY FOODS: Down Home goes Uptown
by Carol Lowe-Clay

An outrageously good cook brings country cooking to its pinnacle. A cookbook that's not fussy, not trendy—simply elegant. Everything from country fresh Pizza Rustica to Crumbed Chicken in Wine Sauce, Country Pork Supper, Sweet Cream Scones with Honey Butter to Whipped Cream Cake with Almond Custard Filling. Over 100 recipes capturing the freshness of the moment!

160 pages, 8x10
Quality paperback, $8.95

DINING ON DECK: Fine Food for Sailing & Boating
by Linda Vail

For Linda Vail a perfect day's sail includes fine food—quickly and easily prepared. She offers here 225 outstanding recipes (casual yet elegant food) with over 90 menus for everything from elegant weekends to hearty breakfasts, and suppers for cool weather sailing. Her recipes are so good and so varied you'll use her cookbook year-round for sure!

160 pages, 8x10
Quality paperback, $9.95

SUMMER IN A JAR: Making Pickles, Jams & More
by Andrea Chesman

"With recipes this simple and varied, it's hard to find an excuse not to preserve summer in one's cupboard."　　　*Publishers Weekly*

Chesman introduces single jar recipes so you can make pickles and relishes a single quart at a time. Plenty of low-sugar jams, marmalades, relishes. Pickles by the crock, too. Outstanding recipes.

160 pages, $8\frac{1}{4} \times 7\frac{1}{4}$
Quality paperback, $7.95

TO ORDER:
At your bookstore or order directly from Williamson Publishing. We accept Visa or MasterCard (please include number, expiration date and signature), or send check to:

> **Williamson Publishing Co.,**
> **Church Hill Road, P.O. Box 185,**
> **Charlotte, Vermont 05445.**

(Toll-free phone orders: 800-234-8791.) Please add $1.50 for postage and handling. Satisfaction guaranteed or full refund without questions or quibbles.